∠ GDEM

Feeling and Personhood

Psychology in Another Key

John Heron

SAGE Publications
London · Newbury Park · New Delhi

SAGE Publications Ltd
6 Bonhill Street
London EC2A 4PU

SAGE Publications Inc
2455 Teller Road
Newbury Park, California 91320

SAGE Publications India Pvt Ltd
32, M-Block Market
Greater Kailash – I
New Delhi 110 048

British Library Cataloguing in Publication data

Heron, John
   Feeling and Personhood: Psychology in
   Another Key
   I. Title
   155.2

   ISBN 0–8039–8728–5
   ISBN 0–8039–8729–3 (pbk)

Library of Congress catalog card number 92–050266

Typeset by Photoprint, Torquay, Devon
Printed in Great Britain by Biddes Ltd, Guildford, Surrey

Contents

Acknowledgements

I wish to record my warm thanks to Luigi Bianchi and Maurizio Righi for their many services in making possible the setting, near Volterra, Italy, where this book was written.

Peter Reason read through the whole manuscript confronting me on points of content, presentation or clarity on almost every page. I have taken account of nearly all his comments. While he is not in any way responsible for the ideas put forward, he has made a very large contribution to improving the manner in which they have been expressed, and I am deeply grateful for this.

My thanks are also due to Mary Corr, Sue Knights, Roberta Skye and forty members of the co-counselling network in Auckland, New Zealand, for much invaluable assistance in refining the many exercises which are included in the book; and to Kate Hopkinson for two days of discussions on several of her papers on a new age paradigm, which stimulated and clarified my thoughts on the imaginal mind.

I am grateful to the Chairman and Committee of the Society for Effective Affective Learning for inviting me to give the keynote address at their fourth international conference, in March 1991, at the University of Reading in England. This invitation was the trigger which set in motion the reflection and writing that has led to this book.

1

Theory of the Person: Preliminaries

Precursors and purposes

This book presents a theory of the person, with a look at some of its practical implications for learning. The 'other key' referred to in the sub-title of this book is feeling, which I distinguish carefully from emotion, and define as resonance with being, the capacity by which we participate in and are compresent with our world. Feeling, so defined, I regard as the grounding level of personhood: within it all other psychological modes are latent and out of it they proceed. The book explores this model and the sort of world-view it generates in some depth (Chapters 2 to 10). It also looks at learning in the light of this model, both learning in everyday living and formal learning in the classroom (Chapters 11 to 14).

The theory is put forward as a contribution toward a science of the person, in the sense that it is based on a wide-ranging phenomenology of human experience and is 'expressed in terms of a self-consistent but limited and approximate model' (Capra, 1983: 416). Its precursors in the wider culture are the philosophy of human relations and of the person (Buber, 1937; MacMurray, 1957); the self-actualization psychologies and their human potential derivatives (Maslow, 1970; Rogers, 1959, 1980); and a little-known line of spiritual philosophy and psychology (Fawcett, 1921, 1931, 1939; Hyde, 1949b, 1954, 1955), as well as the wider and more recent stream of transpersonal psychology (Grof, 1976, 1988; Wilber, 1977, 1983, 1990). There are also precursors in my own recent writings.

In *Helping the Client*, about one-to-one counselling and intervention skills (Heron, 1990), there is the following short passage on the nature of the person:

> The person is a seamless whole, an interacting system which in simplified form has four psychological modes of being: willing is the diamond apex whose facets are cut by the aware discrimination of thinking, which is made wise by the holistic receptivity of intuition, and grounded in the participation in being of feeling . . . . The four psychological modes converge upon enterprise and endeavour. From our felt participation in the world, we open intuitively to grasp a total situation, then discriminate thoughtfully in order to act within it. (Heron, 1990: 17)

In that book I did not say anything further about the ideas thus briefly presented, but moved on directly to practical matters to do with helping the client. The present work makes good that omission and that is the first purpose of my writing.

The Facilitators' Handbook (Heron, 1989) introduced – directly based on the same model of the person – an up-hierarchy account of 'the manifold of learning'. This interrelated experiential, imaginal, conceptual and practical learning, each later form of learning in this list being grounded in the preceding ones. My second purpose, carried out in later chapters of this book, is to develop that learning model further and extend its practical implications.

The immediate stimulus to advance all these ideas was my being invited to give the keynote address to the fourth international conference of the Society for Effective Affective Learning in March 1991, at the University of Reading in England. It seemed to me in preparing this talk that a much deeper account of affect and of affective learning than I had hitherto discovered was needed to do justice to the business of being human. The outline of that talk was the first sketch for this book.

Plumbing the depths of affect took me into the heart of transpersonal psychology and philosophy. So my third purpose in writing is to explore some basic issues in these two closely related fields of inquiry. The account of affect and of the person given in these pages involves some radical transpersonal notions, that is, ideas to do with matters traditionally called spiritual and divine.

It also upsets the ancient yet still current applecart in which the intellect rules over everything else in the soul which is deemed to be less. And that makes a fourth purpose, which is covered more fully at the very end of this chapter.

The book, then, is for readers who are interested in exploring the idea that the nature of personhood is grounded in feeling, in applying this in living and learning, in considering its transpersonal context, and who are seeking to reappraise the traditional role ascribed to intellect.

The part of this book about the theory of the person – which also includes the transpersonal content – is much longer than the account of learning that follows from it. For the rest of this chapter I am going to attend to several issues to do with formulating such a theory.

Sources

The reader is entitled to know something about where the theory comes from. Its phenomenological sources are multifarious, and I could not give any kind of reliable weighting to each of them, but the primary ones are: friendship, including all its special instances of personal and family relationships; the exigencies, tribulations and failures of being wounded; attention to my own emotional healing and development through the practice of co-counselling and other personal growth modalities, especially those involving breathing and body-work; the use of a variety of psychic and spiritual practices, both in private and in groups; experience of running workshops concerned with personal and transpersonal development, professional development, educational theory and practice; personal and transpersonal development work with private clients; reflection, study and discussions with colleagues in the fields of psychology, medicine, education, philosophy and religion; research in altered states of consciousness, in humanistic medicine, in group dynamics, and with co-counsellors in personality dynamics, using the methods of co-operative inquiry; certain outward travels that were also inward journeys; what feel like unseen presences being active in stimulating the flow of thought while I am writing; and for over a year preceding the writing of this book, living on an isolated promontory of land where I had the space, time and opportunity to dialogue with nature, its local creatures, and the planet, the sun, moon and wider universe on its different levels.

There is a story about this last item. In 1976 I attended a weekend seminar with Tarthang Tulku, the Nyingma Buddhist luminary, at the Nyingma Institute in Berkeley, California. In a private talk, he casually suggested I might find it fruitful to spend thirty minutes every day speaking out loud in an isolated place in the midst of nature, giving voice to whatever it was in me to say in such a circumstance. I noticed that the proposal made an immediate appeal. At the same time I thought it was disconcerting, impractical and rather mad. I have since learned its deep wisdom.

To talk out loud to the world, with the world and in the world in a creative way, is quickly to discover what preconceptions and assumptions one is bringing to the dialogue, for the very presence of the whole perceptual field will throw them into relief. The world's own utterance will rearrange them in a form more consonant with what it wants to say at this time and in this space, and will interrupt the tyranny of cultural transmission through the written and the spoken word.

Where do ideas come from? Where indeed. If I were to give a very general account using the model presented in this book, I would say that the grounding level is felt resonance with people in their world, in all the different contexts I have listed above, and felt resonance with the world itself; that out of this extended resonance, seed-images, pregnant with meaning, have started to emerge over the last four years; and that these in turn have been precipitated into conceptual and propositional form by the writing of this book. The propositions, while rising out the yeast of past encounters and actions, now call for new lines of endeavour and practice.

Criteria for evaluating any theory of the person

The criteria I think are relevant are rather different from those which appear in standard textbooks on personality theory. One such text gives the following criteria: empirical validity and testability; parsimony of explanations and assumptions; comprehensiveness; internal consistency; usefulness; acceptability among scientists (Liebert and Spiegler, 1990). The first and last of these are problematic if they mean the use of old paradigm research, that is doing research *on* people rather than *with* them (Reason and Rowan, 1981). The second one about parsimony is restrictive if it is introduced too soon and applied inappropriately at the phenomenal level (Spiegelberg, 1960). Here is my alternative set of criteria.

An adequate phenomenal base

By a phenomenal base I mean a set of categories that describe human personality close to the grain of experience: they honour how the person appears to be. Ordinary language, of course, is full of such categories – in terms like memory, sensation, perception, action, thinking, feeling, and so on. But these terms are systematically ambiguous: they overlap in a fruitful yet disordered profusion, so that everyone in society can use them to suit their own implicit personality theory.

Explicit personality theory needs a formal set of categories, a phenomenal base whose terms are selected, carefully defined and organized in the close-up light of experience. Years ago Zener argued that psychology has too narrow a formal base of such categories and needs phenomenally sensitive observers to extend it, in order to provide a more adequate foundation for the superstructure of theorizing and experiment (Zener, 1958).

A formal phenomenal base is adequate, I believe, if it meets three criteria of its own.

Groundedness   Its terms need to be thoroughly grounded, with a good bedrock quality, in deeply contemplated experience. They must be clearly stated and defined, at the same time evoking the grain of direct acquaintance with people in their world. They are terms you can't get underneath: they seem, *prima facie*, to have no prior experiential referent. Such groundedness, however, is always relative to its cultural context, that is, to the prevailing use of language and the nexus of beliefs in which such usage is embedded.

Comprehensiveness The set of categories needs to extend well over the field and not leave anything out that really needs to be in. Many theories rush into upper-level theorizing and experimentation on too narrow a set.

Dynamic organization The set or categories needs to be systematic, with some basic dynamic principles that hold the whole thing together coherently, so that we do not have a mere aggregate of categories or a minimal map of them. What is assumed here is the nomothetic belief that there are principles that manifest in all personal functioning, however idiosyncratic each individual's process may be.

Low superstructure
Too much elaborate theory constructed with ingenuity on top of the phenomenal base is suspect. And there is too much superstructure if the next three criteria cannot readily be applied.

Personal viability
The theory needs to have vital relevance to the reader's own experience. Its concepts should come alive, through personal acquaintance with oneself, one's intimates, friends, associates, students, clients and the wider public. Of course, the reader may lack awareness and development in this or that aspect of personhood. Also while everyone has some kind of implicit personality theory, it is usually inchoate, and will be remote from explicit formalization. But, *ceteris paribus*, this is an important criterion. It leads into the following one.

Experiential validity
This is a central criterion. It means the theory is coherent with a truly radical empiricism: it is well founded in the human condition, open to deep experience and free of either sense organ bias or Absolute Spirit bias. It offers a range of experiential exercises that any willing persons can try out informally, and that can be elaborated more formally as the starting point for a full-blown co-operative inquiry (Reason, 1989).

Co-operative (or collaborative) inquiry does research *with* people, not *on* them: the researcher co-opts the subjects as co-researchers, and joins the subjects as co-subject. In short, all those involved are both co-researchers in devising, reflectively managing and drawing conclusions from the research, and also co-subjects in experiencing and doing whatever it is that the research is about. They cycle several times between reflection as researchers and action as subjects, and use a variety of validity procedures to keep themselves clear of consensus collusion and other hazards of the method. I and others have written about this kind of non-alienating research at length elsewhere, advancing central arguments for it and reporting examples of it (Heron, 1981a, 1981b; Reason and Rowan, 1981; Reason and Heron, 1986; Reason, 1989).

Applicability
The theory needs to be applicable to the human condition in ways that are relevant and effective. It needs to illuminate practice, to offer working hypotheses for living and learning. This is an extension of both personal viability and experiential validity.

Isomorphism
The theory needs to show some significant overlap of basic principles with other, related fields of knowledge.

No theory of the person can fulfil all these criteria to an equal and maximum degree. The theory I am presenting certainly does not claim to do so. However, I have had them in mind in creating and revising the theory, and have sought to honour each of them, at least to some degree and in some places.

The goals of this theory of the person

The goals of my theory-making are simply to provide a seedbed for generating working hypotheses which may be fruitful in living and working, in learning and inquiry, and in helping and facilitating. Some of these working ideas are developed in the many exercises which are appended to the text; some are included in the text, especially in the later chapters on learning. Many more are waiting to be extracted from the loam.

Experiential exercises

In most parts of the book I include experiential exercises. There are one hundred altogether, running through Chapters 2 to 9 inclusive. There are none in Chapter 10, which gives a critical review of other theories. Chapters 11 to 14 cover a wide range of practical learning cycles in the main text, and therefore further exercises seem redundant.

Each exercise is referenced to a particular piece of text, and appears at the end of the chapter in which that text appears. It offers an activity which can ground the concepts of the text in personal experience. The grounding is of two sorts: either in present experience or in recollected experience.

For reasons of space and a sense of balance in the design of this book, I have been selective in choosing which parts of the text have exercises attached to them. But I have put in so many exercises of different sorts, that the imaginative reader, or teacher preparing a student seminar, can use them as a model for generating new exercises on other parts of the text.

Each exercise is designed to be done with one other person. It can be done alone (even just to imagine doing it is useful); but it becomes much more effective when done with the co-operation of another person – whom I refer to throughout as 'your partner'. Having a partner means you get supportive and enabling attention when it is your turn, and provides someone else's report for comparison and contrast with your own. There can be a valuable phase of shared reflection on both sets of data: a review of the concepts put forward in the text in the light of combined experience.

The exercises work well if you follow these guidelines.

1 Use a timer or a clock and keep to equal time. And use the timer for subsections of time within one turn.
2 If you do a lot of exercises with the same partner, take it in turns to go first.
3 During the speaker's turn, the listener gives abundant supportive attention, but does not intervene or comment in any way at all, except to remind the speaker about the nature of the exercise if he or she has clearly got right off track.
4 For all exercises, at the start of your turn, relax into feeling fully present. The rubric often reminds you of this, especially with exercises that involve a review of past experience. But wherever this reminder is not stated it is always implied.
5 When recollecting experience, always recall specific concrete events and evoke them fully with literal description, so that they stand forth in their imaginal presence. Never analyse any experience until it is thus evoked.
6 The shared reflection occurs after both turns. It is an unstructured discussion which assumes that both parties will have roughly equal air-time.
7 This shared reflection, introduced by phrases such as 'discuss your findings' or 'share your experiences', has three basic parts. The first is some summary of what went on. The second is

reflecting on the experience, making sense of it, and relating it to ideas in the text: this includes issues of both viability and validity, which I discuss further below. The third is asking whether the concepts involved have any practical outcomes, whether they can make a difference in action. This last part is especially important and can readily get overlooked in exercises of this sort. But it is really their consummation.

8   Making non-linguistic symbols (drawing, mime, movement, sound, etc.) of the experience before shared reflection is included in several exercises. Please remember that it is an option for all the exercises even if it is not suggested in the rubric.

9   Be free to alter the time structure, the content, the format or the location of the exercise to make it feel right for you. You may well want to take more time on those exercises in which you have a special interest. Change the instructions to make them practicable for your situation and available resources. For example, there is an exercise called 'Compresent rabbit' which is there because I happen to have a tame rabbit living in my garden, but you may need to substitute some other creature, or plant.

Each exercise can be done with a group of pairs: for convenience up to six pairs. After reflection within the pairs, there can be a valuable further phase in which key data and thoughts from each pair are put before the whole group as a basis for group reflection on the concepts in the light of everyone's experience.

Finally, each exercise can be used as the starting point for a longer or shorter co-operative inquiry. This will also involve a group working in pairs, using several cycles of inquiry. The first cycle takes my concepts and the exercise I give for grounding them in experience. The final group reflection phase of this cycle will lead over into the planning phase of the next cycle, in which the starting concepts, now modified by the first cycle, are taken into some altered or different kind of experience. In this way the researchers refine, deepen and extend or revise the conceptual framework by cycling between reflection and experience. For a full discussion of the issues involved in using this kind of research method, and for examples, see Reason (1989).

Let me say some more about the simple exercises for two people as presented in this book. Their main purpose, as I have said, is to relate the concepts of the text to personal experience: to give them some viability, to bring them alive. A further purpose is to explore the validity of these concepts, to see whether they are indeed well founded in experience. This exploration of validity is paradoxical: the validating experience is defined in advance in terms of the concepts that are to be validated.

However, the conceptual definition is only a signpost to an experience that has more fundamental imaginal and affective parameters. The phenomena have dimensions at more basic levels than the conceptual; and it is out of these that conceptualization itself emerges. The experience can declare itself in its own non-linguistic terms, and we can then say whether the conceptualization is well founded in these terms or whether it needs revising. So the signpost may need alteration once we have become acquainted with its alleged destination.

What this means is that when you have or recall an experience in the exercises, you need to bracket off and hold in suspension the concepts that direct you to it. Then you invite it to declare its extra-linguistic form. What is being disclosed is the affective and imaginal morphology of the phenomena. There is a dialectical tension here between the bracketed concepts and the declaration. If you bracket the concepts absolutely out of the way, then there is no determinate experience that you can identify and ask to reveal itself. If you don't bracket them off at all, the declaration is repressed by the conceptual imposition.

So it's a compromise: you bracket off enough to get a declaration but not so much as to make it impossible. This inevitably means that the declaration you get is always relative to your bracketed concepts: there is no such thing as an absolutely pristine revelation of what the experience is really all about. There is no way in which we can avoid the historicity of our knowledge, the fact that even the most revisionary thought is still relative to its cultural antecedents (Gadamer, 1975). I cover these points again in Chapter 8.

The post-linguistic outlook and an ontological rationale

An important point, by no means original, which I make throughout this book is that the ordinary use of language creates a split world, with an arbitrary separation of object from subject. However, I also argue that this effect can be transcended by the cultivation of what I call post-linguistic perception and thought, in which we learn to see a unitive world and describe it in unitive discourse. In such a world subject and object are distinct, interpenetrating and non-separable.

My theory-making does not claim to be cast unequivocally in terms of unitive discourse, it is just moving in that direction. No doubt there are anomalies, such as split-world categories seeking to make a unitive point. But I am convinced that language can be transformed to convey thought which transcends the subject–object split that comes with the acquisition of one's mother tongue.

The wider ontological rationale of this theory of the person stems from a spiritual philosophy and is as follows. Reality, I believe, is both One and Many. The Many are a real Many, a genuine Multiplicity within Mind, spiritual monads, differentiated centres of consciousness within a cosmic presence. Personhood is one such centre, a particular focus of development within the field of universal consciousness, unfolding a unique perspective within it, with people emerging though the progressive differentiation of the person from germinal to transfigured states. In Reality there is no separation between any conscious centre and its setting in universal mind, and since it is part of this unified field, it can participate in all other centres too. The isolation and alienation of the human mind is an egoic illusion to do with the subject–object split born of our use of language, psychological wounding, and deep tensions inherent in the human condition. Dismantling that illusion means that personal consciousness uncovers its true heritage – that it is both distinct within, and one with, a universal presence.

It follows from this that while a person may psychologically identify with the illusion of existing only as a separate self, a person cannot be theoretically identified with such a separate self. Spiritual philosophies which say the person is nothing but the illusory ego suffer, in my view, from transcendental reductionism. The Many are reduced to the One via the concept of illusion: there are no Real Many, only the unreal many, illusory selves that ultimately disappear in the light of the One. The corollaries of this reductionism are, first, that there is no real love between persons, only the collusion of illusory self-interest; and secondly, that salvation is to be found through meditative dissociation from the illusion of being a person. These corollaries, and their underlying transcendental reductionism, seem to me to be profoundly mistaken.

Modalities, perspective, belief and metaphor

The statements in this book are assertoric in the sense that they are presented without qualification as if they are giving some final account of human experience. This is a device of literary style and convenience. In terms of modalities, I have adopted the convention throughout of converting all problematic statements into assertoric statements. In other words, statements that contain terms like 'may' and 'possible', which express what seems or appears to be the case, have all been converted into statements about what is the case. I ask the reader to remember this when he or she gets oppressed by the persistent assertoric mode; and to convert the offending statements into their implicit problematic mode by replacing 'is' by 'may be' and by inserting 'appears to' or 'possibly' before verbal assertions.

The book as a whole inclines more to the problematic mode than the assertoric, while sometimes hovering ambiguously between the two. The theory given here is not at all a dogmatic account of what there is, but, as a contribution toward a science of the person, it can variously be called a construct, a conjecture, a model, a map, a perspective. The last of these terms is the most fitting. It implies a viewpoint, a transaction, which needs complementing with a thousand other overlapping and disparate views to achieve any social viability.

The same point can be made in terms of the traditional distinction between belief and knowledge. A belief, as against mere opinion, has some supporting warrants – intuitive, intellectual and experiential – but the warrants are not sufficient to justify a claim to knowledge. My theory is thus only a belief, and falls far short of fulfilling a claim to knowledge. At the same time it is not mere abstract speculation.

It is a working belief and a lived belief. It is experientially, phenomenologically grounded and applied. It is the formal, explicit equivalent of what everybody has and uses: an implicit, working belief system about personality, however inchoate, which is the basis of self-management and social interaction. It is a peculiarity of the human condition that we must conduct many of the intimate and demanding aspects of our lives on the basis of reasonable belief rather than on any secure claim to knowledge.

The belief system of this book is elaborated in terms of certain central metaphors: the up-hierarchy, the spiral, the cycle. The up-hierarchy metaphor in particular is a major artifice. Hierarchy as such originally meant rule or dominion in holy things, being applied to orders of angels, and to the organization of priests in successive grades. Later its use was generalized, especially in logic and science, to mean persons or things organized in grades or classes one above the other. Socially, today, it means downward control, through successive levels, by those above over those below.

So the up-hierarchy metaphor turns the traditional concept upside down and implies generating influence, through successive levels, from what is below to what is above. It is a model of emergence and influence from the immanent, rather than emanation and dominion from the transcendent. It carries from the original concept the aura of holy things, but it is about their immanent order. It also carries the overtones of a systematic interaction of beings.

I expect it will be said that throughout this book I push the up-hierarchy metaphor too hard, viewing too much through its lens. Time will tell, together with close attention to the phenomenology of those domains of experience which I have viewed in the light of the metaphor. However I believe it is a fruitful and invaluable antidote to the extraordinary dominance of the down-hierarchy metaphor which still pervades every aspect of our intellectual, educational, cultural and social life.

The ancient Greeks launched western culture with the model of the intellect as that which differentiates humans from animals. The cultivation of intellectual competence is the supreme end of man (not woman, since for Aristotle women were a lesser order of being); and the incidental function of reason is to control and regulate emotion and the passion. The model of intellectual supremacy and control has run higher education – and thence the whole of education and child-raising – since the founding of universities on Aristotelian principles in the Middle Ages. It is a model which has had a remarkable run: through the Greek version, the Roman version, the medieval version, the Renaissance version, the age of enlightenment version and the modern science version, together with concurrent revisions of moral, legal, and political thought and practice.

And it is a model which has run its course, delivered its goods and is becoming transparent with its own inherent limitations. The primary limitation, manifest in every domain where it rules, is that of exploitation and abuse as a consequence of control and domination. The central source of all this, I believe, is in the psychological domain: the intellect exploits and abuses its affective base by controlling, and not acknowledging its origin in, affect; by denigrating and misrepresenting the nature of affect; by inflating its separatist power by leaching the formidable energy of affect while denying the fact.

When this internal psychological abuse is acted out we get the exploitation of children by controlling parents; the exploitation of women by controlling men; the exploitation of students by controlling staff; the exploitation of data by controlling physical science researchers; the exploitation of subjects by controlling social science researchers; the exploitation of human attention by the controlling media; the exploitation of workers by controlling management; the exploitation of management by controlling owners; the exploitation of consumers by controlling capitalists; the exploitation of citizens by the controlling state; the exploitation of the underdeveloped nations by the controlling developed nations; the exploitation of planetary resources by controlling multinational companies; and so on and so forth.

The up-hierarchy model of the psyche grounded in affect, presented in this book, seeks to redress this long-standing abuse.

2

Theory of the Person: Overview

This chapter gives an overall map of the theory of the person. It distinguishes between the person and the psyche; portrays four modes of the psyche and its three basic polarities; uses the metaphors of the up-hierarchy and the cycle as descriptive models; looks at feeling as the basis of personhood; distinguishes between the person and the ego; considers the person as a spiritual monad; and closes with an account of the psychological modes in terms of contracting and expanding spirals of development from birth to adulthood.

The psyche and the person

By 'the psyche' I mean the human mind and its inherent life as a whole, including its unexpressed and unexplored potential, as well as what is manifest in conscious development. By 'the person' I mean the psyche in manifestation as an aware developing being in whom all its modes are brought intentionally into play. A person in this sense is clearly an achievement – of both education and self-development.

From these definitions it follows that the psyche includes both the potentials for personhood and the actual person, as well as pre-personal developmental states prior to realized personhood. 'The psyche' is simply a convenient generic term to use when talking about some of the basic structures and dynamics of the human mind.

Four modes of the psyche and three basic polarities

My basic construct for the psyche portrays it as having four primary modes of functioning which are all in play to some degree at all times in waking life: affective, imaginal, conceptual and practical. They are distinguished from each other in this model only in order to appreciate better how they are interwoven in psychological reality.

The affective mode embraces feeling and emotion: I distinguish between these two in a very fundamental way, which I will clarify shortly. The imaginal mode comprises intuition and imagery of all kinds, including the imagery of sense perception. The conceptual mode includes reflection and discrimination. And the practical mode involves intention and action. I continue with the modes after the next section.

The theory also proposes three dynamic polarities which inform the modes: individuation and participation, ground process and reorganization, life and mind. I pay most attention to the first of these, and look at three secondary polarities that derive from it: figure and ground, subject and object, projective and receptive.

Individuation and participation

Within the psyche as a whole and within each psychological mode there is, I propose, a basic polarity between an individuating function and a participatory one. The former makes for experience of individual distinctness; the latter for experience of unitive interaction with a whole field of being. These poles do not exclude each other; instead the two functions interact along a continuum in which one is most dominant at one end, and the other at the other end.

I believe that a deep contemplation of the dynamism of the psyche, in oneself and others, reveals the radical nature of this complementarity. Each of the main psychological modes is involved in it, having an individuating pole and a participatory one.

There is also considerable concurrence of thought on the basics of this matter. 'Virtually all personality theorists of whatever creed or persuasion assume that personality contains polar tendencies' (Hall and Lindzey, 1957). Koestler used the word 'holon' for subsystems which exhibit the polarity of part and whole in the hierarchic order of life. This was his basis for a generalized theory of autonomous tendencies and participatory tendencies in biological, social and mental development (Koestler, 1964, 1978). Systems theorists agree that these two polar tendencies are a basic complementary dynamic that is characteristic of systems phenomena, whether organisms, societies or ecosystems (Capra, 1983). The same principle is found in Hindu psychology. Bhagavan Das postulates a polarity of the primal Shakti, or creative power within the psyche, as a will to live as an individual, and a will to live as the universal (Das, 1953).[1]

Polar forms of the modes

I now give an introductory account of the four primary modes, stating the two polar functions within each; and for each mode I state its individuating function first, followed by its participatory one. This account will be elaborated in later sections and chapters.

Affective mode

By the term 'emotion' I mean the intense, localized affect that arises from the fulfilment or the frustration of individual needs and interests. This is the domain of joy, love, surprise, satisfaction, zest, fear, grief, anger, and so on. Thus defined, emotion is an index of motivational states.

By 'feeling' I refer, with special usage, to the capacity of the psyche to participate in wider unities of being, to become at one with the differential content of a whole field of experience, to indwell what is present through attunement and resonance, and to know its own distinctness while unified with the differentiated other. This is the domain of empathy, indwelling, participation, presence, resonance, and such like.[2]

Lawrence Hyde made a distinction between the more intense and agitated character of emotion and the creative aspect of feeling by which 'we place ourselves in communion with what we find outside ourselves'. He variously called this empathy, heterocentric evaluation, and identification with the being of things 'in the mode of love' which at the same time enhances our own sense of identity (Hyde, 1955).

There is a correspondence with the views of Susanne Langer, who distinguishes between emotivity and sensibility. Emotivity is what is experienced as autogenic action, processes going within the organism, especially the constant functioning of the central nervous system. Sensibility is what is felt as impinging influence, as 'contact with the plenum of external events': the interdependence of the organism with the rhythms of the environment and other living dynamic entities. And these two notions also correlate, respectively, with her two basic polar principles of the individuation of life rhythms as differentiated organisms and the involvement of such individuated entities in wider and wider wholes (Langer, 1988).

There the correspondence ends, since Langer is giving a reductionist account of feeling as a special phase in the evolving complexity of living forms; whereas I hold that feeling is *sui generis* and cannot be explained exclusively in biological terms. It is basically a concept in transpersonal psychology, as we shall see.

Imaginal mode

By 'imaging' I mean the capacity of the psyche to generate an individual viewpoint, a unique outlook on life through the use of imagery – in sense perception, memory, anticipation, dreams, visions, imagination, extrasensory perception. Such imagery yields a distinctive, personal window on the world. The point I shall develop in later chapters is that the continuous image-making power of the imaginal mind is deeply involved in the generation of perception, through the creative role of primary imagination in perceiving the world.

By 'intuiting' I refer to the immediate, comprehensive knowing whereby the mind can grasp a field, a system or a being as a patterned unity, apprehend it in terms of figure–ground and part–whole hierarchies, see its connections with other patterns, and know what it signifies, what it means. This is the domain of intuitive grasp, holistic cognition, totalistic comprehension, metaphorical insight, immediate gnosis.[3]

Conceptual mode
By 'discrimination' I mean the ability to categorize things in terms of classes, to distinguish between one particular and another in perception, to identify similarities and differences. It depends on the use of concepts that come with language mastery. The perceiver makes relevant distinctions to service the pursuit of individual needs and preferences. This is the domain of defining, differentiating things, and picking out what is salient. It includes the conceptual component in perception.

By 'reflection' I refer to the process of thinking about experience in general terms. It uses concepts to deal with the relations between classes and between classes of classes. The intellect is seeking to formulate a conceptual model that is inclusive and comprehensive. This is the domain of models, generalizations, laws and theories.[4]

Practical mode
By 'action' I mean this piece of behaviour performed by this person. Such action is the result of individual choice and excludes mere unintended movement. This is the domain of the will, of individual acts and personal responsibility.

By 'intention' I refer to the purposes which a person has in mind when performing an action. Intention is the meaning of an action, and relates it to a wider context. This is the domain of plan, design, policy, purpose, and so on.[5]

Table 2.1 sets out the basic scheme. It is to be read from the bottom upwards, since it is set out in the form of an up-hierarchy, a metaphor which I explain in the next section. The individuating modes establish the person as a distinct focus of experience; the participatory modes take the person out into the wider reaches of

Table 2.1   *Individuating and participatory modes*

	Individuating	Participatory
Practical	Action	Intention
Conceptual	Discrimination	Reflection
Imaginal	Imagery	Intuition
Affective	Emotion	Feeling

being; both functions are always interacting, the poles representing the dominance of a function, not the exclusion of its opposite.

Like centre and circumference, the poles are involved in and require each other. The participatory modes include the individuating ones, and the individuating ones presuppose the participatory. Thus strong emotion presupposes felt resonance within a wider situation. Feeling at one with a scene will include some emotional state such as tranquillity. Focus on details of imagery rests on a tacit intuitive grasp of the whole field. Holistic intuition always relates to an idiosyncratic pattern of imagery. On-the-spot discrimination implies a tacit and unstated theory. General reflection is based upon particular discriminations already made. Action presupposes intention, however inchoate. Intention itself is consummated in action.

What the table does not bring out is the liberating place of balance between the poles, where the intentionally distinct and autonomous person participates with full awareness in the greater scheme of things.[6]

Also the distance between the poles is less, I think, as one moves from the affective mode, through the imaginal and conceptual to the practical. The polarity is most pronounced and dramatic at the affective level: the reach of feeling is illimitable, emotion has a distinct focus. Whereas action and intention are closer together; and the most inclusive intentions are, for any one person, necessarily more circumscribed.

The practical mode, the most contracted, accentuates the individuating tendency; and the affective mode, the most expanded in terms of feeling, strongly features the participatory. While emotion in the affective mode is, as we shall see, the foundation of individuation, action in the practical mode consummates individuation. All the other individuating functions – emotion, imagery (especially perception and memory), discrimination – tend to be drawn towards action in the practical mode to service it.

Thus, as I discuss in Chapter 4, is born the ego, which is a busy contraction together of action, discrimination, imagery and emotion. A point I shall repeatedly make is that the individuating modes, *per se*, are not necessarily egoic. They only become so if developed at expense of the participatory, by relegating the parti-

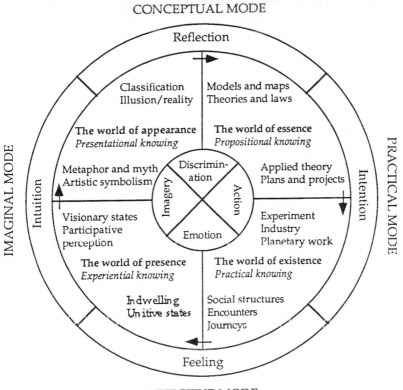

Figure 2.1 *Modes, worlds and forms of knowledge*

cipatory to unnoticed background status. Whereas the whole, transegoic person has all eight functions in a more comprehensive conscious balance: action and intention, discrimination and reflection, imagery and intuition, emotion and feeling.

Figure 2.1 gives an overview mandala of the four modes, with the participatory modes round the periphery, and the individuating in the centre. Remember that 'imagery' in the centre includes all perceptual imagery as well as memory, imagination and every other kind of image process. The modes are portrayed here in a syncretistic model, as involving transactions with the four worlds of presence, appearance, essence and existence, thereby generating, respectively, experiential, presentational, propositional and practical forms of knowledge.[7]

These four worlds and forms of knowledge are explored in Chapter 8. The arrows indicate the cyclic nature of inquiry and

Table 2.2   *Features of an up-hierarchy*

Latency	What is higher is tacit and latent in what is lower
Entelechy	The lowest level is the entelechy or formative potential of higher levels
Emergence	The higher levels emerge out of the lower
Possibilia	There are many different possible forms of emergence
Reduction	The higher levels are a reduced precipitate of the lower
Autonomy	Each level has a relative autonomy within the total system
Support	What is lower grounds, supports and nourishes what is higher

learning. Inquiry is discussed in Chapter 8, and learning in Chapters 11, 12, 13 and 14.

The modes as an up-hierarchy

The first of several related metaphors for the four modes is that of an up-hierarchy. Such a hierarchy works from below upwards, like a tree: something that has roots, a trunk, branches and fruit. The modal up-hierarchy has certain important features, which are shown in Table 2.2.

In an up-hierarchy it is not a matter of the higher controlling and ruling the lower, as in a down-hierarchy, but of the higher branching and flowering out of, and bearing the fruit of, the lower. The basic up-hierarchy of the modes is shown in Figure 2.2.

I give here a sketch of topics developed more fully in later chapters. The ground of the psyche is the affective mode in its most expansive form as feeling, which is the root and fundament of all the other modes and contains them in tacit or latent form. All the

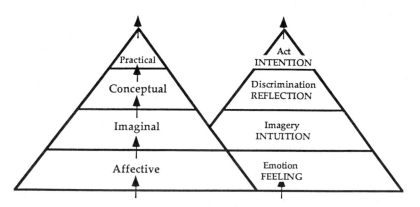

Figure 2.2   *The up-hierarchy of the four modes*

capacities of the psyche are in solution in primordial affect. It is the entelechy or formative potential of the whole.[8]

The deliverance of creative imagination is heralded by a presentiment, a felt resonance with future being as an inchoate process within. Elaborate conceptual models expressed through pages of carefully argued text start life as inspirational seed images into which fullness of meaning is packed, its propositional structure latent, not yet unfolded, but felt to be there. Metaphor and analogy at the level of pattern – of pure form and process – precede and beget propositional thinking. Action in all its human range and variety delivers its skills on the basis of the mastery of experience that language and thought bestow.

As one mode emerges out of another below it, so the lower modes nourish and support the higher. Imagination that is grounded in a developed life of feeling is thereby enriched. Thinking that crops out of wide-ranging imaginative vision is empowered. Action fed by wise discrimination is fruitful.

Each mode is a reduced and relatively autonomous precipitate of its generating ground. The imaginal domain contracts the omnipresence of the affective domain and can become relatively dissociated from it: the world we feel is deeper and wider than the world we perceive, and our percepts can separate off from that felt world. The conceptual domain is an exudate of the imaginal: language is a contracted set of imaginal symbols intuited to mean all kinds of relatively autonomous notions. All action presupposes the belief systems of the conceptual mode, but is not bound by them and can make forays beyond their immediate reach. And action, as activism, can draw all the other individuating modes around it into the separated ego, which functions in dissociation from the participative modes (see Chapter 4).

The up-hierarchy metaphor points to what is going on in the psyche all the time, even if this is in a tacit, distorted and unacknowledged form because of blocks and deformations. In its unimpeded form it portrays a dynamic programme for the continuous functioning of the psyche in an integrated person. In later chapters I shall look at its fruitful implications for methodology in living, inquiry and learning.

Other functional polarities

There are at least three secondary polarities which can be regarded as offshoots of the individuating-participative polarity, each one relevant to a particular mode, although still active in all the others. In each case the poles do not exclude each other; rather the two functions interact along a continuum in which one is most dominant at one end, and the other at the other end.

Focal–global

Here the psyche is attending either to some particular figure in some given field, or to the ground or context in which it is embedded. Thus in the imaginal mode of imagery, one may focus mainly on the house in the middle of the valley, or globally take in the valley as a whole with little attention paid to the house. In the middle of this continuum, of course, the mind is attending to both figure and ground, both house and valley. This is a part–whole, figure–ground, point–plane polarity.

Subjective–objective

When functioning subjectively the psyche is attending to its own processes, and when manifesting objectively it is relating to the content of its presenting world. Hence in the conceptual mode of reflection, there is the contrast between thinking about the state of one's psyche, and thinking about the state of the world. All this, as we shall see, is very much an artefact of the use of language. Ambivertive reflection is at the mid-point, where one thinks about both one's psyche and the world in an integrated way.

This subjective–objective polarity is the original home of Jung's two modes of relating to the world, introversion and extraversion. The former, he says, 'sets the self . . . above the object', the latter 'sets the subject below the object'; and 'every human being possesses both mechanisms as an expression of his natural life-rhythm' (Jung, 1977). Jung's feel for the dialectical interplay of these poles was lost by subsequent conventional research, which kept on looking for a single introversion/extraversion dimension, which, of course, it never found (Carrigan, 1960).

Projective–receptive

Here the psyche is putting out its own energy and direction when projective, and being open to what is present and what emerges when being receptive. Thus in the practical mode of action, we get the difference between taking an initiative and following someone else's. At the mid-point, in co-operative practice, each person blends leading and following.

Modes and polarities

I suggested in the previous section that these three secondary polarities can be regarded as offshoots of the primary, each one

Table 2.3 *Resonance between modes and polarities*

Psychological modes	Functional polarities
Practical	Projective–receptive
Conceptual	Subjective–objective
Imaginal	Focal–global
Affective	Individuating–participative

relevant to a particular mode, although still influencing all the others. So another way of considering all four functional polarities, the one primary and the three secondary, is to see each of them as being particularly at home in one of the four modes, as shown in Table 2.3.

Individuating–participative

Feeling, as I define it in this psychology, is the participative mode *par excellence*. Through feeling I indwell the world, participate in its being, resonate with how it is. I perceive a cat in terms of visual, auditory and tactile imagery. When I feel it, I participate in its unique presence through the immaterial qualities – inscrutability, poise, containment and grace – that pervade its perceptual imagery. And while thus identifying with its presence, I am at the same time aware of my own distinctness, individuated by an emotional state that correlates with my participative experience.[9] This participatory feeling and individuating emotion is the hallmark of the affective mode.

Feeling is the ground of emotion. By our felt participation in a situation we appraise it as fulfilling or frustrating our present need and this engenders our emotional state. In this general sense, emotion arises from a felt apprehension of one's context; although in egoic states feeling is virtually subliminal as we preoccupy ourselves with emoting. But there is a more radical grounding of emotion in feeling. For we can regard the capacity for feeling as a need to exercise it, that is, as a need to participate in our world. And the fulfilment of this need gives rise to our most basic individuating emotion of all, delight or joy. This is the creative paradox at the heart of feeling. Feeling participation in the world individuates us with delight.

The need to individuate when consummated in action, gives rise to the emotion of zest, the exhilaration of achievement. But the heart and core of individuation is found in the emotion of delight or bliss, when the need to participate is consciously fulfilled, for here the polar tendencies are most intimately independent.

In some situations, the feeling process will be inclusive. You may empathize so fully with another that your participation in their reality and way of being in the world is the ground experience, and your emotional state of sympathy is embraced within that. At other times, the emotional state may be exclusive: you may be so annoyed about the cattle from a neighbouring field that have trampled down your garden fence, that this blots out the felt resonance with the scene that enabled you to notice the invasion.

In general it seems to be the case that heightened experiences of felt participation and resonance include awareness of the individuating emotional states that correlate with them; whereas heightened experiences of agitated and distress emotion, especially, tend to obscure or push into unconsciousness the states of felt resonance that are their necessary ground.

It is also important, I believe, not to confuse emotional states with separatist states of personal being; and in general not to confuse the individuating tendency as such with tendencies to egoic alienation. Emotional and individuating states of the psyche *can* become highly egoic and separatist, especially in early stages of personal unfoldment, but this is because they get activated at the expense of conscious participatory development. They are not inherently so, and when grounded in participatory states, they manifest the inalienable distinctness of the person who is unitive within a much wider whole.

Thus you may be in an extravertive mystical state, feeling at one with a whole field of manifest creation, with your emotional state one of ecstatic bliss. The bliss is distinctive bliss, entirely free of separation: it is your ecstatic note amid the orchestrated Many with which you are at One.

Emotion is the primary, basic locus of human individuation. Emotional fulfilment grounds the person in their own distinct being.[10] This being may get enveloped in thick coats of distress and egoic alienation, but sooner or later, I believe, true individuation emerges from the cocoon through the emotions of self-esteem and the delight of loving, emerging in the context of participative feeling in the world.

Focal–global

The focal–global, figure–ground polarity is particularly at home in the imaginal mode. All imagery has a basic figure–ground format in our minds: we focus on one part of the imaginal field, the rest of the images becoming the ground to the part we focus on.[11] And there is a deeper sense in which this polarity applies. For imagery and intuition themselves stand, respectively, as figure to ground: the imagery as whole is the figure in this second and deeper sense, and intuition provides its ground of signification and meaning.

Thus in a dream we may have an immediate intuition about the signification of the dream imagery, about where and what and who and why, even if these details are not clearly evident in the imagery itself; and later we may have an intuition about the meaning of the dream as a portrait of a process going on in the psyche.

The imagery of perception, behind the screen of the concepts affixed to it that come with language, is perhaps figure to a deep ground, the gnostic intuition of its source in archetypal reality (archetypal in the Platonic and Plotinian sense not the Jungian). To this arcane theory, I return in later chapters.

More superficially, perceptual imagery is a figure to an everyday ground of intuited meaning: the common or garden intuition of the conceptual framework, born of language, that identifies percepts as houses, trees, and every other kind of thing.

The ground of memory imagery is often the intuition of the significance the remembered experiences had for me at the time. Or it may be a deeper insight into the connection between past experience and present reality.

Subjective–objective

The subjective–objective polarity has its natural home in the conceptual mode, the domain of thought and language. When the psyche subsumes the imagery of perception under the concepts that come with language – seeing things as things of this, that or the other named kind – then we get a bifurcation of the world into a subject making a discriminatory judgement about an object. The person tends to get set over against the world, and we reify, hypostatize our perceptual images, seeing them as outside us. We become alienated from our continuous generation of them. It is as if they are coming at us, rather than we are producing them.

This subject–object split is very much a by-product of the use of language and the conceptual power it bestows. Conceptualizing perception, which is what we do all the time once we have a language, disrupts its transactional, participatory nature. The concept drives a wedge between the psyche and its world, breaking up the original synthesis of perceiver and perceived.

Concepts give much independent scope to the human psyche. They are represented by the arbitrary spoken sounds and written signs of language. They are not in bondage either to percepts or to their originating archetypes. They can be shaped into innumerable belief systems, each of which may refract a different aspect of human experience of the world. But the kind of world they talk about, a world of separate subjects doing business with separate objects, is an artefact of the talk itself.

The subjective–objective polarity is evident not only in the psyche–world relation, but is reflected within the conceptual mode itself, in the polar distinction between discrimination and reflection. Discrimination, which is the conceptual element in perception that classifies percepts in terms of the distinctions that come with language, is the process that tends to set up the notion and the experience of separate subjectivity. The conceptualization of percepts detaches the psyche from them, obscuring its role in generating them, and turns the mind into a disconnected centre for noticing what is going on. Reflection, on the other hand, which thinks in earnest about the world, formulating theories and laws about things, tends to reinforce the notion of the world as object, as other, as over against the subject.

The challenge of what I call post-linguistic perception, thought and knowledge is to cultivate a syncretistic set of categories that enables us both to perceive the world unitively, rather than in terms of a noxious dualism, and to talk about it through the use of effective unitive discourse. For what I call the world of presence, that is, the world-view parented primarily by the affective and imaginal modes, is one in which the psyche awarely participates in generating the imagery of perception. The psyche feels at one with a perceptual field which has no separative enclosures, and in which all the while subject and object are distinct yet non-separable within a unified field.[12] So described, this is a transpersonal or adult not a prepersonal or childhood state. These issues are discussed in later chapters.

Projective–receptive

This polarity has its home in the practical mode. The exercise of the will is always moving to and fro between the poles of the imparting will and the receiving will, between giving and taking, talking and listening, exercising and resting, leading and following, being creative and appreciating the expression of others, in short, between projecting energy and information out and receiving energy and information in.

As mentioned in connection with Table 2.1, the practical mode as a whole inclines more to the individuating pole. So there is another dynamic which suggests that the participatory pole is most evident in the affective mode and successively less so as you move through its secondary derivatives – the global, objective and receptive poles; and that the individuating pole, while it originates in and has its primary home in the affective mode, becomes more accentuated as you progress through its secondary derivatives – the focal, the subjective and the projective poles.

Ground process and reorganization

There are, I believe, two more basic polarities within the psyche as well as the individuating and participatory functions. One of these is what I call ground process and reorganization. Ground process is the psyche's basic way of being, and one symbol I use for this is the up-hierarchy of the modes. Such process is its given state, its inherent way of interrelating its modes. It also has the capacity for reorganization, that is, for rearranging its basic process, for assuming different forms of relation between the modes. This is for purposes either of psychological survival, or of learning and growth.

This is a bit more basic than the systems theory concept of the polarity of self-maintenance and self-transformation within any organism (Jantsch, 1980). That model puts adaptive survival under maintenance, and only new development and learning under transformation; whereas I am separating out ground process on the one hand from all forms of reorganization on the other.

There is some overlap between my view and Douglas Fawcett's philosophy of divine imagining, which sees two primary imaginal powers in the scheme of things: one is conservative, providing the enduring bedrock of form and structure; the other is innovative, an additive creative dynamic interweaving with the conservative (Fawcett, 1921, 1931, 1939). My ground process is like his conservative dynamic, but by reorganization I refer to a capacity that is not only innovative or additive, since it may also be regressive and detractive; it is a more general principle.

In order to characterize the modes in terms of this second polarity of process and reorganization, I shall introduce the metaphor of the cycle and represent process by a basic cycle and reorganization by a reversal cycle.

The modes as a basic cycle

We can translate the up-hierarchy metaphor of the modes into another one, that of a cyclic process, and see the psyche as involved in a flow of its life through the four modes in a continuous rhythmic pulse. This pulse is the heartbeat of inner need, its rise and fall, consummation and cadence, as it moves round the cycle. Derived from the up-hierarchy and its ground in affect, such a cycle starts from the affective mode, and proceeds through the imaginal, the conceptual and the practical to return to the affective, and so on. This cycle, in this sequence, I call the basic cycle. Together with the up-hierarchy it characterizes the ground process of the psyche.

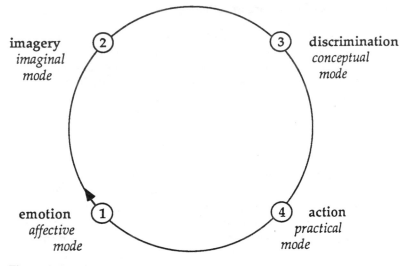

Figure 2.3   *The basic cycle*

Let's have a look at a basic cycle of individuation – the cycle that maintains a certain level of egoic being and behaving. So it will involve the four individuating functions of emotion, imagery (including perception and memory), discrimination and action, in that order; the participatory functions are minimally or tacitly involved. Emotion, the starting point of the cycle, I have defined in terms of fulfilled or frustrated need. This cycle is shown in Figure 2.3.

To give an example, the basic cycle is grounded in the emotional need for more fulfilment or less frustration – say a need for outdoor activity. This gives rise to an image or selective perception of what will meet the need – an image of gardening; and discrimination is exercised in relation to this image or percept – looking round the garden to see what action to take to reach fulfilment or avoid frustration. Then the cycle starts again with the next emergent need.[13]

The basic cycle is grounded in the overall emotional pattern that the person has acquired in their development and starts from some immediate, active component of it. This conservative egoic pattern is a systematic way of being fulfilled or frustrated in life. The emotional need felt now is an index of how the pattern seeks to influence behaviour in order to maintain itself. And the influence is first exerted through an image or selected percept. Once this image is launched the cycle is well under way: discrimination and action are simply means to the envisaged goal.

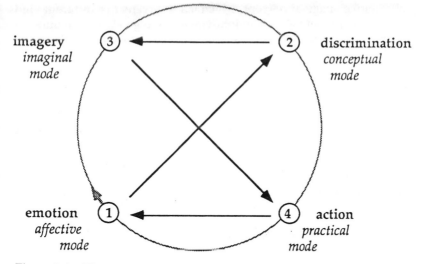

Figure 2.4 *The reversal cycle*

The modes as a reversal cycle

I proposed earlier a basic polarity of ground process in the psyche and a capacity for reorganization. Now there may be many ways in which the psyche can reorganize itself, but in this book I shall focus on just one of them, which I represent by what I call a reversal cycle. This reverses the central sequence of the basic cycle: it goes from the affective to the conceptual, to the imaginal to the practical; instead of from the affective to the imaginal, to the conceptual, to the practical. I think this reversal cycle is mainly used to change the content of the basic cycle, its range and degree of adaptation and establish it at a new level of functioning. It's a learning cycle.

The reversal cycle goes against the grain of the basic cycle. It is 'unnatural', revisionary, a reversal of the established, conservative scheme of things. It interrupts the ground process of the psyche, so it requires alert inward discrimination and motivation to get it launched. I can give no deep rationale about the form of the reversal cycle; it just seems to fit what goes on.

Let's consider again only the individuating modes of emotion, imagery, discrimination and action. The task of the reversal cycle, Figure 2.4, is to interrupt the first leg of the basic cycle (which moves promptly from emotion to imagery) and go instead from emotion to discrimination. As soon as the current emotional need arises, the person discriminates its nature and its propensity to generate a certain kind of image, and replaces this with an alternative image or percept, which leads directly to a different kind of action and outcome. The innovative cycle goes from emotion to discrimination to imagery to action, instead of the normal route from emotion to imagery to discrimination to action. Figure 2.4 shows the reversal cycle in arrows and the old basic cycle as a faint circle.

The reversal cycle will keep going until there is a shift in the underlying emotional pattern and its associated imagery, so that the basic cycle is re-established at a different level and in different terms.

Take an example of everyday change of external behaviour and its immediate process. Emotional deprivation (1) is about to launch the image of smoking a cigarette. But this image propensity doesn't get off the ground, because the aware person spots it (2), substitutes the image (3) of having a warm hug, and follows this through into action (4), and reaps its emotional rewards (1), which are noted (2) to sustain the substitute image (3), and so on. This way there is the possibility of establishing, eventually, a new kind of basic cycle, in which emotional deprivation generates the image of real rather than substitute fulfilment, followed by discrimination and action to obtain the real fulfilment, going round the cycle as in Figure 2.3.[14]

I shall have more to say about both basic cycles and reversal cycles applied to living and learning, from Chapter 11 onwards.

Life and mind

I have considered so far two basic polarities in the psyche, individuation and participation, ground process and reorganization. The third and final one in my theory is the complementarity of life and mind, which I will set out in some simple postulates. The psyche, the actual and potential person, is alive, but not simply because it is involved with a living organism. Its life is inherent: this psychic life interacts with the living organism, but cannot be reduced to it. The psyche has its own capacity for being a centre of life. Feeling, imagination, reflection and action live.

Complementary to the psyche's life is its mind, by which I mean its capacity to learn and grow. I define the human mind as the capacity of the psychological modes to acquire new awareness, knowledge and skills. The psyche, therefore, exists according to this theory in terms of a dynamic interplay of life and mind. It can have much living with little learning, and much learning with little living. It can fill living with learning, or enrich learning with living. The distinction between psychic life and psychic mind allows us to say, to give but one example, that someone can be vitally thinking but not really learning anything. So while life and mind always go together, there can be a lot of one and very little of the other.[15]

Some theorists, such as Bateson and Capra, have wanted to identify mind with life and both with 'the dynamics of self-organization' in physical systems (Capra, 1983: 315). This is problematic. It makes it impossible to separate out innovative learning from simple survival, without bringing a prior and independent knowledge of this distinction to your study of physical systems. And you can only read mind into matter because you already know what mind is as a precondition of being able to 'read' matter at all. Nor can you identify my ground process and reorganization on the one hand with, respectively, life and mind on the other, since either of the former two can manifest either of the latter two.

I take the metaphysical view that the psyche, personhood, is basically immaterial, whatever bodily vehicles or sheaths manifest and express it. A person is a presence *in* the world, not *of* it; and has immaterial qualities of individuation and participation, of ground process and reorganization, of life and mind. All these polarities are relatively independent of each other, so their terms can combine in all sorts of combinations. Figure 2.5 shows the four modes, individuating and participatory (dot and circle), with the basic cycle and the reversal cycle, and the interdependence of life and mind.

The psyche in relation: the power of feeling

Up to this point the psyche has been presented as an entity with four modes, which are informed by three basic polarities, and which can be construed as both an up-hierarchy and a cycle. I wish now to consider more deeply the role of feeling in its life.

I have defined feeling as resonance with being and other beings and construed it as the grounding level of the psyche. The psyche as feeling *is* its attunement to what there is. It is defined by a distinctive capacity for being engaged with the world. On a systems theory view of the world as one vast interconnected web of dynamic events made of up rhythmic patterns, the psyche too is defined in terms of its relations with other events. What does this mean in more detail?

One thing to suggest is that in deeply unconscious states the psyche through its capacity for feeling interacts with all beings. And one way of maintaining this is in terms of some kind of psychophysical feeling. This is what Whitehead tries to do with his notion of prehension, which I discuss in Chapter 5. He holds that all material events, however basic, are psychophysical and take account of each other in a rudimentary psychophysical way: they

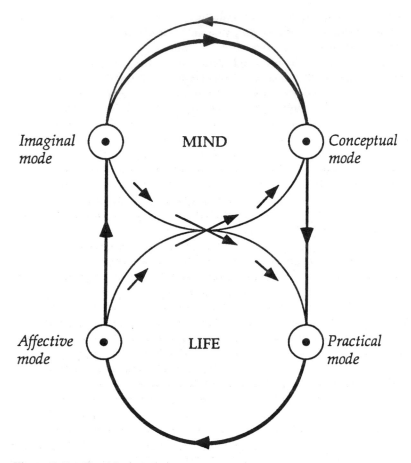

Figure 2.5   *The four modes and three polarities*

'prehend' each other's emotional tone. Since the body is a set of material events interacting with all others, the person, as it were, sits on a great subconscious primitive prehension of everything.

Now it may be there is some kind of psychoid life involved in the atom, indeed some hierarchy of psychic prehension rising through the increasing complexities of inorganic and organic forms, as Fechner and Fawcett and others have believed (Fawcett, 1939). If there is, then feeling responsively interpenetrates all this and is not to be identified with it. My contention is that feeling is a highly refined capacity of consciousness which cannot be reduced to anything other than itself. It is a psychological *primum mobile*. It is a concept in transpersonal psychology, a subtle and universal form of consciousness that is embedded as a potential in the human psyche, and is actualized progressively through various stages of development.

Feeling is One–Many awareness, and while our egoic states may strip it of bliss, and screen it from view, it is always at work below the threshold, making available to us the differentiated field of the everyday mind. It will also reveal itself within that field, to a greater or lesser degree, whenever we allow it to do so. This is the basic premise of this book. One can argue for it up to a point, by presenting a whole web of coherent ideas which are based upon it and which illumine experience. One can provide practical injunctions, simple exercises, which offer an opportunity, it is claimed, to ground the idea in experiential knowledge. One can look for coherence with the ideas and experiences of others. And that's it; or rather it can just declare itself to you.

Feeling as an unfolding potential appears in many guises. One of its most accessible appearances is in an interpersonal field with other people. Consider two people standing, holding hands and gazing into each other's eyes. If they relax, stop talking and gradually let go of emotional agitations, tensions and embarrassments, then they enter the domain of feeling, pure and simple. What such feeling yields is one relation with two terms, one togetherness embracing two people, one meeting comprising an I and a Thou. The unity includes the distinct identities. The reality is in the unifying relation between differential particulars. This is the special power of feeling: it lives and breathes and moves in such a reality.[16]

If you enter this simple experience two things are noticeable. The first is that the feeling of togetherness is mutual, intense, present and gently ineffable. This is primary accessible evidence that feeling is *sui generis*, it does its own thing immediately and directly; it is not a function of anything else or a product of anything else. The second thing is that it also seems to be inclusive of the mutual touching, gazing and physical proximity. And this is *prima facie* evidence that it grounds, upholds and interpenetrates all the other psychological modes. In this instance it interpenetrates tactile and visual perception, and that bodily radar that knows another body is near. And in interpenetrating them it reveals as much of itself as is appropriate to the situation and the kinds and modes of being involved in it.

If two people who are participating through feeling in this experience start to talk, then they may well talk themselves out of the ineffability of the pure feeling state. And if they start to do things together – go for a walk, share a meal, engage in some shared task – this too may dissociate them even further from that state. The

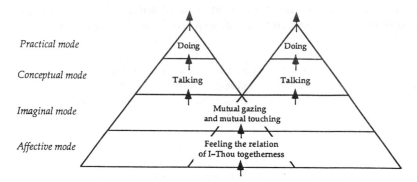

Figure 2.6   *The modes in interpersonal relationship*

more they exercise differential individuation, the greater the tendency to drift away from participatory feeling. We can symbolize this somewhat as in Figure 2.6.

Of course, the drift away from participatory feeling is not inevitable. The field of togetherness can be sustained whatever the two people are doing, in association or apart. But in the ordinary relatively unprogressed life of interpersonal relationship, when people are significantly egoic as described in Chapter 4, the psyche has only a reduced and episodic capacity for participation, and for deeply integrating it with individuation.

So in the normal course of events there is a phasic movement between times of togetherness, times of separate activity and intermediate times of shared talk and action – co-operative occasions which oscillate in and out of participatory and individuated states. Sometimes these polar states are elegantly integrated in depth: luminous conversation, engagement through music, art and ritual provide some of those moments when this kind of deep integration can occur. Hence Buber called I–Thou relating 'dialogic knowing' (Buber, 1937).[17]

The point about feeling as interpenetrative is that, as an active principle of ordinary awareness, it can drop out of the structures – such as gazing and touching – in which it was active, and become passive in them, doing its normal job of upholding all differentiation from unconscious levels. Then the structures become a trap for the psyche, which is void of any principle and experience of true relating. I–Thou becomes more like It–It. Remember, structures higher in the up-hierarchy have a relative autonomy with regard to, and can become dissociated from, the lower ones in which they are grounded.

Another way of saying all this is that full participative unity is interdependent with a full distinctness (not separateness) of individuation. For most of us this is some way down the road. Meanwhile we keep on the move by oscillating in and out of, and by combining, relatively unripe versions of each. Feeling will become active in surface consciousness to whatever degree the egoic structures of the occasion allow. Otherwise it is passive and subliminal so far as the outer mind is concerned, only doing its thing at or below the threshold of human consciousness.

Martin Buber threw a spotlight on the I–Thou relation in a way which caused a great stir at the time. The first English edition of *I and Thou* was published in Edinburgh in 1937, although the original *Ich und Du* appeared in Leipzig in 1923. Karl Heim said that Buber's distinction between the I–Thou and the I–It relationship is one of the decisive discoveries of our time, a Copernican revolution in our way of thinking; and that it must lead to a second new beginning of European thought, pointing beyond the Cartesian contribution to modern philosophy.

Well, there have been one or two more 'Copernican revolutions' since then, but he has a point. What Buber brought out were three things: (1) The personal, distinct I and Thou only exist in their fullness in direct, open, mutual relation. (2) Reality, presentness, wholeness exist only in so far as this relation of meeting exists – he thus stresses the primacy of relation for attuning to the real. (3) I–It knowledge conceptualizes things, separates subject from object, is for our convenience and use and is always a means never an end, and is derived from and depends on the prior reality of the I–Thou relation.

For Buber, immersed in the Hasidic mystical tradition, there was a theological dimension to all this. God is the eternal Thou encountered in everyday life and within the soul: 'Every particular Thou is a glimpse through to the eternal Thou' (Buber, 1937). What he is saying is that in 'the genuinely reciprocal meeting in the fullness of life between one active existence and another' there is a readily available, everyday paradigm case of divine knowing, and that in such knowing the distinctness of beings is a function of the inclusive relations between them.

He also says that the I-self can slip into seeing itself as an It-self, a separated subject cut off from objects and other separated subjects, but that is not what it really is.[18] In this he provides a great antidote to the Buddhist vogue for supposing there is only an It-self and nowhere an I-self. It follows from the Buddhist view that once you have dismantled the It-self you become divine (although, of course, there is no 'you' that can do the becoming). Buber's view engages with a deeper paradox: the I-self can discover its oneness with God through divine encounter, and at the same time relate to God through its distinctness of being.

The power of feeling is evident in relationship not only with other persons but also with rocks, trees, animals and the rest of nature. When the alienating screen of language is transcended, then through feeling we participate in a world of presences, each with its distinctive signature, its utterance, its way of declaring being. I mention this above (p. 23) and again in Chapters 5 and 8. Martin Buber also believed in this kind of relationship with nature, although he met a lot of critical resistance (Friedman, 1954).

Personhood, person and ego

I take the position that a person is a fundamental spiritual reality, a distinct presence in the world. Personhood is the capacity for feeling, as I define it, conceived as a formative potential, an entelechy out of which all the psychological modes and stages of development emerge. The person is progressively actualized through different states, some of which can run concurrently, and I discuss these states in detail in Chapter 3. Being a person is an achievement, it is acquired through a process of learning how to live more fully and awarely. It means conscious use of the four modes, integrating their individuating with their participatory forms. Nevertheless I call all states the states of a person, simply to honour the fact that, whether in potentiality or actuality, it is the deep reality of personhood that we are dealing with.

I make a distinction between the person and the ego. This is much the same as the personalists used to make between the person and the individual. Mounier wrote that the individual is the purely egocentric man, 'the dissolution of the person in matter'. Maritain saw individuality as 'that which excludes from oneself all other men', 'the narrowness of the ego, forever threatened and forever eager to grasp for itself' (Coplestone, 1973).

In Chapter 4, I portray the ego as an alienated part of the psyche that is over-identified with the individuating modes at the expense of the participative; that is the victim of the subject–object split that comes with the use of language; that suffers from the repression and denial of the wounded child; and that is body-bound as a defence against widespread anxieties that arise from radical tensions within the human condition.

The person and the ego are not mutually exclusive at any given stage of development. An ego, I believe, rarely attains total defensive closure. An open ego is not only one in which spontaneous episodes of conscious participation occur, but also one which at a later stage is learning to create apertures between it and the deeper reaches of consciousness. So during a given phase of unfoldment one can sometimes be a person, integrating participatory and individuating modes, and at other times be ego-bound within the individuating modes.[19] All this is described in more detail in Chapter 4.

The actualized person, then, is distinguished by integrating the individuating modes of the psyche with the participative, first in the humanistic sphere and then extending into the subtle and spiritual dimensions, as I explain in the next chapter. The most basic part of all this is that the person is grounded in their capacity for feeling, their ability to enter, as distinct beings, into participative states of union with other entities and with being as such. Indeed, I would go so far as to make the unlimited capacity for participative feeling, as I define it, that which primarily differentiates the person from egos and animals and all other species of non-person.

This is a significant departure from previous accounts. The original and classical definition of a person was given by Boethius in the sixth century AD as 'an individual substance of rational nature'. This was adopted by Aquinas, who spoke of the person as a human substance consisting of a rational soul and a body. Descartes emphasized the self-consciousness of a spiritual substance whose essence is to think. And thereafter idealist philosophers regarded self-consciousness as the chief characteristic of personality. Thus for Hegel, the progress of mind or spirit consists mainly in an advance of self-consciousness.

By contrast, modern personalists, together with the existentialists, put the emphasis on freedom, and on personality as created by the exercise of freedom. For the first time, personality becomes something to be won and maintained. One can become a person, and also one can cease to be a person and relapse into being a mere individual. This focus on freedom is shared by Kierkegaard, Sartre, Marcel, Mounier and his circle, Jaspers, Berdyaev and others. For some, like Sartre, freedom was purely secular, for others, like Marcel, it meant openness to a spiritual relation with other persons and with God (Marcel was much influenced by Buber). Maritain defines personality, rather obscurely, as 'the subsistence of the spiritual soul communicated to the human composite' (Coplestone, 1973). It is characterized by giving oneself in love and freedom. For the English personalist, John MacMurray, the person is an agent, and is constituted by relations with other persons (MacMurray, 1957).

This series of defining criteria, from rationality to self-consciousness to freedom, no doubt reflects the sorts of issue that were at the forefront of social change at each different epoch. The foreground challenge today is the ability to feel at one with our world, including our planetary ecosystem, and this is the new defining criterion of the person I propose.[20]

Person or no person

Is personhood included in realized Wholeness, or is it an illusory prop that we use to help us attain enlightenment, but which is exposed for what it is and discarded when we get there? I have already said that I take the position that a person is a fundamental spiritual reality. I and Thou are not illusions rooted in spiritual ignorance. But I would like to discuss the matter a little further.

The question posed is sometimes represented as an East–West issue, as if in the West we have an inclination to believe in a spiritual monad, an individualized spirit, the spark of the divine in each of us, which is the integrating basis of our personal development; whereas in the East there is a belief in no more than an illusory ego, and when this is dissolved there is only universal Mind.

This is not correct. It is really only in Buddhism, with its doctrine of *anatta*, that the idea of a spiritual monad is rejected, and this in the most extreme and uncompromising way. For the Buddhist there is no permanent deep centre of personhood, only a succession of transient mental states which produce the illusion of a self that connects them. Ken Wilber seems to espouse *anatta* doctrine (1990: 291), and I criticize his attempt to have a spectrum of consciousness without a spiritual monad, or guiding entelechy of personhood, in Chapter 10.

The Hindu view is different. The general trend of thought in the *Upanishads* is that the *atman*, the spiritual self, transcends the *jiva*, the soul or personality that migrates from one birth to another, by inclusion not by exclusion, hence the notion of the *jivatman*. As to the relation between *atman*, the spiritual monad, and *Brahman*, the Absolute, just about every kind of view has been held: they are completely different; they are completely identical; they are different in some respects and identical in others (Radhakrishnan and Raju, 1960).

What this last profusion of views seems to suggest, apart from confusion, is a search for a syncretistic category to define the relation between the spiritual monad and the divine, such as distinctness-in-union. This, at any rate, is the category of description I use to talk about the consummation of personhood in divine reality. And I shall repeatedly reinforce the point that distinctness of being is quite different from separateness of being. Here is Lawrence Hyde on this very issue, and the problem it raises for Buddhism:

> The significance of the monad lies precisely in the fact that it is the expression of *spiritual* differentiation. It is a manifestation, not of separation, but of distinctness – a very different matter. There is no question here of an egotistic centre of consciousness seeking to maintain itself in separation from the rest of the universe. What we are concerned with, on the contrary, is an entity that exercises a function in selection from and projecting into its environment that which expresses its character as an aspect or reflection of the Absolute. We must think of it as a jewel that for the glory of God shines with an ever brighter and more individualized lustre. Buddhist thought, however, would seem to make no adequate provision for such a factor in the cosmic equation. In other words, *it fails to distinguish between differentiation as the outcome of egotism and differentiation as a mode of divine manifestation.*[21] And as a result it is unable to throw any revealing light upon the nature of personality. (Hyde, 1954: 122)

The debate between *anatta* people and monad people can, of course, become more tendentious. The *anatta* people can say that the monad people can't handle the death of the separate self, so are busy setting up a subtle spiritual version of that self. The monad people can say that the *anatta* people can't handle a personal relationship with the divine, so are busy denying any real person that can do the relating. However, both points commit the genetic fallacy of supposing that you can invalidate an argument if you can show that a person has unworthy motives for advancing it. So we just have to look carefully at the mystical logic of the different assertions.

Is Reality both One and Many? If it is Many as well as One, is this an unreal, illusory many, with people overcoming the illusion of being a self, proceeding toward reabsorption in the absolute One? Or is it a real Many, a genuine Multiplicity within Mind, with people emerging through the progressive differentiation of real personhood from germinal to transfigured states? I take this latter view, and explore it throughout this book and more technically in Chapters 9 and 10.

The modes as a developmental spiral

A third metaphor I use in unfolding this theory of the person, after the up-hierarchy and the cycle, is that of a spiral of development for the emerging and growing human being. The spiral may be

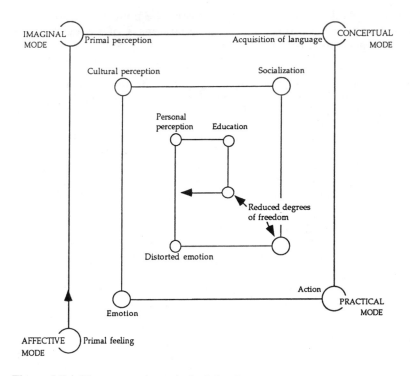

Figure 2.7   *The contracting spiral of development*

contracting or expanding. In either case, the four psychological modes represent nodal points in the turning of the line of life. Thus in a contracting spiral, development is progressively restricted by what occurs at the nodes. This is shown in Figure 2.7.

Round one of the contracting spiral: the outermost
A person is born (bottom left of Figure 2.7) immersed in being. In terms of feeling as defined in this work, there is a felt oneness, a primal fusion, in which the infant does not differentiate between self and context, between body and environment. In terms of emotion as defined here, the child experiences intensely the satisfaction or frustration of needs focused on its various orifices.

There is great openness to the imaginal power of mind, by means of which it generates primal perception of the world (top left), prior to the acquisition of language. We don't know what primal perception is like, since it is screened off from us by cultural and personal perception (see pp. 41–2), but it may well be multi-dimensional, intuiting interpenetrating levels of being. If so, these levels may be known as a seamless intermingling with relatively little differentiation between their different sorts of imagery, or between these and the perceiving self.

Such low differential, unified perception is prepersonal not transpersonal. Transpersonal awareness is of particular beings as well as unitive being; and it is interdependent with an individuated distinctness of personhood that emerges through later development.

The child's imaginal power readily intuits the pre-verbal forms of language so that it can quickly learn its mother tongue (top right). Conceptually, this means that the child who has learnt a language can think in terms of classes, identify something as belonging to a class, and discriminate between one sort of thing and another. This is Piaget's pre-operational thinking (Flavell, 1963). It also means the start of the subject–object split in perception, one of the foundations of the restricted ego.

Conceptual mastery enables the child to become intentional, to defer immediate gratification for more inclusive purposes; and to become proficient in action and gain a wide range of practical skills (bottom right). But the limiting belief systems implicit in the social use of language start to tighten the range of options.

Round two of the spiral
While the primal fusion with the world has long been left behind, there is still some felt sense of the participative glow of the perceived field, as in Wordsworth's celebrated ode, 'Intimations of Immortality'. This is in the background of awareness, while in the foreground more individualized affect holds sway. For on the basis of language and action skills, the child can now experience, identify and express a wide range of emotion, to do with the fulfilment or frustration of its various enterprises. And here it is highly vulnerable to wounding and resultant defensive splitting, repression and denial; although, of course, that can also occur much earlier.

The imaginal power of the child's mind is still considerable. There is an abundant fantasy life and much imaginative play. Recent studies show in just how rich a multi-dimensional reality many children live – with invisible playmates, extrasensory perceptions, out of the body experiences and so on. The perceptual discrimination that comes with the use of language may bring these wider dimensions temporarily into focus. But not for long, since the subject–object split and the restrictive belief systems built into the social use of language impose a selective screen over primal perception, reducing it to cultural perception. Eventually, children see only what the prevailing culture has concepts for and finds acceptable.

While the accessibility of the imaginal power of the mind shrinks somewhat, it is still present enough to enable the child to soak up socialization – the tacit and explicit norms that dictate acceptable behaviour and preferences in society. It is also at this conceptual stage that the child can apply rules in his or her thinking, as in multiplication and division. This is Piaget's concrete operational thinking, still closely bound to perceptual experience; and Wilber's rule/role mind (Wilber, 1990).

Once socialized, the child undergoes a severe restriction on the available degrees of freedom with respect to its purposes and deeds. Its selection of forms of practice is dramatically curtailed. The ego born of language use rapidly becomes a socialized ego.

Round three of the spiral: the most contracted

Socialization and its reduced degrees of freedom cause systematic and unhealthy repression of normal distresses of grief, fear and anger, which turn into distorted emotion. The splitting and denial of the wounded child, which will have developed between conception and childhood, is now fully reinforcing the structures of the restricted ego with compulsions driven by repressed pain. Any prepersonal felt unity of and participation in the world retreats into the unconscious, only to reappear briefly in particular surface structures of consciousness that allow it.

Denied distress further restricts the accessibility of the imaginal power of the mind. Repression and its negative scripting contract cultural perception into personal perception, by which I mean idiosyncratic distress-limited ways of perceiving the world.

This process of the contracting spiral is sustained and reinforced by secondary education. This fosters the development of Piaget's formal operational thinking, in which a person can think in terms of possible and hypothetical relationships, but it does so by means of an alienating authoritarianism.

The imposed curriculum, the unilateral assessment, the lack of student autonomy in learning and exclusion of emotional awareness within secondary and higher education further reduce degrees of freedom for intention and action, as the student steps out into the wider world. The human potentials to be realized are now more circumscribed than ever. Only a fraction of the physical brain is being used to manifest them.

Of course, this whole account of the contracting spiral is in some respects a caricature, as well as being only a cursory, outline map. In particular it takes no account of the fact that some people lay hold of the educational process to develop their powers of reflection to the point at which they acquire some measure of creativity and autonomy. I discuss this point in the next chapter. Otherwise I think the caricature does what it should: it exaggerates real issues.

Contracting and expanding spirals

Pathology of contraction

The contracting spiral model is a metaphor for the limiting effect of current mainstream methods of child-raising, language acquisition, socialization and education. They are methods in which the imaginal power of the mind is unawarely put to negative use: it locks up, and is locked up in, restricted, egoic ways of psychological functioning.

It is the surface structures of the psyche, the states being actualized within it, that are contracting in a way that progressively reduces its capacity to realize its vast potentials. Potentials that were at the edge of actualization in earlier years are repressed, and a host of further unactualized potentials either lie behind this repressive barrier or are simply ignored by virtue of the rigid attitudes and restricted beliefs the person has taken on board from the culture.

Prepersonal and transpersonal

In this account of a contracting spiral of development I am not saying that the psyche of the infant starts out in some sort of transpersonal, spiritual state, which is then eroded and lost until the psyche of the young adult has become a limited and limiting ego, alienated from deeper states of being. For a transpersonal state presupposes mature adulthood: it is a state that spiritually transfigures the awareness of the actualized person. At the same time I do not at all believe that the state of the human infant can be reduced entirely to one of ignorance, animal impulse and Freudian primary process.

Wilber (1990) argues strongly against what he calls the pre/trans fallacy, which elevates the infant's prepersonal state to a transpersonal one. I think he has an important point but he pushes it too hard, stripping the child down to a very minimal, Freudian and Piagetian, prepersonal condition. He gives too limiting an account of the presence of childhood.

In my view, the pre-linguistic and linguistic child up to the age of four or five has – to a greater or lesser degree depending on its history – the capacity for felt participation in its world, and for sensing the imaginal dynamic in perception, both of which yield a primitive unitive experience. It is primitive because it is low in the differentiation of self and other, and of all the distinct beings manifest as other. In terms of the polarity of life and mind which I introduced earlier in this chapter, the child's primitive unitive experience is rich in life but very low in mind.

Martin Buber is interesting on this subject. The child's primitive perception is in terms of only one category, 'the a priori of relation'. It is a relational event which contains its terms in a state of latency: the I is prior to its full self-consciousness, the Thou is 'simply suffered' as a 'total stirring image'. The child who sees the moon 'has in him only the dynamic, stirring image of the moon's effect, streaming through his body' (Buber, 1937). The point Buber is making is that the child has minimal individuation. And that the full depth of participative awareness – an I–Thou relation with persons or nature – is interdependent with a developed, transformed adult individuation. So childhood awareness is definitely prepersonal not transpersonal.

On the other hand, it foreshadows a possible later transpersonal state. And while the child's primitive unitive capacity is usually buried by the acquisition of language and the development of the ego, the fact that it is there at the start of life offers remarkable possibilities for a form of child-raising and education that builds on it rather than buries it.

There are exceptional transformative potentials in the infant and small child – who is incarnated 'trailing clouds of glory' (Words-worth's *Ode to Immortality*), and I think the key word here is 'trailing'. The psyche of the child is very close to the entelechy of its divine potentials. Some of these may vibrate across the borders of explicit and very simple mental structures. Thus a transcendental, unitive flush may surround the primal fusion of the neonate and its world; the extrasensory sweep of the imaginal mind may overflow into childish awareness and play. The work of Grof on perinatal matrices and on systems of condensed experience from early life show how the reliving of early events can have powerful trans-personal overtones (Grof, 1988). But these are *overtones*: for the grounding tone is one of prepersonal simplicity and low-differential unity.

All these potentials presage what can only be fully realized in the transpersonal states of the adult. Further, such potentials can surely be harnessed without being actualized through the practices of child-raising and education in the prepersonal phase, to create a person who, at the appropriate age and stage, is ripe for trans-personal work.

In this case, the potentials remain tacit, not articulated into conscious states, but are called upon from their subliminal resting place to function as an active entelechy, a dynamic formative potential of the person to be. They are evoked to generate a healthy, flexible, open-mesh person, whose egoic structures are porous, and who has within, in due course, the capacity to be self-transfiguring, at which time the potentials emerge into explicit transpersonal structures of consciousness.

Liberation of expansion

An expanding spiral metaphor is shown in Figure 2.8. Here the newborn is at A for affective mode in the centre of the spiral, which expands outward in clockwise mode. The processes of child-raising, language acquisition, socialization and education enhance, elaborate and liberate the affective, imaginal and practical powers of the person. The tacit, formative potential of the psyche is harnessed to generate a powerfully liberated person, who can relatively early in life move on to transpersonal stages.

Cultural perception unfolds primal perception; personal percep-

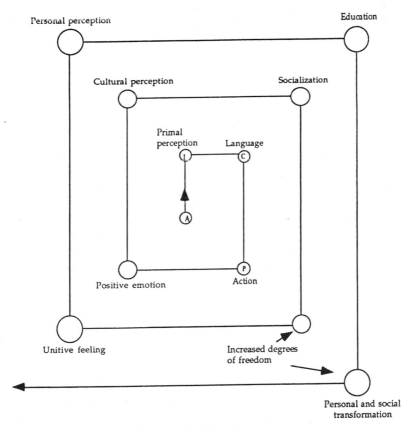

Figure 2.8   *The expanding spiral of development*

tion enriches cultural perception with new perspectives. The affect of childhood progresses relatively early in life into developed unitive feelings of participation in the differentiated network of being. Action expands into increasing degrees of personal and social creativity. What all this means in detail would entail writing a modern equivalent of Rousseau's *Emile*.

The metaphor of a spiral of development for the growing child points to the fact that in its first few years it emerges from a world of feeling and emotion to a world of intuition and perceptual imagery, from this to a world of language, thought and discrimination, and from this to a world of intentions and actions and increasing practical skills – each prior world being the continuing substrate of the one that emerges out of it; and thence round the circuit again in changing but related terms.

Of course, the metaphor is sketched out in relatively gross stages, as though one moves in large chunks of time from mode to mode. In reality there is a continuous cycling through the modes, with each mode always paired with the next one which has a subordinate role, as we shall see later on. What Figure 2.8 brings out clearly, however, are some of the major shifts that occur within the functioning of each mode, and in terms of the effect of one mode on the next, as development goes on.

Looking forward

The remainder of the book picks out certain aspects of my theory of the person from this long overview chapter and considers them in more depth. I have been selective, attending to some of the more basic notions, and by no means everything is covered. The next chapter looks at states of personhood, and rephrases the whole of the developmental process in terms of them. Chapter 4 gives a detailed account of my theory of the ego. Chapters 5 and 6 say much more about the affective mode of the psyche, looking, respectively, at feeling and emotion. Chapter 7 does the same for the imaginal mode.

Chapter 8 introduces a new metaphor of paired modes 'parenting' four distinct and interrelated world-views or 'worlds'. This widens the whole theory out to take account of different forms of knowledge and their interrelation. Chapter 9 considers the person in the context of a One–Many Reality. This ends the part of the book that deals with my theory of the person.

Chapter 10 is an intermediate part that offers a critical examination of the views of Jung, Kolb and Wilber. Chapters 11, 12, 13 and 14 apply the theory of the person to learning.

Exercises

1 Individuation and participation

With your partner take twenty minutes each. Relax into feeling fully present, and for the first half review *any* particular experiences that come to mind in which the individuating effect has been most marked, and for the second half review experiences in which participation has been predominant – whether to do with people, nature, art, ideas, imagery or consciousness. While these principles always interact, one pole is often more dominant than the other. After you have both taken a turn, share any thoughts about these two principles.

2 Emotion and feeling

Take it in turns to stand alone for several minutes in front of a good-sized mirror, with your partner giving attention nearby. As you look at your mirror image, participate and dwell fully in your total presence; notice the difference between feeling your presence in this way and your current emotional state. To intensify the difference, feel and imagine that the mirror-image you is feeling the presence of the you who is looking into the mirror. After you have both taken a turn, discuss your findings.

3 Imagery and intuition

Take turns with your partner to share a recent and well-remembered dream. In recalling the dream, notice how intuition gives a context of meaning in terms of the dream story, indicating what and where and who and how and why, when the imagery itself doesn't make this clear; notice too how it may give a context of symbolic meaning in terms of your current psychosocial dynamics. After both turns, discuss the relation between imagery and intuition in dreams.

4 Discrimination and reflection

Each take a similar but different item from the kitchen cupboard, such as a jar of honey and a pot of jam. Discriminate the appearance of your item, that is, classify and describe its main observable features and how these differentiate it from the other item; then reflect in general terms on the implications of your discrimination. After both turns, discuss discrimination and reflection. Do they exemplify, respectively, the individuating and the participatory principles?

5 Action and intention

Take it in turns to do the following: choose any single and simple action, such as pointing up into the sky, or reaching out in front of you with both arms, and while still doing it imagine and state two quite different intentions that could relate it to a wider social context. After both turns, discuss action and intention. Do they exemplify, respectively, the individuating and the participatory principles?

6   Integration of individuation and participation
Take twenty minutes each. First relax into feeling fully present, then review particular experiences, in whatever order they come to mind, in which you felt elegantly balanced between autonomy and distinctness of being on the one hand and enriching participation in some wider whole on the other. After both turns, discuss whether the shared experiences were mainly in the affective, imaginal, conceptual or practical modes, or in some combination of these.

7   Contemplation of the modal mandala
Each of you gaze at your own copy of the modal mandala, shown as Figure 2.1, for ten minutes while listening to Mozart's Violin Concerto no. 3 or no. 5 (or any other piece with similar formal properties). Let the music penetrate it and drench it. Let your mind drift over it without trying to decipher it beyond what is obviously intelligible. Take it in mainly as an imaginal form, and note what other images it evokes, what associations and free-floating connections you make to it. If you feel moved to do so, make a larger copy of it and colour the various areas without premeditation and in any way that feels right. Then share and discuss what occurred during the contemplation; and talk through the way you have coloured the mandala.

8   Meditation on the ground of the psyche
Take it in turn to guide each other through the following meditation. Play as background music Berlioz's *Harold in Italy*, or Pachelbel's *Canon in D*, and while the music is playing listen, with eyes closed, to your partner read *three times*, slowly and in sonorous tones, the paragraph to which this exercise is attached (except the first sentence). Let the sounds of the words drift through you with the music and *feel* their meaning in *your* universe, while the intellect remains entirely dormant and inactive. Meditate inside this feeling for five minutes. When you have both taken a turn, then share the felt meaning of the words.

9   Participation and distinctness of being
Obtain any good-sized, good-quality colour reproduction of a painting by Piero della Francesca. Resonate with it as a whole, feel

and participate in its immaterial qualities and its complete, unitive presence. Note that the more you enter this participative experience, the more distinct your own being becomes through your own emotional response. When you have both done this for some while, discuss your findings.

10 Formative experience
Take thirty minutes each. First relax into feeling fully present, then review, from early childhood onwards, strong experiences of emotional fulfilment which have been formative in your life, contributing to your sense of a positive identity. After both turns, discuss the role of positive emotion in creating a sense of personal identity.

11 Figure–ground experience
Take fifteen minutes each. Relax into feeling fully present, and divide your time into three equal parts. In the first part describe your immediate perceptual field, in the second part describe a recent event from memory and in the third part describe an imaginary city of the future. As you do so notice the continuously shifting figure–ground format of the imagery. After both turns discuss your experiences of this phenomenon.

12 Subject and object: separate or non-separable?
Each of you choose a different everyday household item. Take it in turns to do the following. Describe your item for three minutes in sentences each of which starts with the same phrase, such as 'That cup is . . .'; then pause and ask yourself aloud, then answer aloud, the question 'Am I separate from this object?' Now commune silently with the object for three minutes and feel the process of your body–mind being involved in generating the image of it; pause and ask yourself aloud, then answer aloud, the question 'Am I separate from this object?' After both turns compare and contrast the outcomes.

13 Basic cycles in everyday life
Read the referenced paragraph until you are clear about the cycle described. Then take ten minutes each to describe one or two sequences of everyday behaviour from today or yesterday in terms of this cycle. After both turns discuss how well the cycle does or does not match your experiences.

14 The use of a reversal cycle
Make a contract with your partner to use the cycle as described in the referenced paragraph, applying it for one day to some minor

habit you would like to change. After each of you has done this, meet and discuss your findings.

15   A week of life and mind
Take twenty minutes each. Relax into feeling fully present, then review the past week and ask yourself how much learning has fluctuated in and out of your living. After both turns, discuss whether the distinction between life and mind as made in the text is viable for you.

16   Two in one togetherness
Hold hands and gaze into each other's eyes, without speaking, and feel free to laugh to release any embarrassment. Let go of all emotional tension and relax deeply into feeling each other's presence through mutual gazing and touching. Expand into the single field of togetherness, its gentle, ineffable timeless unity. Notice how your own particularity is enhanced while at the same time being included in the single field. After some minutes, break the connection, share and discuss your findings.

17   Dialogic knowing
Take twenty minutes each. First relax into feeling fully present, then review experiences in your life, in whatever order they come to mind, in which you have been in a state of dialogic knowing with another person, that is, you have been highly and expressively individuated and at the same time you have felt deeply attuned with and at one with the other. After both turns, reflect together on the nature of this experience.

18   From I to It
Take ten minutes each. First relax into feeling fully present, then review any one or more particular occasions when a valued relationship slipped from an I–Thou state to a state in which both of you or one of you was an It-self. After both turns, discuss what seems to cause the shift.

19   Person and ego portraits
Consider the distinction made in these paragraphs between the person as a whole and the egocentric individual: then take some paper, with crayons or paints or coloured pens, and make one pictorial symbol that shows both your person and your ego. After you have both finished, describe your portrait to your partner and hear their comments on it.

20   Planetary feeling
Take ten minutes each to explore aloud how much you feel, on a
day-to-day basis, the presence of the planet, or nature, as a whole.
Consider what evokes this feeling. After both turns, discuss the idea
of feeling at one with the planet.

21   Differential differentiation
Tune in to this statement in italics then take it in turn to do the
following: give a non-verbal mime of 'differentiation as the outcome
of egotism' followed by a second non-verbal mime of 'differentiation as a mode of divine manifestation'. After both turns, explain
how your two mimes *felt* different, and hear impressions of them
from your partner.

3

States of Personhood

States of personhood

I take the position that a person is a fundamental spiritual reality, a distinct presence in the world. Person*hood* is the capacity for feeling, as I define it, conceived as a formative potential out of which all the psychological modes and stages of development emerge. The person is progressively actualized through different states, some of which can run concurrently, and I discuss these states in detail in this chapter.

Being a person is therefore an achievement of education and self-development, acquired through learning how to live more fully and awarely, integrating the individuating with the participatory forms of the psychological modes. It follows that many people, including children, are potential persons in a prepersonal state. However, I call all states the states of a person, to respect the deep reality of personhood.

Self-psychologists and others have been busy over the past few decades mapping out various stages of development. These have been Maslow's need hierarchy (Maslow, 1970), Loevinger's ego development stages (Loevinger, 1976), Kohlberg's moral sense stages (Kohlberg, 1981), and Torbert's ego development stages (Torbert, 1987). Then there is Wilber's map of the basic structures of consciousness, structures which emerge in stages, and upon which an ultimately illusory self-system climbs to spirit (Wilber, 1990). Just below I make some correlations where appropriate with these various systems, although there is sometimes only partial overlap with my concepts.

I must distinguish between stages of personhood and states of personhood. To talk of *stages* implies a temporal progression with one stage leading on to the next. I prefer to write of *states* of personhood, since this does not raise the issue of what order they occur in for any given individual. While some broad generalizations can be made about stages of development, which hold universally, people have a way of making some very idiosyncratic journeys toward self-realization.

Table 3.1 sketches out eight states of personhood: the minimal

Table 3.1 *Eight states of personhood*

Charismatic person	The psyche is a continuously transfigured, living presence
Self-transfiguring person	The psyche realizes its psychic and spiritual potentials
Self-creating person	The psyche is autonomous in healing and actualizing itself
Creative person	The psyche is autonomous in external behaviour
Conventional person	The socialized psyche adopts cultural roles and rules
Compulsive person	The wounded psyche has defensive splits and repressions
Spontaneous person	The uninhibited psyche expresses its innate impulses
Primal person	Primordial fusion of the psyche and its foetal world

sentence given for each state is elaborated later in this chapter. The table is to be read from the bottom upwards.

The approximate correlations with the different systems mentioned above are as follows. *Primal person*: pleroma (Wilber). *Spontaneous person*: safety (Maslow), impulsive (Loevinger), preconventional (Kohlberg), impulsive (Torbert), body self (Wilber). *Compulsive person*: opportunist (Torbert), shadow (Wilber). *Conventional person*: belongingness (Maslow), conformist (Loevinger), conventional (Kohlberg), diplomat (Torbert), membership self (Wilber). *Creative person*: self-esteem (Maslow), conscientious, individualistic (Loevinger), postconventional (Kohlberg), achiever (Torbert), mature ego (Wilber). *Self-creating person*: self-actualization (Maslow), autonomous, integrated (Loevinger), strategist (Torbert), bodymind self (Wilber). *Self-transfiguring person*: self-transcendence (Maslow), magician (Torbert), subtle level (Wilber). *Charismatic person*: ironist (Torbert), causal level (Wilber).

I must stress again that these are states of personhood, not one-by-one sequential stages. There is no linear progression from the state at the bottom of the table to the state at the top, in the sense that you move in and out of each in strict sequence from the lower to the higher. What you can say is that the bottom four occur, developmentally, before the top four. They comprise the loam, the ground, the humus out of which the top four grow. And within the bottom four, you can say that the primal person – the foetus – appears first, the spontaneous person – the playing child – appears later, and the conventional person, who has learnt the social roles and rules, later still. This is a reliable sequence, to do with basic maturational processes.

When the compulsive person takes root is totally idiosyncratic, depending on when the first unmanageable psychological wounding occurs, which may be before birth, at birth or some time after birth. But it occurs early in life and in our sort of emotionally repressive society it is safe to assume that everyone is wounded. Each of us harbours the compulsive person within our idiosyncratic brood of personhoods. Our educational system has simply not started to come to terms with the implications of this statement.

Before saying more about relations between the eight different states, in terms both of concurrence and non-linear progression, I will give a statement about each. Every statement is no more than a provisional construct. I shall, as I have said, call each state the state of the person, to honour the potentiality for personhood, but the first four of them are really prepersonal (see Table 3.2, p. 66).

The primal person

The primal person is in a pure state of potentiality in which the upper modes – conceptual and practical – are entirely latent, and the lower modes – affective and imaginal – manifest in primordial form as a felt fusion with the foetal world while sensing certain patterned distinctions within it. There is every evidence that the psyche of the primal person is quite extraordinarily vulnerable to trauma, during both pregnancy and the stages of birth (Lake, 1980; Janov, 1983; Grof, 1988).

There is also evidence that the psyche's undisturbed state of foetal fusion has strong transpersonal overtones – oceanic ecstasy, cosmic unity, visions of paradise (Grof, 1988). My own view is that these are indeed overtones, and that the grounding tone is altogether more primal and protoplasmic.[1]

The primal person, in terms of my theory, is spiritually embryonic, containing all the potentials of personhood that manifest in later states. Where does such a being come from? I believe it to be of divine origin, its source being via a descent, an involution, an embedding of the One as one of the embryonic Many.

The spontaneous person

The spontaneous person is the infant smiling, moving, looking, making noises, gesturing, crawling, crying, laughing, walking, playing and eventually talking. In the foreground of its awareness there is a free flow of wants and needs, interests and impulses, with a strong identification with bodily process. If a child is fixated at this natural stage of bodily identification through abuse or neglect, then it acquires a template for being body-bound, which is a basic component of the ego, as I describe in Chapter 4.

In the background the small child has a primitive unitive awareness: it has primal access to participative feeling and the imaginal dynamic in perception. This is underdeveloped and prepersonal since it has a minimally individuated centre, not much psyche–world distinction. It remotely foreshadows the fullness of transpersonal awareness that can be developed when a distinct and transformed person emerges through self-transfiguration, as discussed at the end of Chapter 2.

With language acquisition comes socialization and the formation of the separate ego, which starts to close in on the spontaneous child. But this is for many an open ego, which means the spontaneous child can intermittently emerge and exhibit *all* the modes, both individuating and participatory, in a relatively unfocused, rhythmic, playful, underdeveloped, limited and dreamlike kind of way.[2] Reflection particularly will be at the very early stage of discriminating classes of things and grasping simple rules.

Very powerful formative potentials for transpersonal development may 'trail' around the edges of the light, fluctuating, explicit mental structures of the spontaneous child. The child's mind can suddenly dip, as it were, into the remarkable potentials of its future wisdom and power. These are more like *undertones*: what can be picked up in ordinary consciousness from what is sounding beyond it.

The spontaneous child in its innocence is especially vulnerable to being severely wounded by traumatic oppression of its spontaneity. Its gently manifesting potential is open to every kind of verbal and physical misuse, abuse or neglect. Hence it may be edged off-stage by the appearance of the compulsive person.

The compulsive person

The compulsive person becomes established concurrently with the previous two, and becomes interwoven with the conventional person (described in the next section). The primal or spontaneous person is wounded by alien invasion and oppression, through foetal stress or birth trauma or childhood trauma, or some combination of these. The child's discovery of the individuating power of positive emotion can be treacherously handled by parents and adults, converting it into unbearable pain. To survive, the psyche splits off and represses the oppressed aspects of itself together with the distress at their oppression. (For an elaborate account of splitting, see Rowan, 1990). It erects a false self by identifying with the invading influence, with being a victim to it and with ineffective responses to its victimization – either of self-help or protest.

So the false self becomes in turn oppressor, victim, impotent rescuer and impotent rebel, each of these states generating the next. It is driven by the energy of the repressed components to produce compulsive behaviour – of the oppressor, victim, rescuer or rebel kind – in all sorts of situations where it is maladaptive, that is from the point of view of a valid expression of personhood.[3]

In terms of the four modes, the compulsive person gets locked up in defences against distress emotion and is thereby negatively individuated as the alien self. This is a strong component of the ego, reinforcing its linguistic and socialized structure. Participatory feeling can no longer be trusted since it lays the psyche open to invasive trauma: it is walled off from awareness, only reappearing on occasion when the surface structures of consciousness allow for it.

The great power of the imaginal mind becomes deeply scored by distress-charged recordings of oppression and ineffective responses to it. It then repetitively projects this template, seeing it in all kinds of situations whose patterning need only bear a superficial resemblance to that of the originating trauma. Precisely because this projection generates inappropriate behaviour, it invites more oppressive scoring of the same kind. Imaginal power is thereby locked into creating a self-perpetuating and self-reinforcing prison from which the psyche can see no escape, since intention and action are subject to negative imaginal subversion.

What is the role of wounding in general in the development of the person? There is an apparent divide here between humanistic psychology and sacred psychology. The former sees wounding as an impediment to growth, a barrier to self-realization, needing secular psychotherapy; while the latter sees it as a condition of soul-making, a deep drama that moves us to open 'the doors of our sensibility to a larger reality' (Houston, 1987: 106) and seek therein transfiguring meaning and power.

I think we must distinguish between the wounding of the child on the one hand, and the wider tribulations of adult life through accident, bereavement, disaster, disease, and other deep psychological and social tensions that are inherent in the human condition on the other hand. It is the wounding of the child, surely, which calls in later life for a self-creating healing of the memories in human terms, and which we have a deep obligation to reduce in future generations. The wider tribulations of the adult are those which sooner or later call for transcendence and self-transfiguration, through processes of psychic and spiritual opening and growth. The deep tensions in the human condition that give rise to such suffering are a necessity – in the Greek tragedy sense.

Will we ever be able to conceive a child, and honour it during pregnancy, birth and throughout its upbringing in such a way that it does not get psychologically wounded? As a new age unfolds, I think this may become possible. If so, the issue of wounding will move over entirely into the adult domain of those deep and subtle tensions inherent in this world of soul-making; and the category of compulsive person will radically change.

The conventional person

The conventional person is the psyche undergoing socialization. This means first of all acquiring a language, which gives the child a basic component of the ego. This is a naming subject split off from named objects – a split which blots out the way the imaginal mind is involved in generating perception, and thickly veils the participative process of feeling. This ego then takes on the unwritten rules that prescribe how to behave in different social roles in the surrounding culture. The child learns the norms of its own roles and of others in counterpartal roles, both within and without the family. At the same time, it is soaking up the belief systems and values that permeate the family and its network from the wider culture. The ego gains a social identity and orientation.

This acquisition of language, norms, beliefs and values is a function of felt resonance with parents, siblings and others, allied to the power of the imaginal mind to divine the subtle patterns of these four factors. Social behaviour in the culture, I hypothesize, swims in an imaginal field of such patterns, an invisible ethos or mythos, which is a formative source of behaviour.[4]

The conventional ego thus built up will overlap with the compulsive ego, in that some of the social norms will institutionalize those compulsive behaviours which the individual has in common with other members of the society. However, not all conventional behaviours are compulsive; some are adaptive forms of maintaining social cohesion and order. And not all compulsions are given form by convention; some are private and idiosyncratic. But where the two components of the ego overlap, they will strongly reinforce each other.

As Aristotle pointed out in his Nicomachean Ethics, people need to acquire conventional beliefs and norms before they can become fully rational and moral beings. To become socialized is to acquire a language, an ego, a set of social practices and a social identity as a member of a culture, along with the beliefs, norms and values of that culture. We have first to take this on unreflectively in order to obtain a framework within which we can later establish our own capacity for autonomous thought and action. Socialization is a necessary condition of becoming a person, whatever price is paid in terms of walling off affective and imaginal potential.

The creative person

The creative person is one who has to some degree transcended conventions and compulsions by the development of what Piaget calls formal operational thinking, the ability to think in terms of possible and hypothetical relationships. Such reflexive thinking, when fully cultivated, enables some people to work out their own personal beliefs, norms and values and to act in accordance with them in one or more spheres of life, whether personal, occupational, recreational or whatever. In any such sphere, where such behaviour prevails, the person is being genuinely self-determining.[5] Here for the first time the person appears as actuality in an early form; all the previous states have really been prepersonal.

The purely conventional person is other-directed, whereas the creative person is in some measure self-directed. This does not mean abandoning conventional behaviour, but making appropriate parts of it one's own in an aware and flexible way, while discarding those parts of it that are restrictive and stereotypic.

This is a good example of the relative autonomy of a higher mode that has fully emerged from a lower. When reflection in the conceptual mode is well developed, and becomes full-blown formal thinking, it can function in relative independence of (1) repressed emotional distress; (2) the scored and scarred imaginal mind with its negative formative causation; (3) consequent compulsive behaviour; and (4) the limiting influence of socialized norms, values and beliefs. It will, nevertheless, be rooted in this ground of socialization, however independent its outlook: radical or revisionary thinking is still an outcrop of, and is influenced by, its original cultural milieu.

It is this relative autonomy of the power of reflection that has been a main source of cultural development since the time of the ancient Greeks, give or take a dark age or two. Especially this has been so since the Renaissance. It is also the main claim to fame of our traditional higher education system, still operating on the Aristotelian principle that intellect is that which supremely differentiates human beings from animals.

So creative persons are those who can literally think themselves out of the boundaries set by the conventional person and the compulsive person. They emerge from a prepersonal state – appearing for the first time in their own right with an autonomous viewpoint and genuinely self-directing behaviour. This is usually, however, only in certain areas of life. Other areas may still be run by unreflective convention and by compulsion. And there is a more disturbing phenomenon.

While creative persons have thought themselves into a more self-directing way of behaviour, they have not yet consciously picked their way out of compulsive behaviour and may unknowingly slide in and out of it even in their own chosen field of endeavour. This is a well-known and disconcerting phenomenon among truly creative people. They oscillate, often unpredictably and unawarely, between being creative and compulsive, authentic and inauthentic, flexible and rigid, rational and irrational.

Then there is something altogether more insidious and intractable. A whole creative field of endeavour is a continuous unaware mix of rational and compulsive activity. A good example is traditional higher education itself, which is still in large measure wedded compulsively to teaching at students and making all educational decisions for them.

The ego, with its compulsive and conventional components, is a busy contraction together of the individuating modes of emotion, imagery (perception and memory), discrimination and action, with intention in thrall to the busyness (I discuss this more fully in Chapter 4). Creative persons have an open ego: they have perforated some of its conventionality, and can intermittently and unreliably suspend some of its compulsivity. So when they are being creative, intention is liberated for wider purposes, and there is working access to the participative modes of reflection, intuition and feeling. When they are not manifesting their creativity, their behaviour may be entirely contained within those areas of the ego that are closed; and sometimes when they think they are being creative, they are in reality unawarely compulsive.

The self-creating person

The self-creating person is one who develops further the business of unravelling conventional behaviour through consciousness-raising and social change, seeking to dissociate their beliefs and their behaviour from rigid and unjust social stereotypes. As we have seen, some conventional behaviour does not require changing since it makes sense as a form of social order: it is then rationally adopted, so that while its form remains the same, its motivation is autonomous.

The self-creating person I construe as primarily distinguished by their commitment to take consciously in hand compulsive behaviour, seeking to uncover and resolve the hidden distress that drives it. This may involve regression to traumatic events, with abreaction of the distress emotion, insight into the causes of persistent compulsions and subsequent liberation from them – as, for example, in Grof's holotropic therapy (Grof, 1988). There are many other forms of radical therapy, the best of which, in my view, pay attention to breathing and body-work.[6] The ability to work in this way also deepens and extends the work on dissociating behaviour from conventional stereotypes, especially those that institutionalize socially pervasive distress.

Whereas a creative person is being self-determining, with unpredictable reliability, within some chosen field of endeavour in the world, the self-creating person is also being self-determining about the liberation of their own autonomy from past conditioning and affliction. This involves working intentionally with all the psychological modes and the up-hierarchy dynamic of their interaction. Distress emotion is released, to restore the capacity for positive emotion and aware, participative feeling. This takes the negative charge off the imaginal mind, so that the scoring and scarring of its memory images can heal with new insight. Discrimination and reflection in present time become more flexible and reality sensitive. Action and intention have new degrees of freedom to enjoy.

The self-creating person is also one who seeks to bring into internal relationship the multiplicity of the psyche. For it is not a question of wiping out the many compulsive aspects of the self, but of reducing – through psychological work – the tendency of some of them to hog the stage in blind, rigid or disruptive ways. The idea is then to get all the aspects into awareness and doing some kind of constructive business with each other. It is surely an illusion to suppose that you can simply clean up all your pathology. But you can reduce the distress charge that makes it dominant, then give its residual tendencies a voice in interaction with non-pathological propensities. So we have the voice dialogue work of Stone and Winkelman in which different internal 'energy patterns' are given voice in dramatic interaction with each other (Stone and Winkelman, 1985).

The self-creating person can deepen the whole dynamic of daily living in three related respects: first by becoming a being in whom all the modes, both participatory and individuating, are brought intentionally into play at the humanistic level, especially in face-to-face relations with other people, and in a concern for wider social and ecological issues; secondly by extending the range of creative behaviour, and by seeking to avoid, unlike the creative person, those unaware lapses from authentic into inauthentic performance; and thirdly by giving themselves permission to be and to manifest an aware, interactive and dramatic multiplicity of aspects.

The ego becomes more systematically and sustainedly open, but whereas both its compulsive and conventional components may be significantly reduced, the subject–object split inherent in the use of language, and some deep tensions in the human condition, are still to be reckoned with. I discuss these deep tensions in the next chapter.

The self-transfiguring person

The self-transfiguring person I construe as someone who is dismantling the subject–object split, dealing with the deep tensions I have just alluded to, and cultivating unitive perception of the world – developing the buried capacity for feeling at one with the world and other worlds, and for imaginal participation in sense perception and other kinds of perception. So this includes the creative and humanistic levels but goes much deeper.

This means the person has embarked upon the realization of their subtle energics, psychic capacities and spiritual potentials. They are busy with transformations of ordinary perception and action, extrasensory development and access to other realities, ritual, meditation, prayer, worship, and living in the now (Heron, 1988).[7] And all this is integrated with a creative, expressive life in the world. The ego is opened wider; and may start to dissolve.

It is important to distinguish here between psychic capacity and spiritual capacity. Psychic capacity addresses the subtle dimensions of this world and the subtle worlds in their own right, sometimes divided into lower and higher (Grof, 1988). It is involved in unfolding the imaginal mind into the wider reaches of being. Spiritual capacity addresses the divine as such. It involves a consummation of participatory feeling in unitive states of being.

The subtle worlds, in all their majesty and vastness, have been dismissed as non-existent; subjectivized – that is, regarded as purely psychological in character; castigated as distractions on the way to the Absolute; feared as the work of the devil; or simply left out of account. Materialistic science holds the first of these views, Aldous Huxley (1970) is a good example of the second, Wilber (1977) has at one time espoused the third, Christianity has often put forward the fourth, and Evelyn Underhill (1927) in her sensitive study of the supernatural is an interesting example of the fifth.

None of these views will really do. They all avoid this challenge of a One–Many Reality: that there is a dialectical interplay of the call of the transcendent One and the call of the Many on different levels of immanence. Every world, whether gross or subtle, asks to be known participatively and inclusively. For those thus knowing it, it is neither truth nor *maya*, but an appropriate vehicle of Reality. As such it has a relative autonomy that needs to be honoured fully before one responds to a call to transcend it.

You can also say this is the challenge of the being–becoming paradox. Whatever there is on any level is God, so you had better honour it thoroughly. Whatever there is on any level is becoming God, so you had better transcend it. But the honouring comes before the transcending. No competent modern transpersonal theorist that I know of would be so foolish as to dismiss empirical science as an irrelevance. Indeed modern science has transcended itself by the rigour with which it has done its honouring.

In the same way the time has come for the subtle worlds to be respected by forms of inquiry that are appropriate to them, and for this we need developed psychic competence. So the self-transfiguring person is unfolding both psychic and spiritual capacities, is becoming both adept and priest, occultist and mystic. Lawrence Hyde addressed this whole issue with great elegance in Part 2 of *The Nameless Faith*. He wrote: 'The renaissance of religion will come from the union of a genuine mysticism with the rediscovery and reapplication of the immensely powerful principles of a true spiritual science' (Hyde, 1949b: 195). Elsewhere (Heron, 1988) I have suggested a sevenfold key to self-transfiguration, and this is briefly outlined toward the end of Chapter 4.

The self-transfiguring person is embarking on the transpersonal phase of human development. I must now clarify how I use the term 'transpersonal'. The Latin prefix 'trans' has several meanings. It can mean 'beyond', 'on the other side of', as in 'transalpine' or 'transcend'. Or it can mean 'from one state to another', as in 'transfigure' or 'transform'. So the meaning of 'transpersonal' is currently ambiguous. Some writers quite clearly use it to refer to what is *beyond* the person, as if personhood is something transcended and left behind, or discarded like a dead skin. They confuse the person with the limiting ego, and so mistakenly kill off both at the same time.

By the word 'transpersonal' I refer to the person changing from one state to another, from the state of identifying with egoic separateness to the state of being free of that separateness. In this sense 'transpersonal' means 'transfiguring'. Personhood is not left behind. On the contrary, it enters into its true estate, the heritage which has awaited it all along. Another meaning of 'trans' is 'through', as in 'transparent'. And this is another meaning I attach to 'transpersonal': psychic and spiritual energies manifesting through the person and their full range of creative activities in the world.

So to summarize all this, I do not mean by 'transpersonal' a state that is beyond personhood and implies its dissolution and negation. I mean a state in which personhood is transformed from being identified with egoic separateness to a state which integrates the individuating modes with the participative modes, and is fully creative and expressive in the world; is transparent for psychic and spiritual energies; celebrates distinctness of being within unitive awareness. So the person as actuality is now embarked on the start of its consummating stage.

I believe that every writer who uses the term should make it clear in which sense it is being applied, whether to imply the negation of personhood or to affirm the transformation and transparency of personhood. Otherwise the whole field suffers from disabling confusion.

The charismatic person

The charismatic person I conceive as one whose self-transfiguring development, allied to expressive creativity and spontaneity, has transformed into a continuous dynamic grace and presence. The person marries spirit, subtle and gross matter in a seamless radiating whole. I use the term 'charismatic' here to designate someone who is continuously, not occasionally, transfigured. The person as mystic, spiritual scientist and creative agent, is unified with the world within One–Many Mind. All the psychological modes are transmuted by a distinct presence extending into the depths and reaching the heights, and expressively manifest in the enterprise of the day. The person participates in a field of being which is differentiated into innumerable beings, networks and interrelated levels. There is no ego. Such persons are, presumably, figures of the future.

The emergence of such persons, I imagine, will be marked by their ecumenical and co-operative stance, and their insistence that they are not perfected, have not attained any end stage of enlightenment, and are embarked on a new adventure in a deep mode of cosmic integration. One of the problems with some recent claimants to enlightenment is their social isolationism and their end-of-the-roadism: the 'master' who ignores every other 'master' and the 'perfected one' for whom, having become divine, no further development is possible.[8]

Concurrence

I return now to Table 3.1 and relations between the states of personhood. I said earlier that the bottom four states are the loam for the emergence of the top four, that there is a normal sequence from primal to spontaneous to conventional, and that the compulsive person could take root at any point in the history of the primal or the spontaneous person.

It is also clear that many of the states can run concurrently, in the sense that a person can move between several over some given period of time. Thus a person may at different times of the day or week be spontaneous, or compulsive, or conventional, or creative. Self-creating persons, when not being self-creating, may be any one of the previous four; although theoretically there comes a time when they have reduced the compulsive person to minimal residues, and conventional behaviour has been transformed from automatic and rigid to awarely chosen and flexible, with some undesirable conventions discarded altogether.

A very interesting and important issue arises with the self-transfiguring person. For it is certainly possible to develop psychic and spiritual capacities without doing any work at the self-creating level, that is without intentionally setting out to dismantle the conventional and especially the compulsive self. So what happens to someone who does this and who, when not being self-transfiguring, is creative, spontaneous, conventional or compulsive?

In particular the question arises: does work on self-transfiguring somehow indirectly dismantle the compulsive self? Can some process of change go on, which, while it is not consciously aimed at dissolving the repressed distress that runs the compulsive self, nevertheless has the effect of doing so? After all, there is the unstressing that can occur spontaneously during transcendental meditation, and the celebrated *kriyas* of Siddha yoga. My own view on this matter is as follows.

Good spiritual practices are those that incidentally precipitate release of stored emotional tension, tell students it may happen and encourage them to allow it until it clears. I have just mentioned two of these. The next in favour are those which, while they do not precipitate any release, teach students how to direct their awareness on stirred-up distress in such a way that it is slowly burnt up in the focused light of consciousness. In other words, instead of incidental catharsis, they go for intentional transmutation. Best of all are those practices which include both these two approaches.

But I do not believe that any of these three can do the whole job. This is in line with the view, mentioned in the section on the self-transfiguring person, that the relative autonomy of every level must be honoured. While the principle of transcendence allows that some things at one level can be resolved from a higher one, the principle of immanence implies that basic distress is to be cleared by working directly at the level at which it was laid in. I made a distinction earlier between the wounding of the child and the wider tribulations of the adult, suggesting that while the latter may call for transcendence, the former requires human resolution.

If this is so, it throws a whole new light on the saints and sadhus and mystics of yesteryear. For there is no evidence at all that they had any concept of repression, or of what I have called self-creating, that is, the intentional undoing, by quite specific practices, of the negative psychological effects of the wounding and splitting of the infant psyche. In this case, their repressed basic distress will have been relatively untouched by their meditative practices. Its compulsive thrust will have remained, displacing itself into the whole spiritual enterprise.[9]

Does this explain the flight to God, the reduction of the Many to *maya*, the relentless transcendentalism, the monopolar preoccupation with the One who is even beyond oneness, the insistence on being God rather than relating to God, the preoccupation with *moksha* or release from suffering, the castigation of life as a vale of endless pain, the pursuit of solitude and isolation, the preoccupation with chastity, the doctrine of *anatta* and the rejection of any kind of personhood, and the fact that the whole business is about as far away from mother as you can possible get? Of course, *ma*, the Sanskrit root of *maya* (illusion), gives us the word 'mother'.

I am certainly not saying here that the unresolved infantile traumas of these mystics totally invalidated their spirituality. There was clearly something remarkable about their attainment. But it was an attainment that was skewed, bowling along with a buried bias. They were the victims of a negative concurrence between self-transfiguration and compulsion.

Integration of the personality

What I mean by integration of the personality is that the individuating modes of the psyche – emotion, imagery, discrimination and action – are brought into aware balance with the participative modes of feeling, intuition, reflection and intention. It seems to me that this is done in three stages, each of which goes further than the previous one.

The first stage is that of the creative person who opens up the participative modes as part of his or her creativity, but often shuts them down again at other times. This is an early stage in what in Chapter 4 I call the open ego. The person sinks a shaft down into reflection or intuition or participative feeling as a function of their creative endeavour, but otherwise has no integrated access to them.

The second stage is that of the self-creating person who is consciously seeking to integrate empathic feeling, intuition and reflection into their new autonomous way of being in the world, and does so primarily within the purview of a humanistic stance. The participative capacities are intentionally developed and exercised in face-to-face relations with other people, in group and team work, in organizational structures, and in the wider concerns of human welfare and planetary ecology.

The third stage is that of the self-transfiguring person who includes all the previous stages and also seeks to launch resonant feeling, intuition and reflection into the wider reaches of being: the hidden depths of the imaginal mind, subtle domains, archetypal consciousness and unitive awareness. This is consummated in the emergence of the charismatic person, who is attuned to the One and expressive within the Many.

Possible progression

There is a possible developmental progression through these eight states, as shown in Table 3.2, reading from below upwards – as long as you don't make it linear: allow for all kind of overlaps, concurrences, retreats and advances, alternative routes. If for practical purposes we ignore the primal person in a state of foetal fusion, and consider only the remaining seven states after birth, then there are three basic stages with a pair of transitional stages between them – although it may not be too helpful to call any stage 'transitional'.

The basic stages are the spontaneous person, the creative person and the charismatic person. Of these, each lower one foreshadows the next higher one, and each higher one raises the lower to a more

Table 3.2   *Stages of personal development*

Charismatic person	Integration of heaven and earth	Transpersonal 2
Self-transfiguring person	*Transitional*	Transpersonal 1
Self-creating person	*Transitional*	Personal 2
Creative person	Cultural transformation	Personal 1
Conventional person	*Transitional*	Prepersonal 3
Compulsive person	*Transitional*	Prepersonal 2
Spontaneous person	Childhood play	Prepersonal 1
Primal person	Basic	Basic

complex level. Nor is the lower one lost in the higher but retains its identity through the transformation. The creative person is also the spontaneous person; the charismatic is also creative and spontaneous.

Thus the creative person raises the imaginal spontaneity of the child to a new level of complexity in which imaginative power is allied with reflective thinking and manifest in social action. The charismatic person raises all this to a still higher level of complexity with the addition of psychic, subtle, archetypal and spiritual capacities, grounded in a felt sense of both unitive being and differentiated being. What each of them is busy with, albeit in a very different manner and with significant differences of content, is the play of creation, or, if you prefer, creative play.

The other four stages are transitional – and transitory. The innocent spontaneity of the child is invaded and wounded and partially (but not totally) replaced by the compulsive, distress-driven person, who in turn is contained (but not cured) within the socialized behaviour of the conventional person; and if the education of the conventional person goes on long enough, with plenty of fully-fledged reflection, there is a chance that the resultant conceptual power will release the creative person – who will appropriate some conventions within his or her own purposes and replace others with new endeavours.

The creative stage is bedevilled by intermittent compulsiveness, and so the person goes on to the next major transitional stage of self-creating – to undo the compulsions and transform residual conventions and become an artist in the fashioning of one's own psyche. Once the basement is cleared, the attic beckons, and there is an extension of self-creating into the transpersonal domains, and so the person becomes self-transfiguring – which is a transitional stage on the way to the charismatic person.

These four stages are also transitory: unreflective conventional states not transformed by the creative person, and compulsive states, run on until they are resolved by the self-creating person. And the self-creating and self-transfiguring states are a generative chrysalis dismantled by the emergence of the charismatic person. What is left is a person who is all at once spontaneous, creative and charismatic.

One of the problems with this schematic table is that it is far too neat and tidy. In reality there are all sorts of developmental anomalies and variations. One of the classic anomalies I have already mentioned: the leap to self-transfiguring while doing nothing at the self-creating level, then at a later time making up the omission. So the table certainly can't be used to describe what always happens. Nor do I think it should be used to prescribe how development should take place: personal destiny is too idiosyncratic to bother with such prescriptions. The table shows no more than a possible progression. It is conjecture only.

As such it shows the various prepersonal, personal and transpersonal stages. On this model, the self-creating person has actualized the fullness of humanistic personhood, when all the modes are integrated within a humanistic purview. The conventional person has actualized the fullness of prepersonhood, and the charismatic person the fullness of transpersonhood, which as a total transformation of the person is also its consummation. What personhood betokens at each of these three phases is that there is a distinct human psyche present and in active manifestation. At the transpersonal level the psyche is undergoing transfiguration from separateness to pure distinctness within the One–Many Reality.[10]

This distinctness of personal being, I propose, is not annihilated at the charismatic stage. Rather it is orchestrated within a wider unity of being. The more it resonates with this extended field, the more its uniqueness is enhanced, like a passage of colour whose tonal quality is amplified as it is apprehended within the whole composition of the painting in which it occurs. Within the One there are Many.

Distinctness of being is thus quite other than separateness of being. In any thoroughgoing analysis of the nature of personhood, they should in no way be confused. The reason they are often mixed up in analysis is that they are frequently conflated in practice at prepersonal and personal stages, when personal distinctness can get lost in alienation from the wider unity of the whole. But at transpersonal stages, distinctness of personal being goes beyond this tendency to lose its way: instead the unique and differential particular shines with unitive lustre. The potential for radiance had always been there, even when obscured by layers of separatist grime.

So another metaphor is the simple one of obscuring mud on a pane of glass. The egoistic illusion of separateness means the glass identifies itself with the mud. When the mud is cleared off, the glass is transparent in the light and is fully present in its distinct particularity.

The entelechy of personhood

What I think is at work throughout all these states and their idiosyncratic stages is the entelechy of unique personhood. What Aristotle meant by an entelechy was the condition in which a potentiality has become an actuality. But there is another usage in which an entelechy is the immanent, formative potential of what is actual. So the entelechy guides the emergence of, and is progressively realized in, the actual entity. And it is in this sense that I use the term.

Carl Rogers made the idea of entelechy a basic tenet of his personality theory. He called it an actualizing tendency. He thought it was inborn in everyone as an 'inherent tendency of the organism to develop all its capacities in ways which serve to maintain or enhance the organism' (Rogers, 1959: 196). 'It is clear that the actualising tendency is selective and directional – a constructive tendency' (Rogers, 1980: 121). It affects both body and mind, and with respect to the latter, it guides people toward increased autonomy, expanded experience and inner growth. Virtually the same idea is found in Maslow, as a self-actualizing need, 'the desire to become more and more what one idiosyncratically is, to become everything one is capable of becoming' (Maslow, 1970: 46).

The entelechy of unique personhood emerges into actuality in different states: the spontaneous, the compulsive, the conventional, the creative, the self-creating, the self-transfiguring and the charismatic, and orchestrates them in an idiosyncratic pattern of development. It is emerging through the wounding and pathology of the compulsive person because, in this epoch at any rate, these are profound sources of the later growth of the self-creating person.

If there is an archetype of the person in the wider reaches of universal consciousness, then the entelechy is its seeded, embedded representative. It is our capacity for feeling working as a deep, formative presence within us, the guiding voice of immanent divinity. It has four prompts for our development. It guides us at different times and in different combinations to individuate or to participate; to stay with the ground process of our psyche or to reorganize it; to be more vital in living or more mindful in learning. These are the primary dynamic principles of the psyche, the three basic polarities, introduced in Chapter 2.

It promotes different cycles of emergence – in idiosyncratic personal forms – over a long time scale. There is experiential evidence that is also available over a short time scale for prompting more immediate processes of change. It asks only to be both asked and listened to. There have been various techniques for tapping directly into it.

E-Therapy was one (Kitselman, 1953): 'Greatness is in us; how can we let it out? . . . greatness can let itself out; it only needs to be asked.' Kitselman then outlines a simple technique for asking E, the inner voice, which will respond in terms of any one or more of the

following: inner ecstatic fire, trembling, body movements, disidenti-
fication from personal history, or an impulse toward some strategic
action.[11]

The experiential focusing of Gendlin (1981) is another. This
basically consists in making a clear relaxed area in the body–mind so
that when the key question is asked there is space for the answer to
be heard.

Jean Houston writes eloquently of entelechy as

> that dynamic purposiveness coded in ourselves, longing for unfoldment
> and expression. It is the possibility of our next stage of growth and
> evolution entering into time . . . . This Entelechy Self is also the
> supreme orchestrator and ground of all one's other selves, and serves as
> the protector and provider of balance and mental health amid the
> complex and polyphrenic structure of one's inner life. It is the Root Self,
> the ground of one's being, and the seeded coded essence in you which
> contains both the patterns and the possibilities of your life. (Houston,
> 1987: 31)

One of Houston's techniques in sacred psychology is to create an
imaginal body, let it take on the mythic form of one's personal
entelechy, then integrate the whole with the physical being.

Wilber has a sort of entelechy in his idea of the ground-
unconscious which is 'all the deep structures existing as potentials
ready to emerge at some future point', these deep structures being
different levels through which consciousness unfolds (Wilber,
1990). But this is not an entelechy self, an entelechy of unique
personhood, since for Wilber there is ultimately no such thing as a
self or a person. So his entelechy is really a collective one, for
humanity as a whole. It has nothing whatsoever to do with a
distinctive personal destiny, for personhood is only a seeming self-
sense which is really not there. I examine this archaic view in
Chapter 10.

Entelechy networks and *skandhas*

This is a highly speculative section that takes account of the
compelling evidence produced by Grof (1988) of so-called past
incarnation memories. Does the subject simply have access to
memories of his or her own past lives, as in simple reincarnation
theory? Or does the subject recall the past life of someone else with
whom there is a deep connection, as in the theory of shared karma
transmitted through the successive lives of different members of the
same affiliated group (Cummins, 1967)?

The latter theory is more holonomic. The idea of holonomy is
that the whole being is contained in each of its parts. And this is the

era of holonomic models. On the shared karma model, which I prefer to call shared resonance, the lives of the past many of the affine group are manifest in the life of its present one incarnate member.

Suppose those whose rhythmic 'signatures' (see Chapter 5, p. 98) are profoundly in tune constitute a particular network comprising a limited number of souls, who appear singly and serially at scattered points in space and time throughout the history of the earth. I will call this an entelechy network, since it is anchored in the entelechy of the one living person.

In the all-inclusive subtle matrix of time those who lived in the nearer and remoter past, those who are yet to be born in the future, and the member of the network who is living now, all vibrate together and exert a formative influence on each other. Thus I respond to what was done and not done in the lives of my predecessors, and to the great promise of unexplored potential in my successors. And all this is interwoven with my own unique entelechy, which therefore seeks to achieve its ends in part through resolving unfinished business from the remote past, in part through responding to unearthed impulses from the remote future, and in part through fulfilling its own intrinsic impulses.

On this view, we are not born as a *tabula rasa*, an empty slate, but as a slate that already carries the signatures of psychic inheritance, in terms of both positive and negative congenital behaviour tendencies, and intimations of future signatures as yet unmade. This is a constructive alternative to reincarnation theory, which suffers from its inherent materialistic implausibility.

The shared resonance theory entails the notion of psychic inheritance above and beyond genetic inheritance, although there may well be some interesting principles that relate the two. But they are distinct. Psychic inheritance is close to what the Buddhists call *samskara-skandhas*, or tendencies of will, which are the karmic consequences of choices made in previous existences. I have appropriated the term *skandhas* (which just means 'groups' or 'aggregates') to designate psychically inherited behavioural tendencies, and have stripped it of any necessary association with reincarnation doctrine.[12]

Negative *skandhas*, psychically inherited tendencies to distorted behaviour, if they are part of the mind, offer a special challenge to self-creating persons who wish to empower themselves by becoming free of compulsions arising from the past. Will they yield to the processes of regression and catharsis extended way back into resonant lives in remote or unfamiliar places? Or should they, once uncovered, lead us on to the methods used by the self-transfiguring person, such as the ritual invocation of those beings, now present in their own subtle domains, whose incarnational inheritance we carry? I have discussed this issue elsewhere (Heron, 1988), so will not develop it here.

Exercises

1   Primal regression
Take twenty minutes each to do the following. Lie curled up on your side covered with a blanket (including your head) and relax into feeling fully present. Your partner reaches under the blanket with one hand and maintains a light pressure on your umbilicus with bunched fingertips, to represent the umbilical cord. Breathe rapidly throughout the exercise. Let your mind drift back to early adulthood, adolescence and childhood; then *imagine* you are in the womb, mid-term in the pregnancy. *Imagine* what it feels like, and as the images and feelings arise describe them to your partner from under the blanket. After both turns, discuss your findings.

2   Your spontaneous child
Take twenty minutes each. First relax into feeling fully present, then review your earliest, most vivid memories of spontaneous expression as a child through play, physical activity, exploration, imagery or whatever – alone or with other children, adults, animals. In the last few minutes explore how much your spontaneous child manifests in your life now. After both turns, discuss the qualities of childhood spontaneity.

3   Your compulsive victim
Take thirty minutes each. First relax into feeling fully present, then review your compulsive victim (or oppressor, rescuer or rebel as you prefer). Identify some noticeable respect in which you tend to fall into compulsive victim behaviour in your current life. Scan your life chronologically backwards from now in roughly five-year intervals, and at each point identify how the same kind of victim behaviour was evident. Without staying too long at any point, see if you can get back to a childhood scenario which launched the whole chain. After both turns, discuss your findings.

4   Your conventional roles
Take twenty minutes each to review the various social roles which you currently occupy in your life: friend, spouse, partner, parent, lover, neighbour, citizen, consumer, employee, employer, pro-

fessional, student, patient, child, etc. Identify those, if any, in which your behaviour is unreflectively conventional, in which you simply do what social norms dictate. After both turns, discuss the formative influence of convention in your lives.

5 Your creative person
Take twenty minutes each to review those occasions when you first broke out of the conventional mould in one or more spheres of your life to think your own thoughts, and when you started to express them and act on them. Also identify what seemed to be the triggers for the emergence of this independence of outlook. After both turns, discuss your findings.

6 Self-creation 1
Take sixty minutes each to do the following. Lie down on a mattress that is on the floor. Relax into feeling fully present. Listen to Rachmaninov's *Isle of the Dead* and surrender to the flow of the music while hyperventilating, that is while breathing much faster and more fully than normal. As you continue to hyperventilate allow the body-mind to release itself of buried tension and distress, through sobbing, trembling, screaming, angry sound and movement. In the pauses between cathartic episodes, verbalize the biographical and perinatal material that is surfacing, and the spontaneous insights that arise about it. The hidden tensions may also manifest as prolonged muscular contractions and spasms. At the end of your time be sure to switch your attention into present time by describing what you can see and hear until you feel you are back. Your partner gives abundant supportive attention throughout.

7 Self-transfiguration
Take twenty minutes each. First relax into feeling fully present, then explore entirely in your own terms what self-transfiguration means to you. After both turns, discuss your findings.

8 Charismatic persons
Take twenty minutes each to talk about anyone you have met who has any claim to charismatic status as I have defined it. Explore what seem to be the strengths and weaknesses of that claim. After both turns, discuss your findings.

9 Distorted spirituality
Take twenty minutes each. Relax into feeling fully present, then explore how your own spiritual impulses have been or perhaps still

are distorted by hidden distress. After both turns, discuss your findings.

10   Stages of personal development

Be seated, comfortable and relaxed. Contemplate, in a freewheeling way, Table 3.2 together while listening to Luciano Pavarotti sing *Recondita armonia*. Notice your thoughts, associations and emotional responses, both negative and positive, to the table. When the music finishes, share your experiences.

11   Entelechy request

Take it in turns to do the following, letting each turn take whatever period it requires. Lie down, close your eyes, take time to relax deeply and become fully present, then ask aloud the entelechy within to prompt you through a session of personal integration. After the request allow for several inactive apparently empty minutes of internal unconscious preparation. Then go with whatever arises within you. If memories occur, process them as you are prompted and stay with them for as long or as short a time as you are prompted. Similarly with impulses to move, make sound, see visions, or be in rapture, or make strategic plans, or whatever. Your partner gives silent, supportive attention. After both turns, discuss the process and possible ways of deepening it.

12   Transtemporal regression

Take it in turns to do the following. There is no fixed time contract, but allow about ninety minutes each. Take the turns on separate days. Lie on your back, induce total relaxation and feel fully present. Identify a major area of intractable restrictive behaviour in your life now. Scan backwards describing instances of this behaviour at roughly ten-year intervals. Take plenty of time over this without going into any memory too deeply; add a memory between ten years and birth; then go to the first three months of pregnancy. Then go beyond conception into the matrix of time, and from now on *develop with faith every faint image that comes your way*. After floating in matrix time, allow yourself to be drawn to a particular person at a particular point in time and space. Bring this person into focus with details of clothing, hair, sex, age. Establish the environment – countryside, townscape – what places look like; feel the epoch and geographical location. Clarify the work of the person, their web of relationships, and basic life predicament. When this last is clear, seek integration, that is, the common theme between your starting point in your own restrictive behaviour and the other person's life predicament. When ready, dissociate back into matrix time and then come gradually back up into present time. Your partner gives supportive attention and prompting through the stages. After your turn give yourself plenty of private time to let insights and associated thoughts surface. After both turns on separate days, discuss the process.

4

The Ego

The occidental ego and the oriental ego

I have so far made only passing reference to the concept of the ego. It is now time to explore this idea more fully. It is important to note at the outset that there is an occidental ego and an oriental ego and that they are, in one important respect at least, very different. The ego in modern western psychology, for example in so-called ego or self-psychology, simply means the person relating to the world in a conscious, realistic, adaptive and self-determining way; this is a good, healthy thing and what well-adjusted living is all about.

In the East, the ego is also the adaptive centre of everyday consciousness that co-ordinates and integrates sense impressions; but it is not at all a good thing, because it locks us into the illusory separation of subject and object, the belief in an isolated, separate self cut off from a world of things. So we have to dismantle it, undo its illusions, by turning about to universal and non-separate experience of the world.

By the ego, I mean something similar to the oriental view, but also something rather different. What is similar is that the ego is the conscious everyday person seeing the world as a world of separate things confronted by separate selves, and that this is an illusory and fundamentally mistaken way of seeing things. What is different is my account of the causes of this state, and what to do about it; and my affirmation of the potential person behind the ego.

The most extreme oriental account of the cause of illusory ego consciousness is the Buddhist one. This says that the cause is ignorance, *avidya*. What we are ignorant of are two basic truths. The first is that there is no separate self because there is no self, only an impermanent aggregate of elements – the doctrine of *anatta*. I criticized this view in Chapter 2 and do so again in Chapters 9 and 10. The second is that there are no separate things each with some sort of permanent core, for there is only ceaseless change and becoming, a flow of forces, movements, sequences and processes – the doctrine of *anicca*. This doctrine is amended and replaced by my account of the four worlds in Chapter 8.

The origin of illusory ego states: language and wounding

My view gives three interrelated causes of the illusory ego states that see the world as a world of separate things confronted by separate selves. Two are social and one is more radical. The first one is about the use of language, a point I make at several places in this book (Chapters 2, 7 and 8). What we acquire with our mother tongue is the ability to handle concepts, class-names. This ability infiltrates into everyday perceiving an implicit conceptual layer which sees things as instances of classes. We immediately judge a perceptual image to be a house, a car, a tree – all concepts we have acquired from language mastery. Perception becomes habitually interpretative and judgmental, applying concepts to percepts in the very act of perceiving.

This judgmental act separates us from our imaginal involvement in generating the percept, so that we see it over against us as an object instead of as an imaging process continuous with our creative depths. And that leaves us in the role of disengaged observing subject, peering at a world that is separated from us. This I call the subject–object split. Once we identify with it, we relegate into relative unawareness our felt participation in the world and the imaginal component in perception.[1] I do not, however, believe this relegation is absolute, but that it allows for episodes of relative awareness – as in moments of interpersonal and group communion, contemplation of art and nature, peak experiences, creativity and free expression.

The subject thus set up by the use of language is quickly solidified by the process of socialization, which builds into it conventional role behaviours and the norms, values and beliefs of the prevailing culture. This conventional subject is a major component of the ego.

A second reason for the alienation of subject from object is the wounding and splitting that occurs in the oppressed child, which I discussed in Chapter 3. The child splits off the valid parts of itself that were so hurtfully attacked, and relegates them and the pain to unconsciousness. It sets up an alienated self, which is compulsively driven by its repressed distress to find some unreal substitute for the frozen potential which was the locus of its wounding. This compulsive self is another primary component of the ego.

The valid parts of the child that have been repressed are grounded in its openness to experience, its ability to feel compresent with its world and participate in the shaping of perception. So these too must be pushed to or beyond the margins of awareness. For they make a child too vulnerable to oppression. Thus the compulsive self sustains a split within the psyche, which also becomes a split with an alienated, external world – with which the child can no longer afford to know itself as intimately involved. Again, I do not think this split is absolute. The capacity for participative feeling can become supraliminal when the surface structures of consciousness allow, on the sorts of occasion mentioned above.

I believe language acquisition, with its attendant socialization, and psychological wounding are the two primary, interlocking, social causes of the subject–object split. They provide the conventional and compulsive components of the ego. The open questions are how to weight these two causes and how to construe their interaction. But it seems safe to assume their universal application.

Everybody acquires a language and is socialized, and everybody in the present state of human awareness of these matters is psychologically wounded to a greater or lesser degree. Everything after that, in our present culture, is a hardening of these two universal processes. The whole of traditional education, which further shapes the conventional self and reinforces the compulsive self, is administered by those who are already well established in the split and who will present everything in terms of it.

The origin of illusory ego states: tensions inherent in the human condition

The first two causes of the subject–object split are grounded – though they become relatively autonomous – in a third and more radical cause, which is to do with the human condition itself, the fact that the psyche is incarnate in a dense medium, in a biological organism on planet earth. The organism has basic physical needs that have to be met regularly. And this gives consciousness a limiting focus on meeting these needs and, more radically, on physical survival issues. In this context the psyche has seven sources of stress, which I conceive to be the following:

The tension between life and mind
There is a deep tension between the urges of life and the aspirations of mind: that is, between the need of the organism to survive and be satisfied, and the need of the person to develop their capacities for understanding, creative expression and relationship. The claims of physical subsistence and satisfaction, where there is deprivation *or* where there is plenty, may be at odds with the claims of personal and social fulfilment. Both body and person may be in need; meeting bodily needs may block personal needs, or vice versa. A great deal of tension can be generated here.

The tension of unlimited potential
The life–mind conflict is compounded by a disturbing tension within the person, aroused by a dim sense of the unlimited potential of the soul, the plethora of possibilities for development. There are boundless capacities within. The expression of some may mean the frustration of others. And there are no built-in programmes: every kind of behaviour has to be acquired by learning. All this generates a subtle and profound anxiety, which makes a person inherently unstable.[2]

The tension of the unknown
Embodied persons appear in a world of strange inscrutability: the unknown surrounds them on every side and deep within their own nature. They need to understand; but this world, the other world and the soul do not yield knowledge lightly. Fear and insecurity result from such basic ignorance.

The tension of material intractability
The embodied person has to act in a world of persistent intractability. The physical realm is resistant, refractory and often disruptive: it can readily frustrate physical effort, both in pursuit of survival and in the realization of personal vision and imagination. Tools have to be made, basic skills acquired, tough material worked. Fire, flood, drought, earthquake, vermin, deterioration, decay, disease, accident: the list of earthly hazards and noxious encounters is long. And this purely physical intractability may be compounded by densities and pressures of a psychic kind in subtle space.

The tension of separation
The embodied person has to cope with radical separation from other embodied persons. Birth is a severance, death is a separation; disease, or injury or congenital defect may involve disconnection; the exigencies of survival and the challenges of personal vision may mean departures and partings. The need to love and be loved can be deeply afflicted by these events.

The tension of other tense persons
The embodied person has to cope with the presence of other embodied persons, all of whom are beset by these same interacting tensions, and respond to them in a wide range of different ways. This, too, makes for insecurity and uncertainty. It is compounded when the influence of earth-bound, disembodied persons is taken into account. There is an inherent social instability in the human condition.

The tension of ultimate alienation

Finally, the embodied person is beset by the subtlest tension of all, feeling at a deep level cut off from cosmic consciousness, the community of the universal playground and the life divine. Wilber sees alienation from Spirit as the only explanatory principle of all illusory self-behaviour (Wilber, 1983). However, in a One–Many universe, I believe that a person has ego tensions both within the Many as well as with the One, hence my sevenfold account.[3]

The emerging person, stretched out by these seven interacting tensions, accumulates, around the focus of consciousness on physical needs, a level of anxiety that intensifies into a preoccupation with the body. The anxiety is displaced into being body-bound. The tensions are both denied and compulsively simplified in terms of meeting bodily needs, which then become exaggerated and distorted into all kinds of minor and major addiction.

To become body-bound is also to identify with the gross impenetrability of the body – the fact that it can't go through solid walls – and therefore to see it as separate from everything else. This obscures awareness of the continuous unitive transaction of the ensouled body and its world through breathing, seeing, hearing, touching, locomotion and metabolism. More generally, the body-bound focus of consciousness is cut off from its continuity with the deep levels of the imaginal and affective mind. As before, this severance is not absolute, but allows for occasions of deeper access when the surface structures of consciousness allow.

Being body-bound is the third major component of the ego, and is perhaps the underlying origin of its conventional and compulsive components, although they all circle round each other and interlock. The adult will be driven to use language and social structures to reinforce the body-bound ego, will see the unrestricted potential of all children as a profound threat to its restrictive defensiveness and will therefore attack them. The infant who is at the early stage of being naturally identified with bodily processes is particularly prone to become fixated at that stage through such attack and so acquires a template for being body-bound.

A model of the ego

If we consider the three components of the ego – the socialized language-fixed subject, the compulsive alienated self, the body-bound soul – these combine to produce one major effect: the development of the individuating modes of the psyche at the relative expense of the participatory modes. As a result individuation becomes distorted in the direction of separateness and rigidity of self.

First, the person tends to identify with the practical mode, especially with physical action. The result of this is, secondly, that the individuating poles of all the modes cluster around the demands of body-bound practice. So, in this driven world of doing, the emotion of the moment, deriving from distorted needs fulfilled or frustrated, selects imagery from the immediate field of perception, memory or imagination, within which the individual discriminates in order to act. Action tends to become a self-perpetuating activism, a distracted busyness that estranges the individual from the fullness of their personhood.

It is as if a restricted surrogate of the whole psyche is precipitated within the practical mode. This usurper is a local and reduced up-hierarchy founded on the emotional tone of the hour. When its modal states become habitual, then we get the limited and limiting ego, as distinct from the person – by which I mean the original up-hierarchy manifest in the fullness of both participative and individuating modes. The ego experiences itself as a separate subject: separate from the world and other people, busy making its way in life on an alienated track.[4]

Figure 4.1 portrays an alienated ego, cohered within the practical mode, and cut off from the conceptual, imaginal and affective modes in their participatory functions of reflection, intuition, imaginal depth and feeling – which become progressively more compacted as they are further down below the exclusive ego consciousness. The ego concentrates the individuating functions of all the modes – emotion, perception (and memory), discrimination and action – within the practical mode, where they gather around

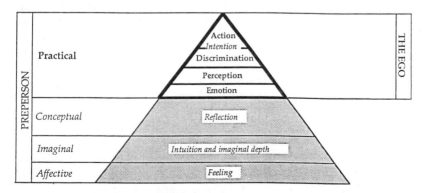

Figure 4.1 *The ego and the preperson*

the conventional, compulsive and body-bound preoccupations of day-to-day behaviour. Intention, the participatory function of the practical mode, is all involved in egoic plans and purposes. The whole figure represents a prepersonal state, not that of an actualized person.

Nevertheless, the alienated ego, because of its limits, has a firm grip on its split world. It is a move forward beyond the innocence and naivety of the spontaneous child, whose state is not trans-personal, but simply the bliss of ignorance – which may have conjoined with it the delusion of omnipotence. By acquiring an ego, the child lifts itself out of its undifferentiated participative world: it shifts from being over-participative and under-individuated to being over-individuated and under-participative. The ego thus constitutes a necessary developmental stage, en route to a later state in which there is a mature integration of individuating and participative ways of being.

But there are egos and egos. It is implicit in this whole account that if you could raise a child without wounding it, and so that its acquisition of language avoided the subject–object split, and you initiated it supportively into the tensions of the human condition, whatever kind of ego it developed might be very different to the ones we know in ourselves today.

The dissipative ego

The ego can also be or become very weak, being invaded by the participatory modes in an uncontrolled way, so that the person is in a neurotic, or a disintegrated psychotic, state. The most positive account of psychotic disintegration, when a person is overcome by a chaotic uprush in which the rerunning of primal trauma is all mixed up with uninhibited and uncritical access to transpersonal states, is in terms of Prigogine's theory of dissipative structures (Prigogine, 1980). The person is disintegrating into disorder so as to be able to reintegrate at a later stage in terms of some more complex and inclusive order. The whole process proceeds from a deeper level of the personality: the entelechy is at work in a process of drastic and profound reorganization of the psyche.

I have been involved in several instances of this kind, and the theory applies well. What the person in such a crisis needs is support and affirmation and a band of helpers to manage the boundary with ordinary life while the process is working its way out. The ordered psyche does indeed re-emerge from its partial dissolution in chaos, but now reorganized, often with what I shall call an open ego, one which is available for the transition to transpersonal states. In short, the stage of self-transfiguration has begun.

The egoic distress barrier

A big barrier between the closed ego and the participatory modes below it is the repressed emotional pain laid down as a consequence of the early wounding that is one of the three main causes of egoic states. The person has to deny this emotion in order to survive psychologically. This layer of hidden distress, until resolved, sustains distorted patterns of attitude and behaviour which tighten the person up in their egoic state. It also keeps at bay those deeper forms of affective and imaginal openness which made the child so vulnerable.

If this distress barrier is dramatically reduced by the work of the self-creating person on regression and catharsis, it does not follow that the ego dissolves. It is just less rigid, obdurate and fixed. There is still the effect of language to deal with, the deep-seated tensions inherent in the human condition, and the activist habits of a lifetime. But it is noticeable that people who have done a lot of work on healing the wounded child within tend to open up to transpersonal development.

The open ego, the strong ego and the extreme ego

The significant point about the ego is that it is closed in upon itself, refusing to acknowledge the participatory modes below, and denying their upward transformative influences. In most people it probably never succeeds in attaining total closure, so that episodes of participatory awareness occur spontaneously when the surface structures of the psyche allow: in various kinds of intimacy and social interaction, in spontaneous ESP and peak experiences, and such like.

And while still remaining egoic in the deeper spiritual sense, it can be open to educative influences from the participatory modes. Indeed, the whole idea of a continuous path of development from egoic to transegoic states requires the notion of the open ego. An open ego is not only one in which spontaneous episodes of conscious participation occur, but also one which is learning to create apertures between it and the deeper reaches of consciousness.[5]

As I have said, the ego moves a person on from the childhood state of being over-participative and under-individuated to a state of being over-individuated and under-participative. And being over-

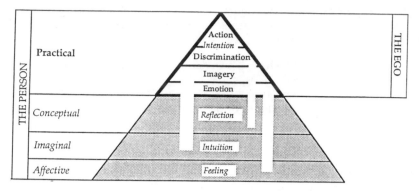

Figure 4.2   *The open ego*

individuated, it seems, is a necessary cocoon, a required precursor
to entering more inclusive states of consciousness. On this view,
persons need to build up relatively strong egos as a precondition of
developing integrated personhood at a later stage. A strong ego will
have a robust sense of a separate self, that is autonomous,
competent, with highly developed coping skills on several different
dimensions of living – intrapsychic, interpersonal, social and political, aesthetic, and so on.

A strong ego in this sense is not at all the same as a very alienated,
distressed and cut off ego, isolated from the main flow of being –
this is an extreme ego. Strong egos may have varying degrees of
spontaneous and learned access to the participatory modes below
them, prior to opening up to full integration. The open ego, at the
stage of learned access, is characteristic of many creative people in
an ad hoc way, and of self-creating people in a more systematic way.
The open ego is illustrated in Figure 4.2. The whole figure
represents the first state of the actualized person; a more complete
state will take the individuating modes down into full integration
with their corresponding participatory modes.

The idea that we all need big, strong, open egos before we move
on to more inclusive states of being is, however, questionable as a
long-term programme for the future of the human race. If my
account of the origins of the ego is correct, then it is a negotiable
structure. There is no need to wound children, to let them learn
language and be socialized in ways that isolate their subjectivity, nor
to let the tensions of the human estate overwhelm them. As I said
earlier, if all these things were handled differently, then a new kind
of ego might emerge. One that is open-mesh, porous, that can be
involved in developing the process of integrated personhood from

Table 4.1 *Different ego conditions*

Dissolving ego	Disappearing, expanding into integrated transpersonhood
Porous ego	Available for integrated personhood from the earliest years
Dissipative ego	Disintegrating into, reorganized from, the participatory modes
Open ego	Cohered, strong, with working access to the participatory modes
Closed ego	Separated, cut off from the participatory modes of the psyche
Extreme ego	Very alienated, distressed and dissociated from people and things

the earliest years. This is the idea behind the continuously expanding spiral shown in Figure 2.8 (p. 45).

Much more speculatively, if there is some kind of holonomic transmission of *skandhas* from present to future generations, as I mentioned at the end of the last chapter, then future persons will be born with a lot of inherent ego development, and can, as it were, move on from there.

Table 4.1 outlines some of the different possible ego conditions.[6]

Illusory ego states: the interacting triad and its resolution

Illusory ego states are to do with the conscious everyday person seeing the world as a world of separate things confronted by separate selves; they are the states of the subject–object split. I have examined in this chapter a triad of causes: the acquisition of language and socialization, the primal wounding of the child, and cumulative tensions inherent in the human condition. They are shown in Figure 4.3 as a triangle of forces. It seems reasonable to make the base of this triangle the tensions of the human condition, since as we have seen, it may be the origin of the other two sources.

There are, then, three ways of dismantling illusory ego states, by working on each of their three sources. The first is through the revisionary use of language and the cultivation of post-linguistic perception. By the revisionary use of language I mean the use of language to expose the subject–object split that results from its acquisition, the kind of exposure that is given in this book.

Anyone can raise their own consciousness to notice how the conceptual layer embedded in perception makes a judgmental split between seer and seen, separating the perceptual image from its creative source in the imaginal mind and setting it up out there as an object cut off from the perceiving subject. This is to reflect about what has gone on in perception and has become habitual since first

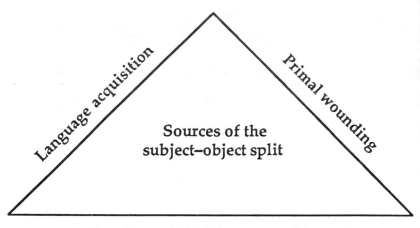

Tensions of the human condition

Figure 4.3 *Sources of the subject–object split*

learning one's mother tongue, and to make it explicit in one's awareness.

This revisionary intellectual activity is a preparation for the practice of perceptual revision, which I call post-linguistic perception. What I mean by this phrase is the experience of perceiving as a transaction between a non-separable subject and object. It is the awareness that I am involved in generating the images of perception, that I participate in the world in the creative act of perceiving it.[7] There is no split, no gap between seer and seen: they are distinct and unified within a seamless whole. A section on post-linguistic perception in Chapter 7 describes three steps in cultivating it.

To be aware of how language use has led us to split the world into separate subject and object does not mean that we go back to the primal, pre-linguistic perceiving of the very small child before it has acquired a language. It is not possible to undo the learning of one's native speech and recover infant perception, except as a purely imaginary exercise (see exercise 1). Nor is it clear that such an amorphous prepersonal view would benefit us, even if we could somehow revive it. Rather we need to honour language, applauding its benefits, while realizing that it has had splitting effects and that we can transcend these. This transcending is the practice of post-linguistic perception.

The second way of dismantling illusory ego states is by healing the wounded child and this is the task of the self-creating person as described in Chapter 3. It involves regression to primal, traumatic events, catharsis of the distress emotion lodged in the memory of them, and re-evaluation of those events by a psyche free of the pain that crippled its original appraisal.[8] The child within, freed of its hurt, reunites with the split and denied positive parts of itself and brings the whole of its being forward to join the adult in a fuller life now. Then all the modes, both participatory and individuating, can be brought intentionally into play in face-to-face relations, in transforming existing institutions and in a concern for wider social and ecological issues.

What also comes forward is the child's primitive capacity to be compresent with its world, its naive participation in generating the perceptual image. This does not and cannot re-emerge as original prepersonal primal awareness, but as a released potential for the adult's personal and transpersonal development, and for the cultivation of post-linguistic perception.

The third way of healing the subject–object split – which I equate with illusory ego states – is by all the processes of self-transfiguration. The tensions inherent in the human condition cannot effectively find their resolution, in my view, through the activity of the creative or the self-creating person. Their cumulative effect calls for resolution through the agency of deeper powers within. Here the person is working at those levels at which the human condition itself is generated – the subtle levels within universal consciousness. This is the domain of psychic and spiritual capacity developed on the path of self-transfiguration.

I have elsewhere suggested a sevenfold key to self-transfiguration, working in the heights, in the middle ground, and in the depths, of the soul. It includes transcendent encounter with the divine Thou; invocation of archetypal powers and presences; a turning about of the mind to universal Mind; manifestation, in everyday action and association, of a creative and self-creating lifestyle; grounding of the soul in the manifold rhythms of the body and the world; evocation of the subtle energies within the body and the world; opening to impulses from the immanent divine life – feeling as entelechy – deep within the embodied soul (Heron, 1988).

Endpiece

The model of the ego presented here does not regard it as something which is destroyed in the process of more integrated development. Rather it is transformed and progressively dissolved by expanding and deepening so that it becomes contiguous with the whole person: the individuating functions which it gathers to itself go home to their own modes and integrate with the participatory ones. So emotion is integrated with feeling in the affective mode,

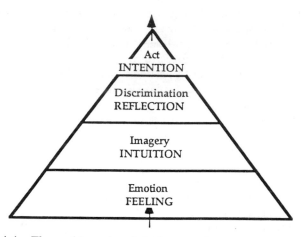

Figure 4.4   *The up-hierarchy of the integrated individuating and participatory modes*

imagery with intuition in the imaginal mode, discrimination with reflection in the conceptual mode, and intention with action in the practical mode. This is shown in Figure 4.4.

Finally, in Table 4.2, I set out the different states of personhood and characterize them in terms of whether they are in fact prepersonal, personal or transpersonal, and also in terms of their egoic states. The table is rigid, schematic and linear, and should not be taken too seriously. I include it here because it gives a convenient overview of what I have been discussing in this and the previous chapter.

It attributes a closed ego to the conventional person, whereas in fact as I have mentioned several times, it is unlikely that any ego is absolutely closed. What 'closed' in this table means is that the ego only has spontaneous episodes of access to deeper levels of the psyche; whereas 'open' here means that it also has working access.

Table 4.2   *Characterization of the states of personhood*

Charismatic person	Transpersonal 2	No ego
Self-transfiguring person	Transpersonal 1	Dissolving ego to no ego
Self-creating person	Personal 2	Open ego to dissolving ego
Creative person	Personal 1	Open ego and closed ego swings
Conventional person	Prepersonal 3	Closed ego
Compulsive person	Prepersonal 2	Closed ego, may be extreme ego
Spontaneous person	Prepersonal 1	Open ego
Primordial person	Basic	Pre-ego

I remind the reader of the point I made in the previous chapter, that I do not mean by 'transpersonal' a state that is beyond personhood and implies its dissolution and negation. I mean a state in which personhood is transformed from being identified with egoic separateness to a state which integrates the individuating modes with the participative modes; is transparent for psychic and spiritual energies; celebrates distinctness of being within unitive awareness.[9]

Exercises

1 Pre-linguistic perception
Find a place, indoors or out, where you can move about on your knees without discomfort. Take ten minutes each to do the following. Get on your knees, crawl around and imagine you are not yet two years old and have not yet learnt to speak. Don't try to remember how you perceived the world then, but simply *imagine* perceiving it like that now, and let your body express this through sound and movement. After both turns, discuss your findings.

2 Your unlimited potential
Take ten minutes each to affirm the depth and range of capacities latent within you, and of the possibilities for development and expression in your current world. After both turns, discuss your findings.

3 The human condition heptad
Take it in thirty-five-minute turns to explore this sevenfold account. Relax into feeling fully present. Then spend five minutes on each of the seven sources of stress in the order given in the text. Contradict the underlying anxiety generated by each by affirming a few times the relevant statement from the following list:

1 'I live in the unity of body and mind';
2 'I rejoice in unlimited potential within me and endless possibilities without';
3 'I am exhilarated by the call of the unknown';
4 'I relish the challenge of mastering the physical realm';
5 'My love is enriched by separation';
6 'Interpersonal encounters nourish my learning and growth';
7 'I celebrate my union with the life divine'.

After each set of affirmations, explore whatever is evoked in the way of emotions, memories, associations, thoughts. Then move on to the next item. After both turns, discuss your findings.

4 Ego dialogue
Take it in turn to do the following for twenty minutes each. Relax into feeling fully present. Then give your closed egocentric activist self a first name that feels suitable, and give it an empty chair in front of you to sit on. Address the ego with its new name, and tell it everything you know about it – its qualities, behaviours and quirks. Then sit in the ego's chair, become the ego, announce your ego name and correct any errors in the description, underline what was correct and add anything extra that was omitted. After both of you have taken a turn, discuss whether the nature of your ego relates in any way to the textual account.

5 Your open ego
Take twenty minutes each. First relax into feeling fully present, then identify particular instances in recent time when your ego has yielded to spontaneous incidents of participation; and when you have intentionally created apertures that open on to wider reaches of being. After both turns, discuss the nature of the open ego.

6 Your ego conditions
Take twenty minutes each to contemplate Table 4.1 and review occasions when you have been in any one or more of these six ego conditions, then describe what it was like. After both turns, discuss the ego's variability of structure. What does the table omit?

7 The object suspended within the percept
Put several different items, organic and inorganic, on a table in front of you both. Take it in turns to pick one up, hold it in your hand, feel yourself involved in generating the tactile and visual images of it, so that you and it become non-separable yet distinct. In this state say 'Here is my percept' and continuing to feel this state say '. . . which I choose to call a glass'. Let the named object be included within your felt participation in the percept. After several turns each, discuss your findings.

8 Self-creation 2
Take forty minutes each to do the following. Relax into feeling fully present, then identify with your child within somewhere between the ages of four and seven. Be that child now. As that child speaking in the first person, talk directly to the bad mother, the good mother, the bad father and the good father, addressing each in the second person. Take ten minutes for each in any order that feels appropriate. Express everything that has been denied outlet: frozen needs and longings, hurts, fears and deep resentments, appreciation and

love. Allow the catharsis to flow freely; verbalize the insights that emerge.

9 Colour code

Make copies of Table 4.2, take a copy each and have to hand a wide range of coloured crayons, pencils or pens. Take one column at a time and colour each of the eight boxes in it with the same or different colours as you are moved. Ignore rows, and treat each column as relatively independent of the others. Talk about the outcome with your partner, and hear their feedback.

5

The Affective Mode: Feeling

In ordinary language the word 'feeling' is the most inclusive of all the mental words. It can be used to refer to physical touch and bodily sensations, to urges, wants and wishes, to general psychological states of being, to emotions and moods, to thoughts, opinions and beliefs, to aesthetic experiences, to intimations, hunches and intuitions, to psychic and extrasensory impressions, to spiritual attunement and responsiveness. It is as if we know that all the ramifications of our mental life are somehow or other rooted in and branching out of the fundamental nature of feeling.[1]

The nature of feeling

But what is this basic feeling? I define it as resonance with being, which means that I indwell the world, participate in its qualities, am attuned to how it is. I am in communion with what is manifest here and now, and while feeling at one with it, I am at the same time aware of my own distinctness. The imaginal mode generates the imagery of perception, whereas feeling is the ground and matrix of perception: it attunes us to that being with which the perceptual process is involved.

The nature of this being is both Many and One, a vast interrelated network of beings of different sorts, each of whom is a particular focus of being, emerging out of it from an infinitude within. I also call such beings presences, distinct manifestations of an all-inclusive presence. A distinct presence is a mystery that cannot be known by definitions, but only by attunement, resonance and empathy in direct acquaintance and encounter. It has its immaterial qualities, its way of being, which manifest a signature, a gesture, an utterance, a unique style, which we can only feel by participating in it. It is, when named, a person, a rock, a flower, an owl, a tree. It is always particular, interrelated with other particulars in a total present seamless field.

If I look at a tree, perception clothes its being in form and movement, a play of colour, light and shade. When I feel it I participate in those qualities that are manifest in and through the perceptual imagery: its rootedness, uprightness, silence, dignity, receptive communion with its world. Within all I participate in the uniqueness of its presence – the ground of all these qualities. So the tree is a presence, manifest in certain immaterial qualities of being, which are clothed in perceptual imagery. It is the presence, and the qualities of being, which I feel.[2]

Feeling, therefore, involves us with that being of the tree which is the ground of its perceptual appearances. While perception is clearly involved, feeling is deeper than perception, interpenetrating it and resonating with being. We might also at the same time be busy conceptually and practically, reflecting on the tree and walking round it. But the bedrock capacity for being engaged with the mystery of this being we call a tree is feeling pure and simple. It cannot be identified with any of the other components of our mental life such as sensation, perception, mood, intuition, ESP. It underlies, permeates and contains all these and is also *sui generis*, that unique capacity of the psyche for empathic resonance with the other.

Feeling is deeply and deliciously paradoxical. It unites us with what is other while telling us that it is other and that we are other to it. It celebrates unity in diversity, identification with what is different without loss of personal distinctness.[3] It is a sweet intoxication with the Many in the One and the One in the Many, with each in the One and each in the Many. It always deals 'with the totality of any system' and its underlying pattern (Alexander, 1979: 289). It is at home in the inexhaustible interpenetration of every single being with every other single being. It cavorts with illimitable inclusiveness, while enhancing each differentiated particular.

This notion of feeling resonates, in my belief system, with the idea of the body of bliss, *sambhoga-kaya* or *ananda-maya-kosa*, in Buddhism, which is the innermost, finest sheath of consciousness, interpenetrating the four other sheaths – consciousness-body, thought-body, pranic body and physical body. It 'is the body of the highest, universal consciousness, nourished and sustained by exalted joy' (Govinda, 1960: 148). You can't identify feeling with such a body, since feeling is a modality of consciousness, but you can suppose that it manifests through such a body.

At the same time, I hold that feeling is deeply immanent, the grounding level of the psyche. It is not remote, far away, to be attained through some kind of deliverance. Precisely because it interpenetrates everything else in human consciousness feeling is involved in every kind of everyday experience. Unless we resonate with what is other there is no perception. We may bury this resonance and the uplift it bestows beneath the subjective–objective split. We may disattend from it, relegate it to relative unawareness, but it is there, servicing our every psychological move. In feeling, we live and move and have our being. Through it, we live, whether we choose to notice it or not, in a one–many integrated universe.

Feeling and the person

Participative feeling as I have defined it is the absolute hallmark of personhood, not reason. It is that which primarily differentiates the person from egos and animals and all species of non-person. The claim of the Greeks, sustained to this day as the premise of our educational system, that reason is the prime differentiating feature of the human being, inaugurated in our history a supreme phase of dissociated intellectualism, in which separate subjects think about and control a world out there. The phase has now peaked and the knowledge generated by it is starting to transcend its split-world premises. The electron, to give the classic example, is no longer an independent object: its properties depend on how a subject observes it.

As the edifice of alienated reason collapses, what is uncovered is the mode it had pressed underground – feeling, as that which initiates us into endless multiplicity while forever celebrating our unity with it. Persons are distinct centres of consciousness with an unlimited capacity to feel their world through continuous empathic resonance.[4] Such feeling enhances personal identity while deepening its unity with the world.

This feeling underpins, contains in solution and is the ground and source of all the psyche's other modes of functioning. Feeling determines the sweep of a person's imaginative vision and thus provides the imaginal material out of which intellectual thought proceeds and upon which it gets to work, as Lawrence Hyde ably shows (1955: 54). It is the entelechy of our personhood, its formative potential. It is the source that precipitates and nurtures each stage of actualization. It prompts us to individuate, to participate, to stay with our ground process or to reorganize it, to attend more to living or more to learning, weaving these in serial and concurrent patterns, as the rhythmic dialectic of our life requires.

It initiates us into the whole differentiated network of particular beings within being-as-such. The notion of a person as a distinct entity capable of continuous development, interacting with all kinds of other entities in a multiple universe with many dimensions, presupposes feeling as the grounding capacity which makes such growth and learning possible. Feeling alone brings us into relation with the distinct yet interconnected other. I develop this point further in the next section.

☞ To define persons primarily in terms of their capacity for feeling is not to define them by what they are in themselves, but by their relations with the rest of being, that is, by their resonant and rhythmic interconnectedness with all other beings. This accords with Bateson's important precept that nowadays relationships should be used as a basis for all definitions (Bateson, 1979).

Feeling as the ground of our apprehension of being

This feeling in its most radical form does not have to be cultivated, pulled like a rabbit by some meditative magic out of an internal hat, it only has to be noticed as the *sine qua non* of everyday living as a distinct being in a multiple world. It is through felt acquaintance that we know what sorts of being and level of being we are relating with.

Feeling as I define it is a necessary condition of ordinary perception. If the imaginal mind in its depths generates perceptual imagery, then feeling attunes us to the manifold of beings with which that imagery engages. We do not know that our imagery is imagery of the other, engages with anything, unless our unitive feeling tells us of our mutuality of otherness with what there is. The subject–object split which comes from the conceptual, discriminatory layer in perception – the restless seeing of things as objects of different sorts out there over against us – may cause us to disattend from the grounding level of feeling our world, to such a degree that it seems to disappear totally from consciousness. But the felt acquaintance is always there.

It is feeling which distinguishes between dreams and waking life, because by its nature it is attuned to the differentiation of being into different kinds and levels of the particular. So feeling authorizes intuition to understand dream images as portrayals of our inner life, and as distinct from the perceptual world of life awake.

It is feeling which registers the great imperceptible ambience – the other reality – within which earthly life is lived, and which can commune with the presences who dwell in it.[5] The monopolar bias of the eastern meditative tradition has often dismissed this vast unseen multi-dimensional multiverse and the radiant persons within it as seductive distractions from the path to the One. This view is extreme *maya* doctrine: the insistence that all distinctions of any sort are rooted in a noxious primary dualism between the One and the Many. The Many thus become illusions, and the more subtle the

Many are, the more they are to be seen as a seduction from return to the One.

Feeling, in contrast to One-focused *maya* doctrine, is the great affirmer of immanence, of the validity of the One–Many distinction, of unitive dipolarity. It celebrates every level of being, when known inclusively, as neither *maya* nor truth but as a vehicle of the Real. It is the vibrant antidote to compulsive transcendentalism and mono-polar reductionism. It is the answer to patriarchal spirituality in which male autocrats of the inward life debar the Many from genuine communion with the One.

Feeling asserts groundedness. It insists on particularity. It sub-verts improper generalization. It revels in networking, communion and relationship. It has a remarkable capacity for self-sacrifice in upholding the psyche even as that psyche tramples underfoot the very process by which it relates within a world.

Feeling, I proposed in Chapter 2, will become active in surface consciousness to whatever degree the structures of the occasion allow. Otherwise it is passive and subliminal so far as the outer mind is concerned, only doing its thing below the threshold of human consciousness. I will now look at some of those instances where feeling does to a greater or lesser degree rise above that threshold to initiate us into its nature.

Feeling and the communion of touch

Communion takes us to the heart of feeling. The simplest most obvious kind of communion is in mutual touching. The word 'to feel', in one of its basic everyday usages, means 'to touch'. When two persons relate through touch they enter one field of being with two distinct centres. Mutual touching reveals the true unitive nature of a boundary. When you and I touch, with aware sensibility, can you or I tell whether that boundary is mine or whether this boundary is yours? Can you feel which boundary is which? The boundary, surely, is ours: it unites us. Yet at the same time it differentiates us. It sustains a mutuality of otherness: we are both distinct in our unity.

In an embrace there is a mutual suffusion across our common boundary, each feeling the being of the other. We interpenetrate and become each other without any loss of distinctness. The whole paradox and delight of feeling is brought out in this most grounded of its instances. We are not talking about emotion here, for emotion is only secondarily involved as I described in Chapter 2 (p. 23). Nor are we talking about eroticism and sexuality. We are simply and solely talking about feeling. In a mutual embrace, we feel, in the radical sense of my basic definition, ourselves to be a dual-unity through feeling, in the touching sense, a shared boundary.[6]

Feeling and mutual gazing

Mutual gazing is the other very grounded instance of communion. In mutual gazing I perceive your eyes, that is, have perceptual images of their colour and form: but I *feel* the quality of your gaze which is distinct from and interpenetrating your eyes (Heron, 1970). If we relax, let go of emotional tension and allow the reciprocal feeling of mutual gazing to emerge fully, we enter ever more deeply the timeless present.

I direct my gaze and at the same time feel the direction of yours, while you are doing the same. These four processes are distinct yet interfused, transforming each other all at once. This is the power of shared feeling in the now. We are dynamically deepening our oneness while remaining entirely distinct. We participate in a felt togetherness while rejoicing in our otherness. We are attuned at the level of our presence, our ground in immanent being.[7]

Group communion

One of the dictionary definitions of 'communion' is 'spiritual intercourse'. It is what goes on in an intensive and integrated group whose members have been in continuous association for a common purpose which entails openness, honesty and authenticity. Here is Lawrence Hyde exploring the concept of what he calls an 'organic' group.

> That we are concerned here with a principle which is at the same time evasive, powerful and essentially mystical is indicated by the marked difficulty of finding appropriate images to convey its nature. For at its root lies the infinite mystery of love, expressed for ever in the overcoming and yet preservation of distinction in unity. It is a question of clutching at any words which can aid us in our embarrassment: William James' 'compenetration', inclusiveness, togetherness, collectivism, symbiosis, solidarity, interfusion, interpenetration. We can see the idea we are wrestling with expressed on the theological plane in the term 'circumincession', which is defined as 'the perfect mutual penetration of the three persons of the Trinity'. And finally we have a most interesting Russian conception of which much is made in Orthodox theology: '*sobornost*', the nearest English equivalent to which is 'conciliarity' (French, *conciliarité*). (Hyde, 1949a: 190)

Writing in the immediate aftermath of an appalling war, Lawrence Hyde must indeed have felt the need to grapple with a notion that had for so long evaded so many. Today in a dawning era of systems thinking and holonomic models, the idea seems much less elusive. The idea of holonomy is that the whole being is somehow contained in each of its parts. And it is now suggested that this may be a universal property of nature (Capra, 1983). In a hologram, the whole is encoded in each part. Pribram (1979) developed a holographic model of the brain to explain why visual memory has no precise brain location. Bohm (1980) has a physicist's view of the whole of reality enfolded in each of its parts.

Thus in an integrated, open and committed group, communion is holonomic. The whole group is within each person, and each person pervades the whole group. The group manifests the integration of personal distinction with collective compenetration. Thus it is so often that the destiny of the whole group manifests at a given time through the individual concerns of one person. The ground of all this is feeling: one underlying, unified field of feeling with many distinct foci.[8] 'This ocean of shared feeling is the place where we become one with one another' (Alexander, 1979: 294).

Hence the importance of training group facilitators to resonate with this field at their own feeling level to establish a dynamic basis out of which images and concepts of appropriate interventions can emerge.

Feeling and rhythm

Human beings are compounded of rhythms: of repose and action, of sleeping and waking, of ingesting and excreting, of inhaling and exhaling, of the systole and the diastole of the heart, of the intestines, of neurological and metabolic functioning. Personal development is rhythmic, with oscillating phases of new learning and consolidation, of interests, social and cultural needs that wax and wane. Such development has its own cycles and periodic recurrences for learning, growth and change. Interpersonal life is rhythmic, with comings and goings, togetherness and separation, communication and communion, unity and alienation, concord and discord.

Personal identity is rhythmic. Each individual has characteristic rhythmic patterns of breathing, gesture, movement and speech, fixed rhythms manifest in handwriting and fingerprints, all of which manifest an 'inner pulse' or distinctive personal rhythm (Leonard, 1978).

Rhythm characterizes the whole of nature.

Rhythmic patterns seem to be manifest at all levels. Atoms are patterns of probability waves, molecules are vibrating structures, and organisms are multidimensional, interdependent patterns of fluctuations. Plants, animals and human beings undergo cycles of activity and rest, and all their physiological functions oscillate in rhythms of various periodicities. The components of ecosystems are interlinked through cyclical exchanges of matter and energy; civilizations rise and fall in evolutionary cycles, and the planet as a whole has its rhythms and recurrences as it spins around its axis and moves around the sun. (Capra, 1983: 327)

Berendt points out that not every numerical value is a tone, but every tone is a numerical value; and that nature prefers numbers which are also tones. Basic harmonic values of the overtone scale are found everywhere from planetary orbits to 'stars and elementary particles, crystals and leaf shapes, plants and the bodies of human beings and animals (and their sexuality), architectural forms, the geological structure of the interior of the earth, the elements and their periodic table, the spin of the particles, the structure of the atoms and the molecules and nucleic acids' (Berendt, 1987: 91). It is sound, harmonic pattern, he maintains, which is the formative causation of the manifest world. 'It is a matter of interpretation whether we experience the numerical proportions that are found in so many phenomena . . . as harmony or as rhythm' (Berendt, 1987: 119).

The idea of the formative power of inaudible, archetypal patterns of creative sound or vibration is basic to the esoteric systems of Kundalini and Tantric yoga in India, and to the *Vijnanavada* and *Yogacara* doctrines of Tibetan Buddhism.

Now feeling, as resonance with being, is the most basic capacity of the psyche to be in synchrony with all harmonic rhythms, audible or inaudible and subtle.[9] It works with and through physical hearing, clairaudience, and with and through other sensory or extrasensory modalities. And it is also distinct from these and cannot be reduced to any of them. Its home is the inmost sheath, *ananda-maya-kosa*, the body of bliss. It resonates to the signature of a presence through all its manifest harmonic rhythms, and within and beyond all these to its distinctive source, its infinitude within.

Through feeling the psyche resonates with a given range of differential rhythmic vibrations, and through this resonance it orders it into a field of distinct particular presences, it identifies with these beings and, in the other sense of the word, identifies them as other – both from itself and each other. Given all the different kinds of rhythmic vibrations mentioned in this section, there is perhaps no limit to the potential capacity for feeling to compenetrate the experiential world. If rhythmic pattern is indeed a basic concept in a unifying description of nature, if it is that with which the imaginal mind is fundamentally engaged in bestowing perceptual forms, then feeling is the attunement to it which brings alive the presences of the world.

Entrainment

What follows from all this is entrainment, also known as mutual phase-locking, in which people share rhythms, vibrate in harmony. When two persons are having a good conversation their brain waves will suddenly oscillate in unison. The same occurs between a lecturer and his or her students, but only when all concerned judge the occasion was a good one; and between preachers and their congregation, parents and children, wives and husbands. Rhythm sharing in human interaction has been identified in many different cultures, from Americans to Aborigines. Heartbeats between therapist and client can coincide. Women sharing the same room for some time may find their menstrual cycles become synchronous. (Leonard, 1978).

Entrainment is a basic experience for musicians in a group and for sensitive listeners to them. The members of a chamber music quartet or quintet are in a complex unitive field of mutual attunement: they don't follow each other, they move along together in a state of continuous simultaneous resonance. This is even more evident in the sophisticated improvization of a group of jazz musicians.[10]

The same tendency is evident in animals and things. So-called 'alpha animals' are locked in phase with each other – in schools of fish or flocks of birds. Such a group is 'more like a single organism than an accumulation of individuals . . . it is as if each member of the school knows where the others are going to move . . . . The fact that they never collide fits this hypothesis' (Partridge, 1982). Similarly, a close formation flock of birds flying at high speed can make a sudden change of course all at once without one bird banging into another. Indeed collisions seem to be virtually unknown among animals of all kinds.

Any two frequencies that are relatively close to each other will, when brought near to each other, become precisely synchronous. Pendulum clocks side by side on the same wall will swing exactly together. When two oscillators are within range of each other's frequencies they will suddenly lock on to the same pulsation. When two heart muscle cells with separate rhythms of contraction move closer together, before they touch there is a jump to rhythmic unison.

It is an open question whether entrainment in animals and things is anything to do with some more primitive version of feeling as I define it. What distinguishes feeling in persons, I believe, is that it is an unlimited capacity for empathic resonance; and that it unifies a person with the felt field while enhancing their distinct identity.

Feeling and hearing

Hearing in the perceptual/imaginal mode of the psyche is very close to feeling in the affective mode. Feeling, as resonance with being, is a capacity *sui generis*, but its prime representative within perception is hearing.

Hearing, of all the perceptual modes, is the most comprehensive and precise in its capacity to differentiate. Hearing registers ten octaves, and seeing the equivalent of just one. There are three times as many nerve connections between ear and brain as between eye and brain. Whereas seeing can only compare and estimate, hearing can measure and can quantify unerringly. Seeing cannot tell us that one colour is twice the wavelength of another, but hearing can immediately tell whether an octave is correct or not; and those with absolute pitch can hear a note and exactly specify its frequency as 'G sharp' or 'A'. Listening to music, said Leibniz, is 'the concealed art of computation for a soul unaware of its counting'.

Whereas seeing can scan repeatedly to check and recheck its estimates, hearing has one chance only: the accuracy and reliability with which it can identify and measure is remarkable. I can sit in a noisy place and identify and locate accurately a whole variety of different sounds coming at me all at the same time from all around.

Because hearing is innately computational, is dealing in numbers, and because numbers can be developed infinitely, and because hearing is dealing with space, time and direction, it initiates us into spatial, temporal and directional infinity. It also reaches into the inaudible: we can hear the undertones of tones beyond our range of hearing, and the overtones of tones below the audible range. So hearing by its nature suggests access to states beyond ordinary consciousness: it reaches across the threshold into the unknown. Hearing also transcends physical time: to listen comprehendingly to speech or music is to live in a transcendent, extended present which incorporates the past, present and future within which the speech or music is unfolding in ordinary time. Hearing clearly operates within archetypal parameters: 231 notes can be registered in an octave, but we hear them as the basic seven notes of the scale plus the semitones. There can be as much as a 40 per cent discrepancy between the actual note sounded and the note heard. All the above data are from Berendt (1988).

Such data are suggestive, but the phenomenology of hearing is more relevant. Hearing is the most total gateway for feeling as I define it. If I sit under the cypress trees in the upper garden and close my eyes, hearing gives the most complete compenetration of the world around. It is multi-directional, yielding the location of bird, insect and frog sounds in every direction, high and low. Without the bias of looking in only one direction, I can encompass and suffuse the whole space around, being in it and of it and other than it. And this aural encompassing evokes an imaginal 'seeing' of the forms and the lay of the land, and this 'seeing' can be simultaneously multi-perspectival and multi-directional, and not necessarily from this point where I am sitting, but more likely from this, that and the other bird's point. So I am the form of the space and the soundings of the space and the presences (birds, frogs, trees) within the space, and where I am sitting just happens to be the centre of this spherical compresence which shades off into a penumbra of infinite directionality.

It is feeling within the hearing, or rather feeling that has always had hearing within it, that is the foundation of this microsmic One–Many knowing of the garden world.[11]

Feeling as the source of all the other modes

In Chapter 2, where I used the metaphor for the modes of an up-hierarchy, I proposed that the ground of the psyche is the affective mode in its most expansive form as feeling, which is the root and fundament of all the other modes and contains them in tacit or latent form. And I sketched out there the argument that the other modes emerge out of feeling. I give here some further accounts of that view.

The ordinary language account

At the start of this chapter I pointed out that the term 'feeling' is the most inclusive of all the mental words: we use it to cover the whole gamut from sensation through emotion to thinking and intuition, branching out somewhere in the middle to sympathy and empathy. It is as though the implicit phenomenology of everyday life knows well enough that we are intrinsically feeling beings, and this feeling runs through every mode of psychological life.

The *Shorter Oxford English Dictionary* (1985 edition) gives the following definitions of the transitive verb 'to feel', and I have italicized definitions which seem especially to bring out the all-pervasive nature of feeling in our mental life: to examine by touching; to touch with the hand; to search by handling or touching; to examine by cautious trial the nature of the ground; to perceive by the sense of touch; *to perceive through those senses which are not referred to any special organ*; to perceive by smell or taste; *to perceive mentally*; *to be conscious of*; *to experience*; *to be consciously*; *to undergo consciously*; to be sensibly affected by; to have sympathy with, compassion for; to think, hold as an opinion; to believe on grounds not distinctly perceived; to have a conviction of; to seem, to be felt as having a specified quality.

Then come the definitions for the noun 'feeling': the general sensibility of the body; the condition of being emotionally affected; an emotion; plural emotions, susceptibilities, sympathies; capacity to feel; susceptibility to the higher emotions; tenderness for the sufferings of others; pleasurable or painful consciousness; what one feels in regard to something; *a fact or state of consciousness*; a generic term comprising sensation, desire and emotion; the element of pleasure and pain in any state; an intuitive cognition or belief; the quality in a work of art which depicts the mental emotion of the painter; the general tone of a building or style of architecture.

It is important also to remember that the broad-ranging definitions I have italicized include special applications to the extrasensory. It is part of the common usage of the verb 'to feel' that we feel a presence, an atmosphere, an energy, a presentiment, a foreboding, a visitation, an omen, a descent of grace, the communion of saints, a synchronicity of events, a common bond, a friendship beyond time and place, a telepathic rapport, and many more cognate experiences.

It is therefore a peculiarity of the word that it is equally at home in the most concrete sorts of experience such as physical touch and bodily sensations of hot and cold, and the most subtle kinds such as rapport, grace and the presence of God. Now this is, of course, equally true of such terms as 'to know' and 'to be aware of'. But the word 'feel' is more inclusive. For it both presupposes awareness and adds to it the notion of participation. So when I say 'I feel your presence' I am saying not only that I am aware of you but that I am qualitatively engaged with your being.

Another way of putting this is that terms like 'know', 'be aware of', 'be conscious of' can readily be kept on the subject side of the subject–object split. So if I say 'I am aware of the sunlight', I can hold on to the idea that my awareness is this side of the split, and the sunlight is out there on the other side of it. But if I say 'I feel the sunlight' I have made a transactional statement of being involved with the sunlight in a way that makes the subject–object split start to look illusory.

Thus the verb 'to feel' is the great subversive element in the dominant use of language to separate subjects from objects. Its compendious and wide-ranging application gives the lie to egoic illusions of separateness. It is as if every time we use it we give evidence that we do not believe at the bottom of our hearts what we hold to be the case at the linguistic top of our heads. Bishop Ridding had the last word on this when he said in a sermon 'I feel a feeling which I feel you all feel.'[12]

It is also interesting to note that in ordinary speech the word 'feel' is readily used as a synonym for 'think'. 'I feel there is another important point to be made', 'I feel the argument is fallacious': common statements like these seem to imply that intellectual understanding is permeated by a substrate of feeling out of which rationality crops, as the earth's crust does from its fiery core.

This leads us on to the fundamental argument that all use of language presupposes that we agree about its rules and the meanings of its words. But how can such agreement in use get started? The first language users could not use language to agree about grammar and vocabulary: to get language started they necessarily had to agree about its use in some other way. Well, they could make all sorts of non-verbal signals to each other. But then they have to agree about what these signify, so we are back to the same problem: how did the first sign language users agree on what the signs mean?

One solution to all this is that there is a pre-linguistic mutual understanding between people, a participative compresence with each other, a felt unity without loss of personal differentiation, which is not only the ground of agreement about the use of any sign or spoken language, but also contains latent within it the vocabulary format and logical structure of any language.

Thus the issue about agreement in use relentlessly takes us back to the origin of language – with its inherent logical structures and the whole panoply of conceptual thought which it makes available – as a formative potential within the participative field of human feeling. It is unfolded out of feeling. It was always implicit and latent in feeling. It presupposes the mutuality and unitive scope of feeling.

There is a final point to make about ordinary language, which is this. How do we understand what another person is saying to us, when we are having an everyday conversation? After all, one sound after another comes out of their mouth, and this may go on for quite a long time before they come to a halt to hear our response. I think we really do need the up-hierarchy here to make sense of how we make sense when the other speaks.

At the grounding level of my awareness of you, I empathize with you, I resonate with your being as you talk to me. In short, I feel your presence. On this basis, I grasp in my imagination a total image of how you are presenting yourself, your posture, gesture, facial expression and stream of vocal sounds. It is out of this total image that I abstract the conceptual content of your speech. Then I make my reply.

There is an interesting exercise I do in workshops, which is to pair people up and ask one of them to talk at length about some topic of the day which is of interest and concern to them. The listener is invited only to empathize and image, but not to abstract conceptual meaning, not to attend at all to what the person is saying, but only to their presence and how they are saying things. Then the listener replies immediately after the speaker has stopped.[13] It is a general finding that the replies are remarkably cogent and get to the pith of what the speaker had said. In other words, the presence and presentation of the other are pregnant with conceptual content, and you can divine what that content is without explicitly attending to it.

The account from artistic creation

If you look through Rosamund Harding's *Anatomy of Inspiration* (Harding, 1942), and consider the direct accounts poets, artists, musicians and scientists give of their own experience of creative inspiration, you get a composite picture something like the following.

First there is a felt creative presentiment, a mood that is pregnant, that portends some creative emergence. Goethe was particularly clear about this. He knew there was a poem coming on because of the pure feeling state that presaged it. In this phase of undifferentiated affect, the image of what is to be is still inchoate, imperceptible: it is entirely latent as a pregnancy of feeling.

Then there comes the image, the first birth of differentiation. It is important to note that this is an image, not a verbally based concept. This image may build up serially; often it comes all of a piece. Either way it is inclusive of everything that is to follow. It is a seedbed of all subsequent differentiation and complex elaboration. It has abundant conceptual and numerical information latent within its imaginal relations. This conceptual datum is only present as a pregnancy of imaging.

Mozart liked to compose sitting in a moving carriage, since this got him into the right kind of creative feeling. Then, on some of his creative occasions, there would arise, out of this mood, an aural image of the whole piece of music. This image of the complete work came all at once, a simultaneous delivery of a complex seriality of sounds. It contained latent within it a staggering amount of computational information, which Mozart would later deploy in chords, harmonic sequences and a sophisticated wealth of compelling musical logic.

The scientist, too, may receive an original theory first of all as a single image loaded with latent meaning, which is later expressed in pages of complex verbal and numerical argument. It unexpectedly floats before the mind's eye; or it appears in a dream. Friedrich von Kekule's highly acclaimed discovery that benzine and other organic molecules are closed chains was the outcome of a dream in which he saw snakes swallowing their tails (Koestler, 1964). Sometimes an ordinary perceptual image suddenly becomes pregnant with latent theory – as in the stories of Archimedes in the bath, and Newton looking at the falling apple. Indeed, the scientific enterprise as such is based on the assumption that all perceptual imagery has latent within it the whole body of scientific knowledge.

In the third phase, the pregnant image gives birth to the conceptual and numerical information and logical structure that is contained within its imaginal format. This can involve a lot of labour: the working out and working through of the germinal idea. 'Conventional words or other signs have to be sought for laboriously,' said Einstein (Hadamard, 1945: 142). Or this phase can, as it was for Mozart, simply be a matter of transcribing serially what was grasped simultaneously.

What is now shaped into explicit concepts conveyed by words, numbers or notations is full of potential practice. Application is present as a pregnancy of conceptualization. All is now readiness for action. The poem is ready to be published and declaimed, the music is ready to be performed, the scientific theory is ready to be put to the experimental test.

So the fourth and final phase is that of application: the poetry reading, the musical performance, the experimental work in the laboratory. And somewhere within its bosom this application harbours implicit developments that transcend it. So the embryo of future creativity is present as a pregnancy of application, and the cycle is off again.

In Table 5.1, reading from below upward, we have a creative up-hierarchy in terms of a series of pregnancies and births, the

Table 5.1   *The up-hierarchy of creative stages*

Psychological mode	Stage of creativity	Sequential pregnancies
Practical mode	Application	Pregnant with new creativity
Conceptual mode	Explicit conceptual form	Pregnant with application
Imaginal mode	Germinal image	Pregnant with concepts
Affective mode	Creative feeling	Pregnant with imagery

originating pregnancy of feeling containing all subsequent pregnancies and births as latent within it.[14]

The painter, sculptor and musician do not have a stage three in terms of the concepts that come with language but they have it in terms of the logic and vocabulary of spatio-temporal and qualitative ideas that are embodied in non-linguistic symbolism. These are the ideas of colour contrast and colour harmony, of symmetry and asymmetry, of composition of shapes in space, of varying qualities of line, of rhythm, harmony and thematic development, and a host of others the meaning of which is only properly portrayed by their exemplification within their respective arts.

There is a classic polarity of creative delivery at the interface between stages two and three, the germinal image and its development into fully explicit form. In the Dionysian creator, while the germinal image is felt to be all there as soon as the first part of it appears to the mind, it only reveals itself in its entirety when the artist has finished the explication of it. It unfolds itself progressively, step by step, as the process of embodying it goes on. The artist knows that he or she is pregnant with something that is fully formed within, but the birth occurs serially stage by stage through the creative expression. Only when the work is done is the fullness of the germinal idea revealed

For the Apollonian creator, the germinal idea is revealed in its fullness before any act of explication commences. Mozart, already mentioned, was a supreme example of this kind of delivery.[15] Both types, of course, can change their minds, abort the first pregnancy and start again with a new germinal idea.

The account from human development

This has been covered in earlier chapters. The human person begins physical existence in a state of felt primal fusion with the mother, within which state is latent the capacity for perceptual imagery, which emerges into explicit differentiation at birth. Perceptual and motor competence develop for two years and contain the potential for language and concept mastery, which emerges into explicit form from the age of two onwards. Such mastery has within it, in turn, the potential for a wide range of skills of all kinds, which continuously emerge once basic language mastery is complete. So once again we follow the up-hierarchy route from the affective mode to the imaginal, to the conceptual, to the practical.

The account from the nature of the artistic image

I am indebted here largely to the work of Susanne Langer, especially to her immense *Mind: An Essay on Human Feeling*

'Works of art,' she wrote, 'exhibit the morphology of feeling.' 'What the created form expresses is the nature of feelings conceived, imaginatively realized and rendered by a labour of formulation and abstractive vision.' The artistic image 'reflects the forms of feeling from which it springs' (Langer, 1988: 41–4).

Langer's basic concept for understanding the world of living form was the 'act', by which she meant an event, a dynamic pattern, which went through a rhythmic cycle of acceleration, consummation, then cadence. All acts are involved with other acts, with their subacts, their superacts, and with further acts through the relation of induction. There is thus one vast rhythmic concatenation of acts, an intricate dynamism of life, which when it reaches a certain level of articulation, concentration and intensity, becomes felt. Feeling for Langer is simply a complex concentration of the interdependent rhythms of a whole network of living dynamic patterns.

So feeling in its own nature is at one with the internal logic of living rhythms and patterns: the tensions, the relaxations, the risings and fallings, the pushes and pulls, the inductions, the inhibitions, the delays, consummations, variations of pitch and pace, differences of scale and proportion as varying oscillations of movement mark out the given spatial field. It is this logic, which is part of life and therefore part of feeling, that is 'the morphology of feeling' and that the artistic image reflects. The artist simply projects into the image the formal properties already inherent in the rhythmic life of feeling.[16] In this sense the artistic image is latent within feeling and emerges out of feeling.

I do not agree that feeling just *is* living process at a certain level of complexity, for I hold that it is *sui generis* and cannot be reduced to any kind of exclusively biological account – which is what Langer wants to do. Apart from this basic disagreement, I find her account persuasive in its whole tenor. I certainly hold that feeling is resonance with the interconnected rhythmic patterning of life and the wider world, and that it thereby participates in the internal dynamic and structural logic of what there is, and that out of this attunement is precipitated the artistic image. But I also think this image is informed by archetypal content from the deeper reaches of the imaginal mind, and I discuss this further in Chapter 8 (pp. 165–8).

Susanne Langer

Langer, in the work just cited, had a purpose wider than to give an account of the artistic image. She wanted to show that feeling is the mark of mentality, that mind *is* feeling. 'The thesis I hope to substantiate,' she wrote, 'is that the entire psychological field – including human conception, responsible action, rationality, knowledge – is a vast and branching development of feeling' (Langer, 1988: 9).

I have to confess to a deep ambivalence about Langer's way of going about this substantiation. She was a philosopher committed to honouring the outlook and findings of scientific biology; she wanted to remain entirely within the context of natural history and to explain mind without resorting to 'metaphysical assumptions of non-zoological factors'. I am a philosopher and a psychologist committed to honouring the outlook and the findings of transpersonal experience.

So I find her biological reductionism misconceived and laboured; at various points it just seems to lose its way in a plethora of conceptual networking, and she doesn't seem to notice, or can't afford to notice, that it has lost its way. Nor was she able to finish her great task. When writing the final parts, she was in her eighties, too old and blind to put on the coping stone, an epistemological theory of knowledge and truth, and had to settle for a more modest concluding essay on the concept of fact.

Yet the work is immensely impressive. She is affirming and exploring, as I see it, a deep and fundamental truth about the human mind as an up-hierarchy rooted in feeling, with the higher levels of the hierarchy grounded in and emerging out of the lower. The importance of the points made frequently transcend the general reductionist intent. It is as if she is making a very powerful statement that has to be listened to, whatever your metaphysical assumptions.

So let me have the impertinence to summarize the thesis of three large volumes in a few short paragraphs; I should say that in so doing I have relied entirely on the abridged version (Langer, 1988). As explained more fully in my preceding section, feeling for Langer is living rhythmic process at a certain level of complexity. It has two forms: emotivity, which is feeling what goes on in the organism; and sensibility, which is feeling the impact of the external nexus. Feeling is involved in the two interdependent processes of life: individuation, that is, individual differentiation, and involvement with wider wholes. All of this correlates with my own views.

When, in the human organism, a high level of complexity is reached, the abundance of the life process within us, through both sensibility and emotivity, reaches such a pitch that it starts to become unbearable over-stimulation. As a defence against this the organism generates dream images, into which is displaced the uncompleted consummation of this over-stimulated process.

The next stage of mental development is as follows. A dream image is culled from its dream context and suddenly recollected in the midst of waking perceptions. Because it stands out in this new setting, its pure form is noted; and then its sameness of form with perceptual images. And because it is imbued with the felt displacement charge of the dream whence it came, it transfers this charge to the perceptual images which are similar to it in form. This sense of significance imbued in the percept and linking it to the dream image is the first primitive act of ideation.

Now Langer has to get language off the ground. To do this she postulates ritual dance based on wordless communion. Communion is a concept she introduces to explain the mutual bond between animals, which do not communicate in the sense of the transmission of ideas. Communion is not upheld by signals but by physical contacts extended by smell and, in some species, by sounds and movements which pass on bodily feelings. It is a mutual awareness, a sense of safety in nearness and numbers.

So primitive people dance in a state of wordless communion. Because they have primitive ideation, imbuing perceptual images with the charge of dream images, their dance takes on the form of ritual, to seek safety in union through fear of the charged perceptions of the world. They make vocal sounds during the dance; through repetition of the dance certain sounds come to belong to certain steps and gestures, and everyone would know which sounds and gestures go with which steps.

The argument is by now predictable. An association is formed by everyone in the dance between a certain gesture, such as waving a spear, and a certain vocal sound; so people start to reproduce the same sound when in ordinary life they handle a spear. And so slowly people use sounds as symbols of things, as meaning things. Language is born when one person knows, by the sound another person – from the same dance group – makes, what that other is thinking about. From this comes the beginning of reflection, systematic memory and reason.

This whole process starts from the dynamic dialectical logic of the life process being inherent in feeling and being displaced thence into the dream image. From there it goes into the perceived image and from there into the word and its associated meaning. From there it can be elaborated as logic and the dialectic of reason. In its very different way, this mirrors my up-hierarchy from the affective through the imaginal to the conceptual modes.

A final word about the origin of selfhood. The sense of self is grounded in *Lebensgefühl*, the continuous feeling of life processes in the body, and when these displace into dream images and the dream images drift over into the primary imagination of daily life, then this accumulation of cerebral imagery means the *Lebensgefühl* is concentrated into a feeling of selfhood, *Ichgefühl*.

From all this you can see how Langer seeks to maintain the impetus of her biological account of mind. It only seems to work because all sorts of mental concepts, which have not been thus derived, are surreptitiously introduced along the way. These include the *defensive displacement* of tension into dreams, the *recollection* of dream images, the *recognition* of similarity of form, the *transfer* of significance from dream image to percept, the mutual *awareness* of communion, the *association* of sound with gesture, the *knowing* of what another person is *thinking*. So as with all reductionism, it has to presuppose the notions it is seeking to reduce in order to make the derivation appear plausible.

I see feeling not as identical with living process but as a profoundly distinct capacity permeating living processes, having within it all other mental capacities in latent or potential form, and as a guiding entelechy that prompts the emergence of these capacities into explicit functioning. What emerges is what was there all along, so you don't have to try to show that it is some kind of biological business going on. The most you can say is that different levels of emergence may correlate with different phases of bio logical development.

I pay great homage to Susanne Langer. I reflect this in my sub-title for the present work, which echoes that of her seminal work *Philosophy in a New Key* (Langer, 1951). In writing *Mind: An Essay on Human Feeling*, she devoted years of her life to advancing a radical thesis, 'one of the most audacious philosophical visions of recent times', as the author of the foreword to the abridged version wrote (Langer, 1988). She really did grasp that deep within feeling was the logic of art and the logic of the discursive intellect. In some very important sense, she inaugurated a new epoch in philosophical awareness, and I doubt whether I would be writing the present book, despite its radical difference of outlook, if it had not been for her.

Whitehead's prehension

Whitehead is another modern philosopher of great stature who has a related belief in the pre-eminence of affect. He makes a certain kind of primitive feeling basic to his whole world-view. He calls this prehension. His philosophy is one of process: he does not think of objects doing their particular thing, but sees everything as events that flow into each other. In this he was directly influenced by modern field theories of physics and by the notion of energy flow in electrodynamics.

Prehension is a primitive perception involved in all energy relations between events, that is, in all basic physical transactions everywhere. Whitehead (1926) quotes with approval the famous passage from Francis Bacon in *Silva Silvarum*: 'It is certain that all bodies whatsoever, though they have no sense, yet they have perception: for when one body is applied to another, there is a kind of election to embrace that which is agreeable, and to exclude or expel that which is ingrate; and whether the body be alterant or altered, evermore a perception precedeth operation; for else all bodies would be alike one to another.'

Whitehead's version of this is that all energetic activity of any sort has an emotional intensity; there is a universal integration of energy and emotional tone. Whenever there is an energy transaction between two events this is also an emotional transaction. Prehension is a 'taking account of' this emotional transaction. So the prehending event takes account of the emotional intensity of the prehended event and re-enacts it in its own emotional state. The universe is one vast mesh of dynamic events taking account of, and taking on, each other's emotional tone as they flow into each other.

Prehension in the human organism has immediate access to this great mesh, and is the primitive base of perception: a direct participative, emotional rapport with the environing field of events, rooted in the 'withness of the body' which is continuous with the rest of the natural world. The organism then simplifies these physical feelings of prehension into patterns of 'sensa' – colours, shapes, and so on – which are projected on to the appropriate part of the environment. The result is ordinary perception. And it is veridical because there is structural similarity going through the chain from the original external dynamic events, the physical feelings that prehend them, and the sensa abstracted from these feelings (Whitehead, 1926, 1928, 1929, 1938).

On this view each of us has a substrate of participative physical feeling which meshes in with the universal interflow of prehending events. Whitehead actually thinks it is possible under certain conditions to revert to this primitive prehension of the world, and that such reversion underlies much poetic experience. It occurs 'when the perception of the pressure from a world of things with characters in their own right, characters mysteriously moulding our own natures, becomes strongest' (Whitehead, 1928). This is indeed like my notion of felt participation in a world of presences.

I should add, in passing, that the idea of primitive, unitive engagement with the world is an important notion in the phenomenology of Merleau-Ponty. He argues that all language and discursive knowledge presupposes the pre-objective, pre-predicative world. This world is perception, consciousness–world union, which is anterior to every distinction including that of consciousness and nature. It is an unformulated consciousness of the totality which is the world and which is also the body, since the body is coextensive with the entire field of possible perceptions, i.e. the world (Merleau-Ponty, 1962). Despite the great difference in language, this whole notion echoes the pervasive, primal prehension in Whitehead's philosophy.

Leslie Paul (1961) goes to town on Whitehead's theory and boosts its mystical potential. He talks of the 'ineffable bed of sentience which is the basis of our presence in the world and to the world'. There is a 'primary cosmic sensitivity', a generalized feeling common to the whole universe, which gives an understanding of the interrelated web of being in which the organism is suspended. Human perception is simply an advanced form of this. It codes incoming signals from the world and decodes them as percepts; and it knows what the incoming codes are about by means of the primal, generalized feeling and understanding, which is prior to the nervous system and its reports.

I am in tune with the general tenor of this approach; and I am quite sure I owe a great deal to Whitehead's philosophy. But I do not think the nature of participative feeling is physical: this makes it altogether too primitive and fusion-like. Nor do I think you can explain perception as being abstracted out of such physical feeling. If this feeling knows enough about what is going on around it to provide all the information for constructing percepts and for validating them, then it is already an efficient perceptual process in its own right; so why have a redundant superstructure? Both Whitehead and Paul have a contradiction here: on the one hand it seems we need the full perceptual apparatus because there is something rather obscure about primitive prehension; but on the other it is just this primitive prehension which guarantees that perception is veridical.

I find it more plausible to suppose that feeling is a form of consciousness in which all the other psychological modes, including the imaginal mode, are latent. It resonates with the universal interflow of events. Grounded in this resonance, the imaginal mode emerges to shape perception through primary imagination. The imaginal mind thus pours its imagery on to the centres of being with which feeling resonates. Feeling does not validate perceptual imagery. It tells the imaginal mind where to put it and what quality of presence it is encompassing. Imaginal mind emerges to celebrate, articulate and play with the grounding resonance of feeling, not to make clearer something that was a bit obscure about it.

In short, my view is a transpersonal one. Feeling is a high form of consciousness embedded in the organism as a profound entelechy, interpenetrating and responding to all levels of energy. It is a lofty estate in humble form, grounding the whole human enterprise. It manifests first as a physical, felt primal fusion of the foetus and neonate; then as the very primitive, unfocused participative awareness of the small child; then after the subject–object split it goes underground, sustaining the whole perceptual field from below the threshold of explicit awareness, only appearing above ground in certain special forms of human experience. The creative person taps into it for their creativity; the self-creating person brings it intentionally above ground for integrated humanistic living; and the self-transfiguring person invites it to reveal its all.

Jean Wahl

Much of the philosophical tradition has neglected the idea of participative feeling, but by no means entirely. There is Hegel and his feeling for the whole, Bradley and his notion of a felt totality, William James's idea of felt acquaintance, Bergson's *élan vital*, Santayana's 'animal faith', Langer's ideas, and of course the prehension of Whitehead.

Jean Wahl, with his dialectical existentialism, brings this alternative tradition to a head in his theory of the concrete (Wahl, 1948, 1953). He affirms that what is given – in 'extra-linguistic vision', in that immediacy of perception which is found behind the screen of language, in 'the now and here as they are felt which language can describe only imperfectly' – is not parts outside parts, but felt wholes. In such perception we feel rooted in the world, which is at the same time a participation in and a communion with the world. We have an intuitive awareness of becoming as 'concrescence', in which part and whole are present contemporaneously and emerge in simultaneous growth. This unity can hardly be defined, but it can be felt and felt vividly. In the immediacy of perception there is a 'silence of ecstasy where mind achieves a union with its own highest point, which is at the same time the highest point of the world'. In this direction, he thinks, lies the philosophy of the future, superseding modern ways of thought. 'Immediate vision remains the goal of the philosopher.'

Exercises

1 'Feeling' in *your* use of language
Take five minutes each to express all the different kinds of mental
states that you are in as you speak and that you are comfortable in
prefacing with phrases such as 'I feel', 'I feel that', 'It is my feeling
that', 'I have a feeling that'. Then let the exercise extend beyond
your present state of mind to any state of mind that you could
preface in this way. After both turns, discuss your findings.

2 Arboreal presence
Go together into the garden or a convenient park and each choose a
secluded tree. Feel the unique presence of your tree: empathize
with its gesture, resonate to its silent utterance, attune to its total
style of life through all its qualities of being. See it and listen to it,
move round it, stand near and far from it, touch it and embrace it,
talk with it, sing with it – all the while participating through feeling
in its being as a whole. Then meet and share your findings: try
presenting the felt presence of your tree and its qualities through
sound or song, or through posture, gesture and movement, or by
drawing and painting, or through poetic metaphor. After this
presentational symbolism, see if there is anything else you want to
say about the unique signature of your tree.

3 Dinner date
Make a dinner date with each other to celebrate your friendship. As
you talk and share and exchange experiences with each other, feel
the difference within the unity of friendship and the unity within the
difference. At the end of the meal, reflect on the feeling of
celebrating unity in diversity in this way.

4 Feeling the world
Take five minutes each, in each other's presence, to do the
following. Stand in an isolated open space with a view out over the
landscape and intone the declaration 'I feel the world'. Don't let the
words get in the way: vary them, play with their sound, abandon
them if they block rather than release. Feel your continuity with the
whole perceptual field, visual, auditory, tactile. Find the posture
and gestures that integrate your being with the statement. Dance
with the feeling if moved to do so. After both turns, share your
findings in further movements without speech. Let this develop into
a dance together. Then say anything you need to say about the
experience.

5   Unseen presences
Take ten minutes each to review particular occasions, at any time in your life, when you have felt a subtle communion with invisible presences. Describe what the feeling was like. What did it tell you about who these presences were and what they were doing? After both turns, discuss your findings.

6   Dual-unity embrace
Embrace your partner and let go of all emotional and physical tensions. Without speaking, participate through the embrace in a state of mutual attunement and resonance, so that you feel there are two beings in one togetherness. Notice how the frontal boundary becomes a shared permeable membrane that unites you in dual-unity. Feel this state and enter deeper and deeper into the timeless moment. After some minutes disengage from the embrace without words and make a line drawing that symbolizes the experience. When both drawings are finished, take it in turns to describe how the drawing relates to the embrace.

7   Mutual gazing
Sit opposite each other, relax into being present and enter the state of silent, mutual gazing for fifteen minutes. Feel free to laugh, smile and let go of any embarrassment and emotional tension, without speaking, until you settle into the timeless moment of dual-unity. Break the spell after some minutes and take it in turns to symbolize the experience by a sound or combination of sounds. Then discuss your findings.

8   Group experience
Take twenty minutes each to describe experiences of being in any kind of group where you have felt this sort of holonomic communion. After both turns, discuss your findings.

9   Breath resonance
Sit immediately opposite each other and relax into feeling fully present. Using all the cues of sight and sound, *feel* your partner's breathing rhythm, and as you participate in it gently bring your own breathing rhythm to synchronize with it. Breathe now together feeling the shared rhythm, while also deepening into mutual gazing. Disengage after ten minutes and make a line drawing of the feeling. Explain your drawing and its relation to the experience.

10   Mutual kinaesthetic resonance
Make a space in the room and prepare to move in complete

empathic resonance with each other. Improvise a very slow, gyrating dance together, each of you moving in simultaneous resonance with the other, neither of you leading or following. And within your own body, let every part move in simultaneous resonance with every other part, no part leading or following any other. Let the dance take over and dance you both in whatever tempo it chooses. After the dance brings itself to a close, discuss your findings.

11 Feeling the wind
Stand together where the wind is blowing through the trees and where this is the only or the primary sound. Participate in, *feel*, the sound of the wind, and as you do so ask yourself where you are. After fifteen minutes or so discuss your findings with your partner.

12 Participative subjectivity
Sit opposite your partner and gaze at each other until you relax into a state of gentle ineffability. Then take it in turn to do the following: repeat five or more times the statement 'I feel your gaze-light' and pause for some while between each utterance. Feel what you are saying. At the same time consider this question: do you or do you not participate in the subjectivity of your partner? After both turns, discuss your findings.

13 Disattending from content to presence
Take it in turn to do the following: while your partner talks for five minutes on a topic of concern, you pay no attention to the content of the talk, the meaning of what is being said, and give your attention entirely to feeling their presence, bearing, manner of being and tone and rhythm of voice; then give your response to what your partner has said. After both turns discuss your findings.

14 Your creative cycle
Take it in turn to spend fifteen minutes exploring one or two examples of your own creative cycle in any field of endeavour from gardening to social action. How are its stages similar to and different from the up-hierarchy of creative stages given in the text? After both turns, discuss your findings.

15 Your creative style
Take another fifteen minutes each to explore the same or different instances of your creativity in any field. Review each instance and see whether it is Dionysian or Apollonian in its creative style. After both turns discuss your findings.

16   Cézanne and van Gogh

Collect three or four good-quality colour reproductions of paintings by each of these artists. Participate in them, feel them. Then discuss together whether you find it plausible to see these images as projecting 'the morphology of feeling' in the way that this is defined in this and the preceding paragraph.

6

The Affective Mode: Emotion

Feeling, the participatory form of the affective mode, interrelates us with the network of beings; emotion, the individuating form of the affective mode, gives each of us a locus within that network, highlighting a distinctive being that has differential experience from every other. Putting it in terms of just one link, feeling attunes us to a unique presence and its qualities of being, emotion is our state of fulfilled or frustrated need that correlates with that felt connection. The statement 'I feel your presence and it fills me with delight' makes clear the distinction between feeling and emotion which I am advancing in this book. In Chapter 2 (p. 23) I explored the way in which feeling is the ground of emotion. In this chapter I present a model of emotions and emotional processes.

Emotion, motivation and appraisal

Emotion I have defined in Chapter 2 as the intense, localized affect that centres around the fulfilment or frustration of individual needs and interests – the domain of joy, love, surprise, satisfaction, zest, fear, grief, anger, and so on. Emotion, also, is always associated with a vital element of appraisal: it is a function of what we intuitively feel the situation to be – supporting, or opportune, or threatening, or frustrating.

So emotions are related to both motivation and appraisal. J.N. Findlay saw this, saying that our emotions at their core incorporate both a practical policy and a presumption about what provokes them. This presumption means viewing the emotional situation in a certain light (Findlay, 1961).

The definition of emotion in terms of meeting needs sees it as an index of motivational states, and immediately raises the question of what these states are. What are those basic needs whose fulfilment or frustration gives rise to emotion?

I think we can distinguish needs at four different levels: bodily needs, personal needs, entelechy needs, and spiritual needs. The single term need, here, denotes something qualitatively different at the bodily level and at the other three levels. What I call personal needs, entelechy needs and spiritual needs, can be construed as passive actualizations of the individuating-participatory dynamic, unfolding its unlimited potential for distinctness in unitive resonance with being.

Bodily needs are for food, water, excretion, air, sleep, exercise, sex. Their fulfilments and frustrations are experienced in terms of sensations of pleasure and discomfort or pain. Since the body is also a necessary medium for meeting personal needs, its fulfilments and frustrations can involve the personal emotions; the pleasures of sex can involve the emotion of joy, the pains of hunger can involve anger at social injustice. But while bodily pleasures and pains and personal emotions can overlap, there is no necessary connection between them. Personal emotion is *sui generis*: it is not reducible to the dynamics of bodily needs.

Personal needs

By 'personal needs' I mean something more compendious than the phrase conveys. I intend it to include the needs of the whole person in relation with other persons within their shared planetary context. It refers to the person not only in their psychosocial setting, but also in their ecosystem environment as a member of Gaia (Thompson, 1987).

In previous writings I have classified personal needs as the needs to love and be loved, to understand and be understood, and to exercise free choice and to be freely chosen (Heron, 1982). To these I would now add the need to image and to be imaged, although more deeply stated I think this is the need to intuit the meaning of imagery and to be intuited as meaningful imagery. For convenience I use the short version.

Given the depth and range of the imaginal mind, human beings have a profound need to enjoy a flourishing stream of imagery – tactile, kinaesthetic, auditory and visual – in waking life, dream life and altered states of consciousness. Hence, at the most obvious level, the valid claims of spectacle, art, music, theatre, travel and sight-seeing.[1]

These four needs – to do with loving, imaging, understanding and choosing – express the capacities of the four psychological modes, in the sense that to have a capacity is to have a need to realize it. So the up-hierarchy of the modes can also be shown as an up-hierarchy of needs as in Figure 6.1. The grounding level is the need to love: the need to feel resonance with particular beings in the network of being. Loving *is* feeling the resonance – with a person, a group, a

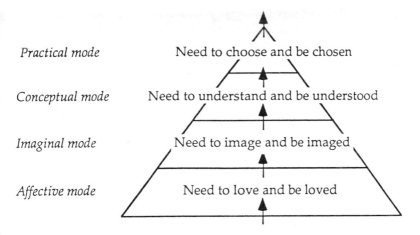

Practical mode   Need to choose and be chosen

Conceptual mode   Need to understand and be understood

Imaginal mode   Need to image and be imaged

Affective mode   Need to love and be loved

Figure 6.1   *The motivational up-hierarchy*

bird, the moon. When this need to love is fulfilled we have the emotion of delight, as I elaborate below (see also p. 23).

What the up-hierarchy is saying is that fully and effectively to meet needs higher in the hierarchy requires the fulfilment of needs lower in it.[2] If we aren't fulfilled in loving, we can't adequately appreciate the imagery of our world; and then we can't achieve a real interest in understanding our world; and without this our satisfaction in making choices is impoverished.

Each modal need has an active and a passive form – to love and to be loved, and so on. When the modes are considered as dynamic needs they partake of the projective–receptive polarity of the practical mode, discussed in Chapter 2, the principle of putting out and taking in; hence the active and passive forms.

Whether these four sets of needs are deficit motives coming out of inner lack or growth motives arising from inner abundance, in Maslow's sense (Maslow, 1955), depends on the stage of personal unfoldment. For the compulsive and conventional person, they are deficit motives; for the creative, self-creating and self-transfiguring person, they increasingly become growth motives.

Basic active personal emotions

If we now think of the fulfilment of the basic active needs, we get an up-hierarchy of emotions, projected upwards, as it were, from the individuating pole of the affective mode, where emotion has its home. This is depicted in Figure 6.2.

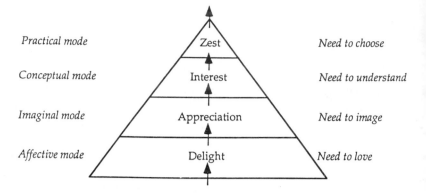

Figure 6.2 *The up-hierarchy of basic active emotions*

Delight

It is impossible to find just one word which will convey the full range of emotions involved in the fulfilment of any basic modal capacity. I have elsewhere defined loving in the following terms: 'To love a person is to delight in, and take pleasure in enhancing, that person's uniqueness' (Heron, 1990: 117). So I choose here the word 'delight' to symbolize the emotions involved in fulfilment of the need to love. What the word does not adequately convey is the dynamic thrust of love to enhance the flourishing of the other.

The chosen word could also have been 'joy'. But as well as joy and delight in, there is a whole family of cognate emotions: affection, regard, respect, raptness, tenderness, fondness, devotion, warmth, ardour, adulation, passion, rapture, liking, cherishing. Our need to love relates not only to other persons, but to our planetary environment and indeed the whole of creation. The fulfilment of this extensive need is also covered by the term 'delight': we delight in flowers, mountains and all manner of creatures.

Appreciation

By 'appreciation' I mean the emotions elicited by a consummation of the need to image, through the perception of nature and all forms of art, and through the creation of images. These are the aesthetic emotions called forth by the spatio-temporal properties of perceptual and all other kinds of imagery: colour, line, proportion, balance, symmetry, asymmetry, measure, scale, depth, tone, rhythm, harmony, melody, grace, strength, dynamic tension and so on. The emotions of a fulfilled imaginal sensibility are of a range and subtlety that outstrip the power of language to symbolize them. Hence they are conveyed by the non-discursive symbolism of drawing, painting, sculpture, music and dance. One cannot give a verbal list of these emotions, but only show a portfolio of their aesthetic representations.

Interest
When the need to understand is realized, we experience interest, extending into curiosity and fascination, the passion for truth, excitement in intellectual discovery, pleasure in the clear communication of ideas.

Zest
Finally, 'zest' is the word I have selected to convey the emotions involved in the fulfilment of free choice and effective action. The affective family here includes relish, gusto, exhilaration, achievement and work satisfactions, creative excitement, and so on.

The emotions higher in the up-hierarchy are all really forms of delight, and the fulfilment of different kinds of loving, for the capacities-cum-needs of the higher modes emerge out of the capacity for feeling or loving. Appreciation is a delight that springs from the love of aesthetic form; interest a delight that springs from the love of knowledge; zest a delight that springs from the love of action.[3]

Basic passive personal emotions

I now turn to explore the passive emotions which arise when the passive needs are satisfied. These are represented in Figure 6.3.

The basic passive emotions have not had a good time for a long while, in both the West and the East. Traditional Christianity, with

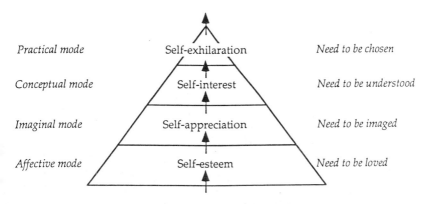

Figure 6.3 *The up-hierarchy of basic passive emotions*

its notions of the miserable sinner and the negative virtues of humility, self-denial and self-sacrifice, regarded them as sinful indulgences. Oriental mysticism has tended to discard them as insidious forms of bondage.

It is only in very recent times that some due estimation is emerging of their fundamental importance as touchstones of the full and proper individuation of the human person. In the One–Many universe, we are all members one of another; we are a holonomic community of souls. Our proper sense of our own distinctness is interdependent with its reflection in the validations and appraisals of our peers.

Self-esteem

Perhaps an emotion as fundamental as delight, since it is so central to the individuation of the human person, is self-esteem, which arises when our need to be loved and delighted in is consummated. All the evidence suggests that it is almost impossible for human beings to feel good about themselves if no one else ever has. And if they don't feel good about themselves, they have no secure and grounded identity around which the structures of explicit person-hood can form. The result is a deformed non-person masquerading as a person.

This is not to say that all self-esteem is necessarily a function of the explicit esteem of others, only that it originates in the latter and needs periodic reinforcement by it. Then it can become autonomous and self-generated.

Maslow acknowledged the interdependence of self-esteem and esteem from others, and regarded self-esteem as more essential. He stressed the point that lasting and healthy self-esteem is based on the deserved respect of others. And, of course, for Maslow, real self-esteem was a precondition of entering the highest develop-mental phase of self-actualization in which one desires 'to become everything that one is capable of becoming' (Maslow, 1970).

For Carl Rogers, self-esteem was a central concept of his personality theory. He called it positive self-regard, a feeling of worthiness coming from oneself, but originating in the positive regard of others. He assumed as a basic tenet of this theory that everyone has a need for positive regard. A person needs to get a lot of it from others, as a foundation for positive self-regard. Positive self-regard can function on its own when feelings of worthiness are well established from the acceptance, respect, sympathy, warmth and love of others. If this develops into fully autonomous and unconditional positive self regard, then the person is in an optimal state for self-actualization (Rogers, 1959). So both Maslow and

Rogers make a very close connection between self-esteem and self-actualization, a view which marks a major turning point in the history of psychology, eastern and western.[4]

Co-counselling, a form of peer self-help personal development, a co-operative tool for self-creating persons, has discovered that the giving and receiving of esteem – validation, affirmation, celebration, unconditional respect and acceptance – is the *central* way of healing the wounded child. It precipitates the discharge of its emotional distress and then releases the denied and buried capacity for self-esteem (Heron, 1979).

Self-appreciation

The other passive emotions are elaborations, in the upper levels of the hierarchy, of self-esteem at the base, but they deserve recognition in their own nature and their own right. Self-appreciation arises when the need to be imaged is fulfilled. This is a need to see a reflection of one's own mode of appearing in the world. The most literal way of meeting it is through the use of mirrors, and of photographs, films, audio-recordings of oneself. What is required as well as, or more than, this is spoken and written appreciation from others about how one presents oneself, on the qualitative impact of one's immediate behaviour.

Self-appreciation is the emotion of proper pride and self-respect in how one thus manifests. It is aesthetic self-regard in how one appears and presents oneself and is an important ingredient in positive individuation. When the image reflected from others is negative, or seen to be negative, this is information to use in the work of self-creating. You either use it to change the image, that is alter your appearance or behaviour; or you use it to alter the way you construe that image.

Self-interest

'Self-interest' is a term that has, in ordinary usage, an entirely negative connotation. It refers to the pursuit of one's own welfare to the exclusion of regard for other people. I wish to rescue it from this bondage and give it a very different kind of meaning. I use it to refer to the emotion of being interested by what one comes to understand about oneself as a function of feeling understood by others.

Like self-esteem starting with esteem from others, so self-knowledge starts with understanding from others, and self-interest is the emotion aroused by such self-knowledge. And like self-esteem, it can become autonomous, so that people feel deep interest when they acquire insights into their own psychological processes, their interpersonal behaviour, the unfolding of their

Table 6.1   *Modes, motivations and emotions*

Mode	Active need	Active emotion	Passive need	Passive emotion
Practical	To choose	Zest	To be chosen	Self-exhilaration
Conceptual	To understand	Interest	To be understood	Self-interest
Imaginal	To image	Appreciation	To be imaged	Self-appreciation
Affective	To love	Delight	To be loved	Self-esteem

personal history, and so on. Self-interest can, of course, degenerate into morbid fascination with the mess within. Again, this is a challenge for self-creating – to heal such wounded self-interest and restore it to its proper estate.

Self-exhilaration

Finally, self-exhilaration is the emotion arising when the need to be chosen is satisfied. This is the need to have the right kind of person seek you out and say 'I want to be with you and do things with you.' When it is met, the emotion is a self-exult.[5]

We can now summarize the modes, the active and passive motivations, and the active and passive emotions, in Table 6.1.

Personal distress emotion

When the basic needs are oppressed, actively frustrated by human or natural intervention, then distress emotion occurs. The person is emotionally pained. If this pain is repressed and not healed, the process of individuation is deformed, and the denied pain gets displaced into a variety of compulsive, distorted behaviours. My experience, with myself and others, is that whether the need is active or passive, its frustration occasions the same basic kind of distress emotion. What is different, however, is the way in which that distress is displaced after it has been repressed.

So while both an interrupted need to love and a frustrated need to be loved cause grief, the repressed grief of the former may be acted out in a different way to the repressed grief of the latter. In an earlier publication I suggested some correlations based on this distinction (Heron, 1977).

Grief

When the need to love and be loved is blocked, through rejection, severe misunderstanding, argument, isolation, parting or death, then we feel grief. Why this should be so is like asking why some reds are crimson. Enjoyment and suffering are the complementary poles of the emotional life. Grief is the suffering of frustrated love.

Genuine guilt is a special variant of grief. It is a consequence of a person doing something hurtful to a loved one and thus impeding the flow of love. It is the emotional outcome of self-interrupted love. Spurious guilt is the result of misguided and oppressive socialization, as when a person is brought up to feel that certain quite innocuous or benign behaviours are wrong.

Boredom

When the need to image is starved for whatever reason, with a severe reduction in the flow of imagery that one can appreciate, a person feels boredom. If the need to be imaged is starved, then we get internal boredom, self-alienation, ennui, ataraxia.

There can, of course, be spurious boredom, which is the result of laziness and lack of resourcefulness; and there can be pseudo-boredom, which is a mask for irritation and anger. But there can also be genuine boredom, as when one is confined to a drab transit lounge for some hours. Also there is the boredom of the creative impasse, which has to be suffered until there is a genuine break-through.

Boredom is a particularly challenging kind of distress emotion, because whatever the external situation, there are always the unlimited resources and hidden depths of the imaginal mind. But there is a time to go in, and a time to go out. If it is the time to go out and there is nothing much there, then there is boredom pure and simple.

I am not sure that authentic boredom has yet been properly acknowledged as a major block to effective individuation through aesthetic or imaginal appreciation. Just as you can't love adequately again until major past griefs have been owned, released and worked through, so it may be that you can't appreciate aesthetically in full until cumulative past boredoms are recognized and processed.

Fear

When a person's need to understand what is going on is thwarted through lack of education or information, through lies and mis-information, then fear is the outcome. Instead of the engaging, individuating emotion of interest in new information, there is the panic of disorientation, of facing the unknown without guidelines, of losing identity because there are no bearings within which to give it co-ordinates.

Of course, there are peculiarly physical fears, such as the fear of bodily pain, of injury and death. But the physiological mechanisms of pain and fear are very similar. Indeed much pain may be compounded by fear. For physical pain is an erosion of the bodily base of personal identity. All pain is potential death, the possible end of the body and can arouse fear of the great unknown, fear of a loss of any identity.

Fear de-individuates the person in a particularly harrowing way, because it creates a vacuum of intent. Its paralytic message is that one cannot do if one does not know. And one cannot do if one is not known; for fear is also the outcome if the need to be understood is unfulfilled: if I am not understood I have the deep anxiety of having no real social identity.

Anger

If I cannot choose freely, and be chosen freely, and I cannot see any good reason for this, then I feel anything from mild irritation to righteous indignation, anger and rage. Anger *per se* is the basic human response to inappropriate and unjust restriction of freedom of choice, whether this is the result of human oppression or of natural disasters. Rage is often anger from an immediate restriction that is heaped up with lots of old, unprocessed angers from the past evoked by the current anger-making situation.

There is the implication here that if I believe that the restriction on my freedom of choice is appropriate and just, I do not feel anger. This is perhaps too good to be true in all situations, but it is true in some, and in others the force of anger is mitigated by this kind of realization.[6]

The dynamics of distress emotion

Because we live in an emotionally repressive society, there is no general awareness about the nature of distress emotion, about what effects it has and about how to handle it. It is important therefore for us to have some working model about these matters, which is not just for specialist use, but for everyone as part of their education.

The following model is based on co-counselling theory and practice (Jackins, 1965, 1973; Heron, 1977, 1979), which, of course, owes a lot to other modern psychodynamic schools. What co-counselling networks have clearly established is the *accessibility* of this theory for peer self-help psychotherapy. People can help each other use it to transform their lives. I give here a summary account of my version of it.

A certain amount of distress emotion is enabling: it is a shock or spur to growth and development. The sadness of parting can make the heart grow fonder; the boredom of imagery starvation can lead to the exercise of creative imagination; the fear of the unknown can be a motive for learning and inquiry; anger can move one to put right social wrongs.

Beyond a certain threshold of tolerance distress ceases to be enabling, goes into overload and becomes disabling. This is especially true of the infant and small child. Faced with some overwhelming combination of grief, boredom, fear and anger, the psyche of the child resorts to the low-level survival 'choices' of repression, denial and displacement: push the pain down, disown it and act it out in some disguised form. At the same time the child has to repress and deny some deeply positive part of its own psyche, and identify with a false, alienated and conformist self.

There is a good deal of ambiguity about the mechanism of repression. Is it some kind of innate affective survival mechanism, which the guiding entelechy kicks into gear when there is too much emotional pain around; or is it a learned response to subtle parental cues which imply 'bury it or else'? I tend to think it is a mixture of both of these.

The next point is that repressed and denied distress distorts behaviour. Once pushed out of consciousness, or more to the point, prevented from crossing its threshold, what were the perfectly valid distress emotions of grief, boredom, fear and anger go sour. They become rank. They coil into twisted forms, which press against the barrier of repression and warp the behaviour of the false self, who thus becomes an unwitting hostage to its own act of repression.

To give but a few examples, repressed anger is acted out as oppressive manipulation of others, fear as devious deceit, boredom as driven sensationalism, grief as clinging dependency. In each case what was authentic distress has turned through repression into something nasty. All these distorted behaviours are compulsive and maladaptive. They get the false self nowhere, which, precisely because it is false, is about the only place it has to go.

The person becomes negatively individuated as the compulsive self. The imaginal mind, scarred with the distress of trauma, projects the template of its scarring on to daily life. The world is pathologically envisaged as a place where continuous repression and alienation of being is required.

What can a person do to break out of this negative individuation? Catharsis is one solution for repressed distress emotion. It means interrupting the distorted acting out, dismantling the repression, finding the core of authentic pain and releasing it: grief in tears and sobbing, boredom in uninhibited, imaginative talk, fear in trembling and shuddering, anger in high-frequency storming movements with loud sound. The real point about this psychophysical abreaction is the spontaneous self-generated insight that follows it: the reappraisal of past trauma with the realization that a deeply valid part of the person was repressed along with the pain, and that this part can now be reclaimed and educated to participate in adult life.

Transmutation is another solution. Whereas cathartic methods activate the distress-charged imagery of early trauma in such a way as to release the embedded pain, transmutative methods transform the imagery in a manner that alters its charge of distress into something neutral or even positive. It is an alchemical process of turning the base metal of inner pain into more refined affect. One method is to invoke a higher order of imagery in the extended reaches of the imaginal mind – fusing myth and ritual – in order to re-vision the afflicted imagery from the standpoint of a greater story, and to transmute its pain by an influx of archetypal power (Houston, 1987; Heron, 1990). Another way is to switch awareness from internal distress to feeling participation in the wider world until the negative energy shifts into neutral or positive effect.

Catharsis in my view is the method choice for the self-creating person, certainly at the outset, and certainly for the very major infantile traumas and what Grof calls COEX systems – systems of condensed experience (Grof, 1988). This approach really does ground autonomy in the discovery of itself. It guarantees that basic work is done at the level at which wounding originated. It prevents a premature shift to self-transfiguring – which leaves a bad odour sealed off in the basement of the psyche, which in turn points the nose of spirituality too high in the sky.

There remains the important question of the relative weight to be given to either catharsis or transmutation in practice. I think both are needed, since they work in complementary and mutually supporting ways; the exclusive use of either has distorting effects. So if you rely entirely on transmutation, there is the danger of deep-seated distress remaining denied, contracted and congealed, causing a distorted, dissociated or inflated kind of spirituality to develop. And if you rely exclusively on catharsis, there is the danger that frustrated spiritual energy will continuously inflate the cathartic process, causing an excess of emotional discharge.

Catharsis is important as the first step, in accord with the principle that some things have to be worked through at their own level. You cannot entirely resolve unfinished business at one level by working at it from a higher one. Not all personal distress can be transmuted by archetypal work; some of it simply has to be catharted at the level where it was laid in. So it seems a sensible idea to start with this; then it doesn't get forgotten or left behind or covered over with transcendental elegance and charisma. Catharsis, and the very personal insight it generates, establishes and affirms human autonomy on a bedrock basis. It is a basic tool for the self-creating person.

Transmutation is important as the second step. Of course, it is going on all the time in minor ways: the imaginative content that informs any culture sees to that through drama, stories, films, rituals and so on. But it can become much more intentional in personal growth work. And it is important because, equally, I don't believe you can deal with all personal and cultural distress at its own level by catharsis. To believe so is to get trapped on the cathartic treadmill, which is yet another version of the materialistic fallacy: the idea that everything has to be worked through at the material level, with something bodily going on. So transmutative work helps clean up the personal/cultural domains while at the same time opening up wider vistas of imaginal, archetypal reality. It is a basic tool for the self-transfiguring person.

Emotional competence

Emotional competence is one of the hallmarks of the self-creating person. It means that a person who has it is able to manage their emotions awarely in terms of the basic skills of control, expression, catharsis and transmutation, plus one or two others.

Our society is emotionally repressive. It has no working concept of the wounded child, no pervasive methods of emotional education and training. Child-raising, socialization and early education have only one guiding norm about emotions: learn to control them in order to be socially acceptable. This norm is tacit only: there is no explicit training in how to control emotions, no real clarity about what it means, only a general supposition that it is too obvious a social necessity to discuss.[7] It does not differentiate between healthy control and unhealthy repression. All too often the prescription to control emotion is misapplied and it then degenerates into suppression, repression, denial and the eventual return of the repressed in distorted form.

The result is that society has no way of dealing with the excess of distress emotion that children build up. Up to the age of five, with a peak after the first stage of language mastery at about three years old, children holding on to an excess of distress will readily displace it into all kinds of acting out behaviours – disruptive, demanding, clinging – both to try to relieve some of the pressure and to try to find some pretext for discharging the underlying pain.

If you interrupt the acting out, firmly but also very awarely and supportively, emotional discharge of pain will immediately occur with an intensity that bears no relation to the issue involved in the little bit of displacement that preceded it. Old-style discipline put a stop to the displacement, but in a punitive way that acted out the parents' own repressed distress: in demanding that the disruptive behaviour cease, it also angrily demanded that the child's underlying emotional pain be repressed and denied.

New-style discipline also stops the disruptive displacement behaviour, but in order to allow the child to release the distress emotion that is producing it. So interrupting the distorted behaviour, which will often mean some direct physical intervention, needs to be done in a manner that is free of any parental irritation or anger. It may involve quite firm holding, but it is a holding that is deeply affirmative of the child's being – as full-throttle catharsis proceeds. A distressed child will seize this opportunity to sob, scream, kick or tremble from anything between a few minutes to twenty minutes. All this time, the parent is gently affirming the child's self-healing. When the emotional release of pain reaches its clearance point for that occasion, the parent gives the child a warm and appreciative hug. The child will dance off to enjoy its world and its restoration to positive emotion.

A child that has been holding on to a lot of distress – because of some enforced period of parental deprivation, or for whatever other reason – may need to go through this whole process many times. It is as if the organism measures out the release in manageable phases and at appropriate intervals. When the next chunk of material is ready to be discharged, it will distort behaviour in some ritualistic manner; the parent interrupts the distortion and the release proceeds to a further point of clearance. Few parents have the nerve to do this. Their own repressed hurt child within is projected on to the child without: the inescapable result is that the repression of the child within the parent is imposed on the living child without.

The wounded child in our kind of society is a universal phenomenon. Its underlying emotional pain is repressed. The adult sustains the repression throughout life, achieving only limited release of the denied distress in the context of permissive intimacy and through laughter, dreams, post-orgasmic catharsis, the catharsis of drama, music and poetry, response to nature, and sport and religion. Some of these experiences may also be transmutative of hidden distress. The pain that is untouched by all this distorts behaviour.

For some this means neurosis and psychosis. For all it means unaware displacement: rational and sensitive responses to situations are all mixed up with compulsive distress-distorted maladaptive responses. And people do not know which is which; they slip unawarely from one to the other. This is because significant amounts of displacement behaviour are socially legitimized; they have become conventionally acceptable. Within the professions they have become correct professional interventions. So rational teaching is mixed up with compulsive teaching, rational medicine with compulsive medicine, rational priesthood with compulsive priesthood, and, in general terms, rational helping with compulsive helping; and the professionals cannot differentiate one from the other.[8]

This is a vast social pathology, a vast malaise. It cannot be regarded as a therapeutic problem, other than in the short-term individual case. It is an educational issue. We need concepts of child-raising and of education at all levels that foster the progressive development of emotional competence, in the same way that at present we foster the development of intellectual competence.

Emotional competence means many things. (1) It validates both positive emotions and distress emotions. (2) It sees the catharsis of distress emotion as evidence of self healing, not as evidence of breakdown. (3) It differentiates distress emotion as such from the disturbed, distorted forms it acquires after it has been repressed and denied. (4) It knows the difference between the catharsis of distress which occurs when repression is dismantled, and the displacement or acting out of distress which is the result of repression still being in place. (5) It can distinguish between catharsis as such and dramatization or pseudo-catharsis, which is the last vestige of acting out as repression falls away.

(6) More generally, it means the management of emotion in terms of the creative expression of positive emotion, the aware non-suppressive control of all kinds of emotion when appropriate, the catharsis of distress emotion at appropriate times and places, and the complementary process of the transmutation of distress emotion. (7) These four basic intrapsychic skills are supplemented by being able to identify, own and accept emotions of all kinds, and to switch and redirect emotional states. These important matters I have discussed in a series of other publications so I will not pursue them here (Heron, 1977, 1982, 1989, 1990). What all this emotional work does, among other things, is to make the affective mode of feeling, as I define it in this book, more accessible.

(8) In everyday living, emotional competence means being able to spot the restimulation of old emotional pain and to interrupt its displacement into distorted behaviour. So old hurt-laden agendas are not projected, not transferred, into current situations. (9) Behind this there is general insight into the main elements of early traumatic experience and its influence on adult behaviour.

(10) It means being able to spot institutionalized and profession-

alized forms of displacement, and to find ways of replacing them with more rational, flexible and adaptive behaviours. This is a crying need in all the helping professions. So the doctor abandons the repeat prescriptions of psychotropic drugs and cultivates an ability to handle psychosocial disorders. The academic relinquishes sixty-minute lectures and develops more skill in facilitating self-directed learning. The priest stops preaching sin and acquires competence in enhancing spiritual self-esteem.

(11) It means being able supportively to confront other people who are unawarely acting out their denied distress in negative and disruptive forms of behaviour. The confrontation does not shirk the behavioural issue: it deals with it straight and true. At the same time it does not attack, invalidate or abuse the person who is being confronted about the issue. The uncompromising feedback is fundamentally respectful.

(12) It means enjoying and expressing positive emotions, and (13) noticing when these are clouded over by distress to a degree that requires taking some time out for catharsis and/or transmutation. (14) It means cultivating celebration and self-esteem as a foundation of emotional life.[9] For an overlapping account of emotional competence and its criteria, see a recent paper by Denis Postle (1991).

Subtle and spiritual emotions

As I said at the beginning of the chapter, what I call personal needs, entelechy needs and spiritual needs, are progressive actualizations of the capacity for feeling distinct, unitive resonance with being. Entelechy needs underlie personal needs, and spiritual needs underlie both.

Entelechy needs are deep, developmental, formative motivations that shape the interplay and sequencing of bodily and personal needs. They have already been introduced in terms of the three basic dynamic polarities within the psyche: impulses to individuate or to participate; to ground the psyche in basic processes or to reorganize it; to be more vital or more mental. I think it is only the self-creating person who starts to be aware of these deep impulses in terms of their rhythmic oscillations and promptings, and to find the satisfactions of according behaviour with them. These satisfactions and correlative frustrations are a refined order of emotional experience.[10] They constitute a class of subtle emotion between personal emotions as such, and spiritual emotions as such. The tense emotion that correlates with frustrated entelechy needs is, in my view, too subtle to be dealt with by catharsis. It calls for transmutation at subtle and spiritual levels.

Spiritual emotions are to do with the consummation of spiritual needs in the full emergence of the self-transfiguring and charismatic person. They are celebrated by mystics of the heart such as the Sufi poet Jalaloddin Rumi who took to the path of illumination through love. On the One–Many view of the universe, where the relation between the enlightened soul and the divine can open at any time, sublime emotion sparks through the vast space within which the attuned soul and the great Other are at one. Such emotion individuates the distinctness of personhood within the embrace of the One. This is ecstasy, bliss, adoration, worship, praise, numinous awe, the continuous lauding of the unitive life. Such spiritual emotions, I believe, are the apotheosis of the individuating process. They are that focus whereby the transfigured person has a relationship with the divine.[11]

Exercises

1 Imaginal frustration and fulfilment
Take thirty minutes each to review your imaginal life. Relax into feeling fully present, then for the first ten minutes share experiences of being starved of imagery of any kind. For the remaining twenty minutes share experiences of being enriched by abundant imagery in perception of nature, places, art, in imagination, dreams or other states. Remember to include all sensory modalities, including touching, moving, hearing, seeing, tasting and smelling. After both turns, discuss your findings.

2 Emotional review
Take thirty minutes each to review your current lifestyle. First relax into feeling fully present. Then move up the hierarchy in Figure 6.1 and ask yourself about each active and passive need whether – in your life now – it is being fulfilled or frustrated and to what degree. Notice the emotional tone that goes with each identified fulfilment or frustration. After both turns, discuss the nature of the up-hierarchy, what if anything it omits, and consider whether higher needs are in any way grounded in those lower in the hierarchy.

3 Forms of delight
Take thirty minutes each to review experiences of the active personal emotions, as shown in the up-hierarchy of Figure 6.2. First relax into feeling fully present. Then evoke any three vivid instances that come to mind, from your whole life, of deep emotional fulfilment, first of delight, then of appreciation, interest and zest as

these are defined in this section. After both turns, discuss these differentiated forms of delight, and consider in the light of your shared experiences whether emotions higher in the up-hierarchy are in any way grounded in those that are lower.

4 Autonomous self-esteem
Take ten minutes each to affirm and celebrate, *without any negative qualifications*, your personal qualities and way of being in the world, and your achievements in life. If any compulsions to be self-deprecating arise, disidentify from them and sustain the celebration of your positive self-image. After both turns, discuss the dynamics of self-esteem.

5 Forms of emotional fulfilment
Take thirty minutes each to review experiences of the passive personal emotions, as shown in the up-hierarchy of Figure 6.3. First relax into feeling fully present. Then evoke any three vivid instances that come to mind, from your whole life, of deep emotional fulfilment, first of self-esteem, then of self-appreciation, self-interest and self-exhilaration as these are defined in this section. After both turns, discuss these forms of fulfilment, and consider in the light of your shared experiences whether emotions higher in the up-hierarchy are in any way grounded in those that are lower.

6 Forms of distress emotion
Take thirty minutes each to review experiences of the personal distress emotions, as defined in this section. First relax into feeling fully present. Then evoke any one or two vivid instances that come to mind, from your whole life, of deep emotional distress, first of grief, then of boredom, fear and anger. This not a cathartic session but one for noticing the *form* of the distress, its quality, intensity, its context and what basic needs and capacities in you were oppressed and thwarted so as to generate it. After both turns, discuss these different forms of distress, and consider further in the light of your shared experiences what gives rise to them.

7 Early emotional conditioning
Take twenty minutes each to review any earliest memories that come to mind of particular instances of being given explicit or tacit messages about controlling emotion of any kind, and especially distress emotions of grief, boredom, fear and anger. In what kind of emotional state was the person who gave you the message? After both turns, share your views on emotional control in our society.

8 Compulsive professionalism
Take twenty minutes each to review standard behaviour within your own profession and identify those typical behaviours that are compulsive as defined in this section. Also explore to what extent your own professional behaviour stumbles unawarely into compulsive routines or sudden irrationalities. After both turns, discuss the extent and social implications of compulsive professionalism.

9 Self- and peer-assessment of emotional competence
Fourteen criteria of emotional competence are given in this section, all numbered in the text. Take thirty minutes each to assess your own emotional competence, working through each of these criteria in turn. Somewhat with tongue in cheek, score yourself out of ten on each criterion, your partner keeping a note of the scores. After both turns, and if you know each other well, give each other feedback on the self-assessment scores, making your partner's scores higher or lower as you see fit. Discuss the difference between self-assessments and partner-assessments. Don't take any of this too seriously.

10 Entelechy emotions
Take thirty minutes each to do the following. Relax into feeling fully present. Then review your current lifestyle, the choices you have made and are daily making, and ask yourself, at the level of subtle emotion, whether you are fulfilling or frustrating the impulses to individuate, participate, conserve, reorganize, live and learn. Consider each in turn while bearing in mind its interaction with the others. After both turns, discuss the nature of entelechy emotions.

11 A personal relationship with the life divine
(1) This exercise is for you to do when alone. Deep in the emotional core of you, give yourself permission to say mentally to the life divine 'I need you, I love you, I want you . . .' with uninhibited extemporization. After a while, let the first-person pronoun undergo transcendental reversal, that is, let 'I need you, I love you . . .' be spoken inwardly to you by the divine I which is the ground and source of the everyday I.

(2) This exercise and the next one are to share with your partner. Try the same silent and deep inward emotional exchange for a few minutes while looking into your partner's eyes. After reversing roles, share you experiences.

(3) Let your partner be the life divine. Speak aloud your need and love to the divine partner; the partner voices aloud the divine response. After both turns, share your experiences.

7

The Imaginal Mode

The psyche in its imaginal mode is, I believe, inherently and continuously creative. At its own level, it generates the imagery of our worlds through perception, memory, dreaming, extrasensory perception, visions, creative imagination. It also gives rise to the conceptual mode as its offspring and outcrop. For in terms of the up-hierarchy model of the psyche, each mode emerges from the one below it in the hierarchy.

In this chapter I will consider first the imaginal mode as the source of the conceptual, together with a brief theory of the imaginal mind and a myth about the first language, then look at the role of the imaginal mind in perception, review a wider range of its other manifestations, and end with an account of intuitive processes.

The imaginal as the source of the conceptual

Fawcett sees imagination as the 'fundamental power' of the psyche, and the intellect as one of its transformations. In the tradition of Schiller, Dewey and Rignano he regards reasoning as imaginative experimenting; and philosophy, after Bosanquet, as a formal embodiment of penetrative imagination. Imagination, he reminds us, is the main source of all new ideas and of all variations in art and science (Fawcett, 1931, 1939). As I discussed in Chapter 5, accounts of the creative process show how a germinal image is the seedbed of conceptual and numerical information, which is later unfolded out of it. Images are packed with meaning prior to any explicit formulation of this meaning in verbal and conceptual terms.

> The imagination is a capacity to sense what you do not know, to intuit what you cannot understand, to *be* more than you can *know*. The imaging capacity of the mind is a transform of awareness from other dimensions of sensitivity. The song you did not hear you may begin to hum. The bacteria you did not see you may begin to envision. This capacity to think in images and then transform them into other dimensions of reference is vital to art, poetry and science. (Thompson, 1987: 8)

Max Planck, the founder of quantum theory, said the creative scientist must have a capacity for generating new ideas not 'by deduction, but by artistically creative imagination' (Koestler, 1964:

147). Hadamard questioned prominent mathematicians about the nature of their creative thinking. He found that almost all of them use mental pictures, mostly visual or sometimes kinetic, and avoid not only the use of mental words but also the use of algebraic and other precise symbols (Hadamard, 1945).

Einstein's reply to Hadamard's questionnaire brings out clearly the pre-conceptual, imaginal nature of the creative process. He says that his thought process uses images of greater or lesser clarity, some visual and some 'of muscular type', and that words and language 'do not seem to play any role'. The 'combinatory play' of these images 'seems to be the essential feature of productive thought – before there is any connection with logical construction in words or other kinds of signs which can be communicated to others'. He makes it plain that while the goal of this 'rather vague play' of imagery is to arrive at logically connected concepts, such concepts 'have to be sought for laboriously only in a secondary stage, when the mentioned associative play is sufficiently established and can be reproduced at will' (Hadamard, 1945: 142).

What Einstein's account brings out, I suggest, is that there is play of imagery in the imaginal mind which is felt to be inherently meaningful and this felt meaning has to be brought to a certain point before it can be expressed in linguistic and logical terms. This imaginal meaning I call archetypal, in the sense that it is entirely independent of and prior to the sense and reference of human words. It is not an artefact of human discourse and the speculation that follows from such discourse, since it is a precondition of these. It is to do with the meaning that is inherent in imagery as such. It can only be divined and received, not constructed; although, of course, the reception and subsequent linguistic translation and manipulation may distort and misrepresent it.

This inherent imaginal meaning is ultimately, I believe, to do with those deep patterns of form and process that interconnect the vast multiplicity and variety of images that make up our different experiential realities. 'Metaphor,' says Bateson, 'was the logic upon which the biological world had been built, the main characteristic and organising glue of this world' (Thompson, 1987: 46). Metaphor is about homology, correspondence in structure, the pattern that connects everything with everything else, like a ground-plan of creation. This may be why profound creative thinkers, like Planck and Einstein, who have the capacity to generate external thought from within their imaginal depths, tend to be convinced theists.

Many forms of creativity training have been developed in recent years. It is noticeable that they all basically seek to free the trainee from the grip of the direct intellectual approach to problem-solving, with its fixed assumptions and head-on strategies, and to release the uninhibited power of the imaginal mind. Brainstorming encourages a free flow of unusual and bizarre ideas, deferring any evaluation of them to a later stage (Clark, 1958). Lateral thinking seeks out different ways of looking at the problem, and imagines a variety of approaches to solving it before pursuing any of them (De Bono, 1975). Synectics, one of the best-developed types of creativity training, emphasizes both emotional and imaginative processes as the source of new ideas and solutions to problems, and stresses the importance of verbalizing these processes before any explicit problem-solving (Gordon, 1970).

Wenger, quoting a study by Reinert, claims that the regular practice of evoking, with eyes closed, a completely spontaneous and undirected stream of imagery and verbalizing it out loud to a listener or tape recorder, can improve IQ, integration on the Kolb Learning Styles Inventory and exam results (Reinert, 1989; Wenger, 1991). It is the combination of this image-streaming and explicit description which has the effect: imaging without describing out loud doesn't work. In other words, to draw spontaneous imaginal power right up into the conceptual mode through the spoken word improves intellectual competence.[1]

Wenger suggests that 'every aspect of every image is charged with meaning, pregnant with metaphor'; and that spontaneous image-streaming, verbalized and followed by intuitive interpretation, can be a fruitful aid to personal development. He also suggests an exercise which supports the thesis that all conceptual thought has a pre-verbal purely imaginal form. If you are studying a difficult area of text that you can't understand, ask your subtle image-streaming faculty to show you a picture that symbolizes its meaning, then hold the picture in mind while rereading the text 'and watch meaning fall into place for you' (Wenger, 1991: 60). This is similar to improving the rate at which you solve cryptic clues in a crossword puzzle by imaging the puzzle as already completed, especially as you write in each solution.

Wengers' idea of conscious image-streaming as an aid to personal development is, of course, rooted in the idea of unconscious image-streaming, that is, dreaming, as such an aid. The practice of dream interpretation in which dream images are translated into words and concepts that illumine some aspect of conscious life is ancient, and has a vigorous modern following. The meaning inherent in dream imagery seems to occur at three different levels at least.

There is the dream that is a metaphor for the internal dynamics of the psyche, often its conflicts, dissociations and distractions. Then

there is the dream that shows the dynamic of the psyche's interaction with mythic images – which I construe as dynamic foci of
meaning in the shared imaginal mind of embodied humanity. These
images are like condensed repositories of cumulative human experience of the basic parameters of life: gender, birth, death, age,
growth. They can be as confused, contradictory and misleading as
human experience itself, and are not, in my view, a reliable guide to
integration of the psyche (Heron, 1988).

Thirdly, there is the rare dream that reveals the interaction of the
psyche with those archetypal powers of transcendent origin that
shape the format of human destiny, and this involves a very
different level of the imaginal mind. Wilber seems to be one of the
few writers who is quite clear about the difference between mythic
images and archetypes in this sense. He points out that Jung is to
blame for mixing them up: 'the fact that certain archaic-mythic
images are *collectively inherited* was confused by Jung to mean that
they are *transpersonally located*' (Wilber, 1990: 255). Jung dealt
with mythic images and tried to give them an archetypal status
which they cannot carry.

A theory of the imaginal mind

This analysis of dream interpretation brings out some basic postulates for a theory of the imaginal mind in general. First, it is
interpenetrative, participative and fundamentally collective.
Secondly, there are two quite distinct levels of its interpenetrative
and collective nature. One of these is a cultural field of embodied
humanity which, more superficially, carries the image patterns
underlying the norms, values and beliefs of a given culture, and
more deeply the mythic images as I have defined them. The other is
a transcendent archetypal field whose images bear witness to the
underlying pattern of creation, and which while it may influence the
first level, is not influenced by it.

So when I spoke of the archetypal meaning of the imagery with
which deeply creative minds are busy, it is this second level with
which their imaging is in touch. And it is clear that in the process of
converting such meaning into conceptual form, the two levels will
inevitably be interfused. As soon as I look for concepts for my deep
images through the use of language, I become involved with the
image patterns of the cultural field, in particular those that underlie
prevailing beliefs involved in language use. Hence the great likeli-
hood that archetypal meaning will undergo all sorts of transformation and possible distortion in the process of giving it conceptual
expression.

A myth of the first language

The hypothesis of these two levels gives us a framework for considering the origin of language, which is really the first birth of the conceptual mode from the imaginal mode. Language is made up of person-made spoken and written images, aural and visual patterns. What these artificial word patterns mean are the natural patterns of the perceptual images that constitute our world. This is the denotation, extension or reference aspect of language.

But word patterns can also be used to mean other word patterns, and are then at one remove from the perceptual patterns of the world. This is the connotation, intension or sense aspect of language. And this is really the birth of the concept, the abstract and general idea: words defined in terms of other words. Once we get a network of such concepts going we have a relatively autonomous layer of meanings that members of a culture can use to discuss the significance of their experience.

What I have called the imaginal cultural field contains the *pattern* of linguistic interconnections that underlie the prevailing belief systems, the conceptual networking, of a culture. But at the birth of the first language no such conceptual networking had yet been established. The sense or connotation of word patterns could only come from the archetypal imaginal field, whose images provide the interconnecting homology or ground-plan of creation. Hence the fable of the first language as the Language of the Birds, or the Language of the Gods, or Court Language, as the key to the double science, sacred and profane (Fulcanelli, 1984).

This myth of a first language portrays it as arcane: it bears witness to the ground-plan of creation and is still almost entirely within the imaginal mode. It upholds a deep symbolic connection between three kinds of pattern: the pattern of perceptual imagery; the archetypal homologic pattern of creation; and the pattern of spoken sounds and engraved images.[2] The idea lingers on in the old tradition of sacred languages, such as Sanskrit and Hebrew, and the belief that the very pattern of their sounds and signs symbolizes the deeper structure of things.

One may surmise, continuing the myth, that the few seers who were raised up to utter the first language taught it to the many whose use subjected it to the exigencies of survival and the tensions of life. The archetypal relevance of its terms rapidly fades as a relatively autonomous conceptual network develops in the cultural field through the progressive interdefinition of words. People can now manipulate this to give expression to their independent learning and inquiry about the scheme of things. So we have the conceptual mode as a deposit of, a relatively separate crust on, the imaginal mode. Language shifts from the archetypal to the conceptually networked meaning of percepts.

While the conceptual mode bestows great freedom for the human manipulation of meaning, it is beset by its tendency to set up the subject–object split. Once this is done, the knowledge generated about the so-called objective world, however impressive, will be controlling and manipulative of, and alienated from, the deeper processes of being, as these can be apprehended by the imaginal and affective modes.

I wish now to look in more detail at the subject–object split, to see how it obscures the imaginal process in perception and to consider how this imaginal creativity in perceiving the world can be restored to human consciousness. I begin this analysis with the basic idea that perception involves a transaction with what there is.

Perception as a transaction

Perception is an interaction between psyche and being: the psyche is involved in shaping percepts, not just passively receiving them. Perceiving a world is a matter of the intelligent construing of forms, as Susanne Langer persuasively argues (Langer, 1951). Even modern neurology now confirms that perception involves processes of structuring and categorizing (Edelman and Mountcastle, 1978; Sacks, 1990). Being, *ens mysterium*, the immanent ground of our experience, is also making its contribution, always engaging us with an absolute otherness, which yet forever reveals its oneness with us. Such being is One–Many, a manifold of other presences, a network of beings that includes persons and all other sorts of entities.

This construing of a world through perception cannot be attributed to the brain alone, for it is a way of giving meaning to experience. Meaning is an irreducibly mental phenomenon: it can manifest through brain processes, it cannot be produced by them. Perceiving, as a mental process of giving meaning by shaping a world, is of a different order of reality to the brain through which it works.

Wilber gives a good lead on this point philosophically, developing clearly the point that 'mind transcends but includes physiology' (Wilber, 1990: 184). Wilder Penfield, the neurosurgeon, who spent years 'striving to explain the basis of mind on the basis of brain-action alone' finally decided that the active faculties of the mind are not in the brain but are 'transcendent functions' irreducible to physiology (Penfield, 1975).

The conceptual layer of perception

One aspect of the psyche's perceptual transaction with being is obvious enough: the conceptual layer that comes from our use of language and gets deeply embedded in the perceptual process. This enables us to see things as trees, or hills or fields or houses, that is in terms of the concepts that come with words. It is the classifying judgement that is built into perceiving when we have mastered our native speech. In the jargon of Kant, the understanding subsumes the sensory manifold under a concept so that there is an implicit judgement by a subject about an object. Elsewhere (Heron, 1981b) I have called this propositional construing. It turns perception into a continuous, unspoken, implicit description of the world in our mother tongue.

This tacit conceptual layer of the perceptual transaction is habitual, long-standing, entrenched in each moment of perceiving; but I do not think it can be called unconscious. It is still supraliminal. Like many such deeply engrained, automatic habits it is relegated to the very margins of awareness – except when some critical act of perceptual discrimination is called for, when it moves to centre stage.[3]

The imaginal layer of perception

The second aspect of the perceptual transaction with being is of a very different order. It is the layer of the percept as such, the actual visual or auditory or tactile image that portrays the world. That this is a construct is evident first of all from the structure of the sense organs, neural connections and cortex, which obviously determine a lot of what and how we perceive. But this does not explain the origin of percepts, only some of the limits within which they manifest. Indeed the bodily basis of perception is only known as a set of percepts itself: the body is a special class of percepts that constitute a gateway for a wider class.

The images of perception are meaningful patterns. Meaning, as I said above, is an irreducibly mental phenomenon. So also is its correlate, pattern: 'contrast and ratio and shape are the base of mentality. Pythagoras and Plato knew that pattern was fundamental to all mind and ideation' (Bateson and Bateson, 1987: 60). Langer argues that perceptual forms are inherently meaningful – in terms of their relations within the total structure of which they are a part (Langer, 1951).

The visual, auditory and tactile images that portray the world are constructs in a radical sense: they are products of the imaginal power of the psyche. This is Kant's productive imagination, which is responsible for synthesizing into concrete wholes the manifold of sensory apprehensions. Without such imaginative grasp of concrete wholes, Kant realized, no coherent experience would be possible. It is also what Coleridge calls primary imagination, which, in his own very different kind of language, is 'The living power and prime agent of all human perception and a repetition in the finite mind of the eternal act of creation in the infinite I AM.' The imaginal mind at work in perception is described by Kant as 'productive' and by Coleridge as a 'power' and an 'agent'. It is a shaping and moulding process: perceptual imagery is being *made* by the psyche in accordance with some unknown blueprint and programme. It is what I have elsewhere named presentational construing (Heron, 1981b); and what Fawcett calls the irreflective consciring that is the basis of perception (Fawcett, 1931).

This imaginal layer in the perceptual transaction with being is, I believe, entirely unconscious. I am not aware of my imaginal mind busy with the generation of perceptual imagery whether through seeing or hearing or touching. I turn what is a continuous process, a transaction, into something out there that I am looking at. I am aware of the image, the product of the process, but not of the imaging itself. I hypostatize, reify, this image into an appearance in the world that is independent of me. The transactional process I bury in unconsciousness.

Identification with the conceptual layer

The method whereby the burial takes place is a form of restrictive identification, which I define as my becoming so preoccupied with the current explicit structure of consciousness that I lose awareness of this involvement, since I have abandoned any viewpoint that would give me such cognizance. This means I cannot locate the boundaries of that structure, which in turn means that I sustain in unconsciousness everything beyond those boundaries.

The structure with which I identify in order to bury the imaginal layer of perception is the conceptual layer, the interpretation embedded in perception that sees things as instances of this, that or the other concept derived from language.[4] If I identify with this layer so that I can see nothing beyond it, then I am lost in the subjective–objective split and become entirely alienated from the active imaginal power of the psyche that is productive of every second of perceptual imagery. To remind the reader of this split I repeat here two paragraphs from Chapter 2.

The subjective–objective split

When the psyche subsumes the imagery of perception under concepts, the class names, that come with language, then we get a bifurcation of the world into a subject making a discriminatory judgement about an object. The subject tends to get set over against the object, and we reify our imaging of the world, and see the images as things outside us – we become alienated from our continuous generation of them. It is as if they are coming at us, rather than that we are producing them.

This subject–object split is very much a by-product, and an artificial one, of the use of language and the conceptual power it bestows. Conceptualizing perception, which is what we do all the time once we have a language, disrupts its transactional, participatory nature. The concept drives a wedge between the psyche and its world, breaking up the primordial synthesis of unit and unity. For what I call the world of presence, that is, the world-view parented primarily by the affective and imaginal modes, is one in which the psyche takes part in generating the imagery of perception, in which the psyche feels at one with a perceptual field which has no boundaries, no subject–object split, and in which all the while the psyche enjoys distinctness without separateness of being. So described, this is a transpersonal not a prepersonal or childhood state.

In the world of presence there are other particular beings of various kinds, different presences, including other persons. But in this world these are not known as objects or alienated strangers. They are known inclusively as participants in a unified field that includes both seer and seen as non-separable and distinct.

Reclamation of the imaginal power in perception

It is possible to disidentify from the conceptual layer in perception, and allow its creative imaginal power to surface into consciousness. In the section after the next, I outline a three-step method for doing this. Perception then starts to be included within consciousness as a process, a psyche–being transaction, rather analogous to breathing. Breathing is a transaction between the body-mind and being. It is both an involuntary and a voluntary activity: some power within me is breathing me, yet I am also somehow involved in the process and can certainly modify its depth and rate.

The imaginal power of perception is shaping the whole sensory field and flowing through me in a creative stream from some archetypal source – of which I get hints and gnostic intuitions as soon as I disengage from the conceptual layer and let the stream flow. It is, I suppose, these intimations of a wider power that are disconcerting to the psyche and lead it to identify with the conceptual layer, so that it doesn't get more reality than it can handle.

But the imaginal stream is not entirely involuntary, for I realize that I am involved somehow as a conscious agent in it, and begin to sense that, as with breathing, there is scope for me to modify the streaming within certain limits. There are thus two classic routes whereby the psyche can practise self-transfiguration and commune, both passively and actively, with a deeper presence: by attuning with full awareness to breathing, and to perceiving. The productive imaginal power in perception can, I find experientially, be let into consciousness to an unmistakable degree.[5]

The imaginal mind and universal consciousness

Once I disengage from the subject–object split and attend to the imaginal mind as a creative source of perceptual imagery, I am in touch with a universal power of consciousness working through me. Here in the very process of daily perception is a remarkable key to the liberation of awareness from the preoccupations of the ego.

For whatever the ego is busy with – whatever its compulsions, guilts, blamings, obsessions, restlessnesses, indulgences – this imaginal force that shapes my world is at work with immaculate thoroughness. If I cease feeding attention into the ego and lie back in this immediate might, I find that perceiving is a universal process focused through my personhood and my participation.

Because it flows through my being, I can turn into it and know it for what it is – impeccable form and pattern-making emerging from a ground of archetypal grandeur, the great range and sweep of cosmic consciousness. This is indeed, to quote Coleridge again, 'the living power and prime agent of all human perception – a repetition in the finite mind of the eternal act of creation in the infinite I AM'.

Douglas Fawcett conceived the universal ground as divine imagining, comprising a dynamic field of imaginals – cosmic powers or agents – which uphold creation and which human imagination at a deep level refracts in generating percepts of its world (Fawcett, 1939; Johnson, 1957). 'The eternal body of man,' said William Blake, 'is the imagination, that is, God Himself.' Frances Yates in her scholarly research on the Renaissance thought of Giordano Bruno and its strong links with the Hermetic tradition, brings out his deep commitment to a magic of the imagination, which empowers the mind by building up within it images that connect dynamically to the archetypal powers of creation (Yates, 1964).

There are correspondences, in my view, between my account of imaginal mind and the Buddhist doctrine of *manas*, intuitive mind. *Manas* is an emanation of universal consciousness, *alaya-vijnana*, also called store-consciousness, in which the archetypes of all things are stored. So *manas* is continuous with universal mind.[6] But it also takes part in everyday thought-consciousness, *mano-vijnana*, which co-ordinates sense impressions, and which can become the focus for restricting ego consciousness.

Manas mediates between everyday consciousness and universal consciousness. The power of *manas* becomes a source of error if it feeds ego consciousness and the subject–object split; it becomes a source of liberation if it turns about to attend to the universal store-consciousness whence it emanates. Perceptual imagery is then seen reflected in its archetypal form in this oceanic reality. This is the Knowledge of the Great Mirror, the Mirror-like Wisdom (Govinda, 1960).

Post-linguistic perception

What I mean by post-linguistic perception is the experience of being consciously involved in generating the images of a world, of participating in the process of forming percepts. It closes the gap between seer and seen, who are thus known as non-separable and distinct within a transactional whole. It does not try to revert to the pre-linguistic perceiving of the very small child, which is neither possible nor useful. Without in any way rejecting language it seeks to transcend the splitting effects of its ordinary use.

I give an outline here of a three-step method for uncovering the imaginal process in perception. This first move is to raise one's consciousness about the way language use sets up the subject–object split. So this is a matter of reading something like this chapter, and being persuaded that a valid point is being made. If you don't find the analysis plausible, and consider, for example, that percepts are a by-product of brain processes, then that will be the end of the matter.

The second step is to get out and about in the world, and while doing so to implant a brand new conceptual layer right inside the very act of perceiving. The old conceptual layer sees the percept as the image of a cat or a house or the moon. The new one knows the percept is projected out of the depths of the imaginal mind. I call it the reversal concept, since it refers to what you know through the great reversal. This is when you turn about in the deepest seat of

ordinary consciousness, away from objects into the coming into
being of percepts. The purpose of the reversal concept is to flip the
mind into the great reversal.

You don't try to get rid of the old conceptual layer, which in any
case is very embedded. You just ignore the habit of seeing things as
instances of class-names, and embed the new reversal concept. So
while looking at the landscape you are saying to yourself things like
'This is all streaming out of the imaginal mind', 'I am involved in
generating my world', 'I feel my participation in creating images',
'Here comes my version of the world', 'I am the percepts I am
creating' or indeed any other inner statement that triggers you to
turn around deep within to face the stream of perceptual imagery
that is your immediate field. Then it is as if all at the same time you
are the percepts and the universal consciousness that is pouring
them forth. It is a unity of three-in-one.

Remember you are not just naively telling yourself that the whole
perceptual field is a product of your private imagination – this would
be the crudest kind of 'new-age' you-create-your-own-reality talk.
Rather you are owning that your own mind is continuous with
universal mind releasing its storehouse of images to clothe the
beings-in-a-world whose presence you feel.

I have found it interesting to combine the embedding of this new
conceptual layer with quite rapid hyperventilation combined with a
sound on the out-breath. You will need to be reasonably isolated to
practise this without alarming bystanders. This does two things: it
brings into consciousness the fear of being overwhelmed; and it also
releases some of the fear through the bodily vibration and the
sound. Remember we usually repress and deny what we are afraid
of. If anything is going to make the separate-subject-ego anxious it
is the streaming luminosity of universal mind.[7]

In and among all this you may well get flashes, great openings,
dazzling intimations, a pre-dawn of what the Tibetan mystics call
the Mirror-like Wisdom. And this is the third step, not that it is a
step you can actually take; rather, *it* takes the step, the underlying
process suddenly reveals itself.

Another version of the second step is to go out and view the world
and all the time imagine that you are looking into an immense
mirror the edges of which you cannot see. And imagine that what
you see in the mirror is a reflection of a small part of your own
cosmic body. You may want to hyperventilate with this one too. It is
a powerful kind of reversal concept-cum-image.[8]

In the next chapter there is a section which looks at how this new
way of perceiving could be applied within the framework of what I
call post-linguistic propositional knowledge (p. 171 ff.).

The range and depth of the imaginal mind

The unconscious imaginal power of the psyche generates imagery in many other domains as well as perception. It is not my purpose to go into any of these in great depth, but to sketch the extent of the territory.

Dreaming

The imaginal mind frequently overflows into consciousness in remembered dreams, the interpretation of which I have already discussed. Dreaming reveals the abundant and effortless energy of imaginal power. A person can be too tired to imagine a hairpin, yet fall asleep and the psyche releases a vigorous and complex stream of dream imagery. Dreams teach us the deep autonomous interaction of intuition and imagery. In a dream the meaning of imagery is relatively independent of conceptual discrimination; and the interpretation of a dream often requires considerable concentration to convert its purely imaginal intuition into verbal form.

Lucid dreaming

And it is now clear that being unconscious is not a necessary condition for releasing the imaginal power of dreaming, since LaBerge (1985) has already shown convincingly that conscious or lucid dreaming can be practised, in which the subject can exercise significant control over the dream imagery.[9]

Out of the body experiences

Beyond lucid dreaming there is a further stage of out of the body experience, in which the imaginal mind is busy generating the imagery of another reality and another body, sheath or vehicle of consciousness through which the person can operate in this other reality (Rogo, 1978; Heron, 1987).

Hypnagogic imagery

There is the vivid hypnagogic imagery that can occur spontaneously between sleeping and waking and may develop for a period into visionary and *clairvoyant perception*. My own experience of this is that it is very quickly cut off by some combination of processes that relegate it to unconsciousness (Heron, 1987).

Idio-retinal lights as a gateway to the imaginal mind

An immediate point of linkage between the imaginal power that works through the sensory field and the same power moving in other dimensions is provided by idio-retinal lights. When the eyes are closed, the visual field, long after all after-images have faded away, will have a variety of vague shapes and colours that correlate with bio-electrical activity in the neural structure of the eye and pathways to the brain.

If you focus on these gently and consistently, pouring imaginal attention into them whatever they are, after a time they will start to become gateways for the appearance of another order of imagery. The whole field transforms into views of landscapes, the interior or exterior of buildings, and so on – of greater or lesser clarity. This imagery can be highly metamorphic, changing from form to form with bewildering rapidity; but here, unlike perception, the psyche has great scope to exercise voluntary control and regulate what goes on. The portrayals can have a surprising and exhilarating quality, as if unfurling out of some wider or deeper layer of being, rather than just one's own memory bank (Heron, 1987). The voluntary–involuntary nature of imaginal power is quite nakedly revealed.[10]

Psychotropic drug experiences
This might is revealed in its dramatic fullness by the use of psychotropic substances such as LSD, which temporarily suspend whatever processes normally keep imaginal energy at bay. Stanislav Grof has perhaps done more than anyone else to lay bare the range of experience that can be unleashed by LSD (Grof, 1976). It covers the perinatal matrices to do with foetal life and the birth process, early traumatic childhood experiences, an array of spatio-temporal, extrasensory extensions of consciousness within this reality, and a further wide sweep of extensions of consciousness within other realities. In all these experiences, the imaginal mind is operating in its polar functions of imagery and intuition. It delivers impressive imagery at the same time as a gnostic intuition of what aspect of being this imagery portrays and what its significance is.

Kundalini yoga
In oriental psychology, imaginal power is called *kundalini-shakti*, the feminine creative power generating everything, consort of *shiva*. In its untutored forms it shapes the content of ordinary consciousness through perception, memory, dreaming, anticipation, fantasy. When tutored through the disciplines of awareness training, as in various forms of yoga, it releases the structures of non-ordinary consciousness having transactions with wider dimensions of being (Krishna, 1970; Mookerjee, 1982).

Intrasensory perception
In the ordinary course of events, regardless of any special training, the imaginal mind penetrates ordinary consciousness with forms of

intrasensory and extrasensory perception to a degree that our culture is only just beginning to acknowledge. By intrasensory perception I mean all those non-sensory apprehensions that are at the very heart of everyday human behaviour. Thus the gaze is to be distinguished from the eyes; and taking up someone's gaze is not the same as perceiving their eyes. Rather there is an imaginal apprehension of the gaze at the same time as perception of the eyes (Heron, 1970).

Similarly, a person's touch is not the same as the texture of, or temperature of, or pressure from, their skin. It is an intrasensory quality that is mediated by these sensory phenomena, and imaginally realized together with them.

It is also a commonplace of human interaction to be able to divine someone's mood and unstated thoughts in ways that are not always reducible to inference from perceived behaviour. It is as if there is an imaginal apprehension of subtle, non-physical aspects of their psyche, together with an immediate intuitive grasp of what these mean.

In all these three instances, the ground of imaginal apprehension is felt resonance with the other, which is the most fundamental component of the transaction.

Extrasensory perception
Spontaneous and unbidden extrasensory perception has been tumbling into the unsuspecting awareness of ordinary people since, presumably, time immemorial; or certainly since the Society for Psychical Research and similar bodies started to collect anecdotal evidence of ESP. Precognition, retrocognition, telepathy, clairvoyance, clairaudience, psychokinesis, out of the body experiences: all these have found a way of avoiding the processes that normally keep them unconscious, in those who are otherwise busy with the demands of everyday life, and who have no pretensions to any kind of arcane training. The sheer quantity of data in this field, together with information about the sorts of sensible people who report it, starts to become evidential. Tyrrell (1948) had a useful theory of the subliminal self to account for all this.

Near-death experiences
Significant numbers of people who are brought back from the very brink of physical death by modern medical technology give remarkably consistent accounts of how death is a transition in which imagery of another reality unfolds in a series of identifiable stages (Moody, 1977; Noyes, 1980; Ring, 1984).

Childhood experiences
At the other end of life, there is mounting evidence of the degree to which many small children live in a multi-imaginal reality that goes beyond the rich fantasy life of creative play.[11]

Three degrees of intuition and gnosis

The imaginal mode of the psyche I have suggested is polarized into two complementary functions, imagery and intuition. Imagery yields a unique perspective on some particular aspect or dimension of being. Intuition I defined at the outset as the immediate, comprehensive knowing whereby the mind can grasp a field, a system, a being as a patterned unity, apprehend it in terms of figure–ground and part–whole hierarchies, see its connections with other patterns, and know what it signifies.

In this definition there are actually three components, three degrees of intuitive knowing. The first is the grasping of some field of imagery as a patterned unity, a figure–ground, part-whole hierarchy embedded in other such hierarchies. The second is the awareness of the pattern that connects this imagery with other and related kinds of imagery. This is the intuition of analogy, metaphor and symbolism: the grasp of homology, the correspondence of basic structures. The third is the apprehension of ontological meaning, an immediate knowing of what kind of being, or what qualities of being, the imagery signifies.[12]

The second of these, the grasp of homology – the metaphor that connects the deep structure of one sort of imagery with that of another – seems to me to be the main business of imaginal intuition. The third one, apprehension of ontological meaning, is really what feeling, as I have defined it, is also about. It is where feeling emerges as the substrate of the imaginal mind.

Exercises

1 Image-streaming
Make a contract with your partner to spend ten minutes each day for one week verbalizing into a tape recorder, with eyes closed, a spontaneous uninterrupted stream of imagery. After the week is over, meet to discuss the process and share what, if any, seem to be its effects.

2 The recreation of sacred language
Meet together at night in an isolated place in clear sight of the full

moon; relax and feel your participation in its image. For ten minutes chant together the word 'moon' feeling a connection between the sound, the perceptual image of the moon, and the archetypal ground of the moon. Discuss your findings.

3   Perception as tacit description

Go for a walk together for ten minutes without talking, just looking and listening. Be extra mindful about your perceiving of the world. Is it not the case that your every act of perceiving is always a matter of seeing something as, or of hearing something as, a certain sort of thing? Do you not, for example, see that thing as a tree, and is it not the case that although the word 'tree' is tacit and latent in your mind, it still delivers the concept of a tree to be incorporated in perception? And is not this a very marginal rather than an unconscious process? After the ten-minute walk, discuss your findings together.

4   Disidentifying from the conceptual layer in perception

Go for another walk together for ten minutes without talking. Just look and listen selectively and slowly, staying with each percept until its verbal tag comes right into awareness. As it does so, notice the whole process of interpretation and judgement embedded in perception. Let this conceptual layer be so evident in your perceiving that you can start to disidentify from it, that is get some mental space right around it. After the walk, discuss your findings together.

5   Perception as imaginal process

Practise the following for five minutes together in a room or garden – moving, pausing, looking, hearing and touching. Relax into the present moment and feel continuous with the world through perception. As you see, hear and touch the world, remind yourself that there is no separation between you and any of your perceptual images: your body–mind is involved in generating them. Feel perceiving in all its modalities as a process, in which the subject–object split is absent. After the five minutes, share with each other what happened.

6   Turning about in the deepest seat

Take ten minutes to do the following meditation together. Relax and feel the deepest seat of the ordinary everyday mind, within and below its preoccupation with immediate mental, emotional and perceptual phenomena. *Turn about* in this deepest seat and notice how this mind is subtly continuous with universal mind. After the meditation, discuss your findings together.

7   Hyperventilation and the transfiguration of perception
Go to an isolated spot with commanding views and do the following
together for ten minutes. Look to the sky while still being able to
see much of the landscape. Relax and feel that everything you
perceive, the perceiving process and you yourself are pouring out of
universal consciousness whose luminosity is within, beyond, around
and all about, dissolving everything in its light while yet retaining
everything as distinct. As you start to cultivate this feeling, also start
to hyperventilate, breathing in and out rapidly with full breaths,
making a sound of shock and surprise on the out breath. Open
yourself more to the feeling as you intensify the sound and the
breathing. Afterwards, share and discuss your findings.

8   The world as mirror image
Stand together on a remote hilltop with a panoramic prospect. Look
to the west, relax and feel your participation in the view, and
imagine that between you and the image of the landscape there is a
mirror of vast scale whose edges are beyond the range of your
vision. Imagine that the landscape which you now see is the mirror
image of a small part of the whole universe which you have become.
After twenty minutes, discuss your findings. On another occasion,
go together to a busy city intersection, find a convenient location in
a vacant recess or doorway, and practise the same exercise. Later,
compare and contrast the effects at the two different locations.

9   Conscious dreaming
Agree with your partner to do the following for a month. Ask
yourself ten times a day, when you are awake, whether you are
dreaming or not; also in bed while drifting toward sleep. This
critical, reflective attitude to everyday consciousness has been found
to be most effective for inducing conscious dreaming (Tholey,
1983). After a month, share and discuss any conscious dreams either
of you may have had.

10   Idio-retinal transformations
Do this exercise together for twenty minutes. Lie back in a
comfortable chair with eyes closed in a place where the external
lighting is uniform (sitting outside in the shade on a sunny day works
well). Keep the eyes closed for the whole exercise. Relax into being
fully present. Watch the after-images wax and wane until they fade
away totally. Now attend closely to whatever vague shapes and
colours next appear in the closed-eyes field. Keep feeding attention
and mental energy into these shapes and colours as they change,
while dissociating entirely from any other mental contents. Sustain

this until the idio-retinal images transform into imaginal scenes before the mind's eye. However vague the pictures, go with them as they develop more clarity. After the twenty minutes, share and discuss your findings.

11   Imaginal world of childhood

Take twenty minutes each to remember how the imaginal mind filled childhood. Recall experiences of the creative imagination of play and games of make-believe, of the magic and mystery invested in everyday places and events, of 'imaginary' playmates, of daydreams and fantasies, of vivid imagery projected out before the open eyes, of visions, out of the body experiences and whatever else. After both turns, discuss what seemed to shut it all down.

12   Three degrees of intuitive knowing

Take fifteen minutes each to do the following. Draw one simple plane figure well inside another one, for example a circle within a square. First, describe the image as a part–whole, figure–ground unity – this is the first degree of intuitive knowing. Secondly, describe the analogies and metaphors that the image evokes ('It looks like a hole in a card', 'I see a face in a window') – this is the second degree of intuitive knowing. Thirdly, describe what qualities of being the image signifies ('It tells me that human experience is dignified by its limits') – this is the third degree of intuitive knowing. After both turns, each with a different image, discuss the differences between these three degrees.

8

The Psyche and its Worlds

The integrated modes as world parents

In Chapter 2 I used the up-hierarchy, the cycle and the spiral as metaphors for the interaction of the affective, imaginal, conceptual and practical modes of the psyche. I now come to a fourth metaphor: the modes seen as interactive pairs, each pair parenting a world. I combine it with the cycle and the up-hierarchy.

What I mean by this is simply that the world is the fruit of a transaction between the psyche and being, and that what sort of a world we are in depends on what psychological modes are primarily involved in that transaction. The model proposes that to generate a distinctive world-view, or 'world', it takes two modes and that within each of these two modes its participatory and individuating poles need to be integrated. These two modes will be active in the transactional foreground, while the other two will be tacit in the background.

Figure 8.1 presents the basic scheme. Around the circumference are the four participatory modes, and in the centre their individuating correlates. Each world is in a quadrant of the circle and is parented by the two primary modes, in both their participatory and individuating forms, overlapping that quadrant. Each quadrant details some of the different sorts of modal transaction within each world.

For each world-view one parent mode is rather more dominant than the other, since from the point of view of an up-hierarchy, one of the pair is the ground and source of the other. Thus the affective mode is dominant in parenting the world of presence, the imaginal mode the world of appearance, the conceptual mode the world of essence, and the practical mode the world of existence.

In their transaction with being, the affective and imaginal modes together create the *world of presence*, the world-view of the mystic and visionary. Feeling is the primary mode and together with emotion, intuition, perceptual and other imagery, generates the experience of participating with comprehensive awareness in a qualitative world of interrelating presences. Presence refers to the unique impact of any particular being, its distinct signature. To use

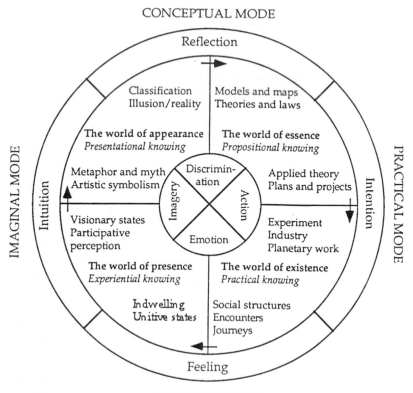

Figure 8.1   *The psychological modes parenting four worlds*

more metaphors, it is the manifest tone of a thing, its immanent speech or utterance, its declarative sound.

A presence, such as we call an owl, manifests through immaterial qualities of being – serene, quizzical, inscrutable, noble, elegant – and these in turn are clothed in perceptual imagery. It is a direct and unique disclosure of being that both grounds and unites all its immaterial qualities and its perceived form. A unified field of resonating presences is a world that can be felt when it is liberated from bondage to restrictive classifications that come with the old use of language. It is a world, however, compatible with the holistic categories of unitive discourse in a new use of language – which I discuss later in this chapter.

Toward the imaginal pole of this bi-modal world there are visionary experiences, and process-engaged, participative perception, with intimations of its archetypal origins; toward the affective pole, mutual resonance, participative indwelling and unitive states attuned to the interdependence of presences – each in each, and all in each and each in all.

The imaginal and conceptual modes, in their conjoint transaction with being, beget the *world of appearance*, the world-view of the artist, poet, phenomenologist and discriminating observer. Here, the imaginal mode of intuition and imagery is primary. Interacting with reflection and discrimination, it yields discernment about the patterns of phenomena, and their interconnections.

In this world it is the manifest formation of the perceptual field that is paramount. We disattend from feeling the unique presence and immaterial qualities of particular beings, to pay regard to the configurations of perceptual imagery that constitute their way of appearing, and to correspondences between these perceived patterns.

At the imaginal pole, there are artistic and non-discursive symbols and linguistic metaphors for the world of appearance and its interconnections; at the conceptual pole, classifying and categorizing with concepts, and distinguishing between illusion and reality in how things appear.

The conceptual and practical modes generate the *world of essence*, the world-view of the inquiring intellect. This world view stems mainly from reflection and discrimination. I use the word 'essence' here in a traditional philosophical sense to refer to universals or general ideas, which we use in various combinations to define the nature of things. At the conceptual pole of this world, these combinations are expressed in concepts and numbers and formulated by conjecture into models, maps, formulae, laws and theories. At the practical pole, the conjectures become theories of application and technology, plans and projects that look forward to action.

The practical and affective modes engender the *world of existence*, the world-view of the doer. Intention and action are primary, and together with emotion and feeling, create a lived world of enterprise and endeavour, in which deeds encounter what exists. At the practical pole, this enterprise includes all kinds of experimental and action research, industry, and planetary work – by which I mean any labour that develops and supports the planetary environment. At the affective pole, it has the nature of interpersonal encounter and relationship, of visits, voyages and journeys: the heart and the will take us forth to meet particular people and places. Between these poles at the centre of the world of existence is the creation of social structures.

The four worlds can for convenience be thought of in terms of four words beginning with 'p'. There is the world of presences, the world of patterns, the world of propositions, and the world of practices. The arrows in Figure 8.1 indicate that each world is grounded on and emerges from the prior one in the circuit. While the metaphor of the up-hierarchy makes the world of presence basic, the cycle image also shows that enterprise in the world of existence can lead over into a new level of experience in the world of presence. Thus in this century, basic experimental work in physics – in the world of existence – is pointing towards a new experiential relation with the world of presence.[1]

The above account of the four world-views is a holistic one: it presupposes that the participatory and individuating modes of the psyche are integrated within each mode. These worlds are therefore the worlds of the integrated person in one or other stage of development – creative, self-creating, self-transfiguring. The closed ego, comprising only the individuating modes in the centre of the figure, has an activist bias exclusively toward the world of existence, giving only a very limited account of it.

Discontinuities between the worlds

The different worlds, or world-experiences, are quite distinct. To feel the world of presences and their immaterial qualities of being is different from being exclusively involved with the world of perceptual form and appearance. And this is different from relating to the world as the exemplification of conceptual models, theories and laws. And all these are different from the world encountered through action and practical projects. When any one world-experience is to the fore, the other three become tacit, falling into the background. When they are all integrated into a fourfold, simultaneous, multi-world-view, then we have perhaps the world of the charismatic person.

A creative person may exhibit anomalies and discontinuities in the relations between his or her four worlds. How this person actually perceives the world as the world of appearance can be quite different from some of their basic belief systems in their world of essence.[2] Thus a committed systems theory theist in his or her world of essence may still have, in the world of appearance, the culture's mechanistic and atheistic concepts embedded in their very act of perceiving the hills, the trees and the High Street. And the same person may generate through their actions a world of existence in which people become alienated objects to be manipulated like things. Again their world of existence is quite different from their world of essence.

Even when there is a good deal of consistency and coherence between the four worlds, they still yield creative discontinuities. For in terms of the up-hierarchy metaphor, each world is a reduced precipitate of the world below it. The great potential variety in the fecund emergence of world from world means that their interaction is always going to be one of *frisson* and surprise.

Epistemological issues

Each world is a subjective–objective reality, a transaction between the paired modes and being. The paired modes do not just create their worlds in some arbitrary way; rather they generate their realities through interaction with what there is. So these realities are relative to being. However, since they are modal versions of it, they can never give any final, purely objective account of it. And since persons are developing, their modal versions of being undergo periodic metamorphoses. Again, for all we know, being itself may undergo periodic changes.

The four relativistic worlds can also be shown as an up-hierarchy, as in Figure 8.2. In this model, the higher worlds are all tacit and latent in the lower, emerge out of them and, while being to some degree autonomous, are grounded in and supported by them. Thus the world of existence is a relatively independent transaction arising out of and based on the conjectures and belief systems of the world of essence; these are partly autonomous transactions growing out of and rooted in the patterns, metaphors and classifications of the world of appearance; and these in turn proceed from their ground in the participation and indwelling of the world of presence.

In terms of a theory of knowledge, the validity of any set of

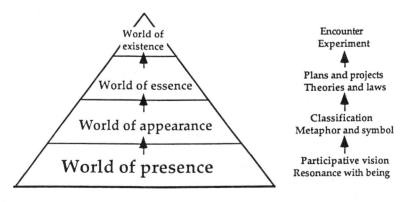

Figure 8.2   *The four worlds as an up-hierarchy*

transactions will partly have criteria internal to its world, and partly have criteria to do with its grounding in a lower world. Within the metaphor of the up-hierarchy, this means that the validity of the transactions that constitute the world of presence will be a touchstone for the validity of all higher sets of transactions.[3]

Within the metaphor of a cycle, however, all the worlds are dynamically modifying each other, as indicated by the arrows on Figure 8.1. Both metaphors are probably needed. For while there is a sense in which the world of presence is a base touchstone, it too is a psyche–world transaction which can be transformed as a result of encounters and journeys that influence it from the world of existence.[4]

The result is a double coherence theory of the soundness of any set of transactions that make a world. It needs to have coherence within itself, and also coherence with transactions in each of the other grounding worlds, and especially with transactions in the world of presence – the world of unitive perception, and participative empathy. But this world too is subject to revisionary influence from the world of existence: like the serpent feeding off its own tail.

What I mean by the coherence of a set of transactions that make a world is the validity of its claims to knowledge. The four worlds generate four forms of knowledge, and to these forms and their canons of validity I now turn.

Experiential knowledge

The world of presence yields what I shall call experiential knowledge. I give this phrase a definition in depth. I mean by it knowledge through participation in, and resonance with, one or more beings in the unified field of being; the knowledge, in short, that comes with feeling as I define it. This is a much deeper version of the traditional accounts of knowledge by acquaintance, which means knowing something by face-to-face encounter with it.

William James made the classic distinction between what he called 'knowledge of acquaintance' and 'knowledge-about'. The former means meeting people, places and things; the latter means having ideas and information and judgement about them. He points out that most languages make this distinction (*kennen, wissen*; *connaître, savoir*; *noscere, scire*). 'All the elementary natures of the world,' he says, must be known by acquaintance or not known at all; and it is 'through feelings we become acquainted with things' (James, 1890, Vol. 1: 221).

But he minimalizes knowledge of acquaintance even while stressing that, without it, there is nothing for knowledge-about to be about. He writes of the '*dumb* way of acquaintance' and again of 'a *mere* condition of acquaintance'; and the real business of knowing starts when 'we can *ascend* to knowledge-about' and generate thoughts which are 'the *developed* tree' of cognition (my italics). So he asserts an unwitting paradox that while it all starts with acquaintance, this is a pretty minimal business until we get some knowledge-about going.

The same basic distinction between the felt qualities of the world and conceptual knowledge-about is found in Bertrand Russell (who gives it a special technical twist), G.E. Moore, Herbert Feigl, Stephen Pepper, and others. But they all imply the same kind of minimalizing as James: direct acquaintance with the qualities of things yields a bare, spare, mere and dumb kind of apprehension. It is as if this is a primitive, necessary evil on the way to the real business of the day, which is propositional knowledge.

I think this is the result of the subject–object split at work, the relegation of felt indwelling resonance with the world into relative unawareness, whence it is exploited and used for what are thought to be higher-order processes. What I mean by experiential knowledge is not some mere apprehension of felt qualities, but an exhilarating participation with differentiated beings – presences – in a unified field of being.

It presupposes a deepened state of awareness, not just an ordinary state in which conscious subjectivity is cut off from the objective world of things. Nor is it the pre-linguistic state of the child's mind, which while it may foreshadow experiential knowledge, inclines more to fusion and is low on differential awareness. What I am evoking, by contrast, is a fully participative and unitive state, in which the seer and the seen are both distinct and one.

It is normally buried, trampled underfoot by the subject–object split, dispatched to subliminal status and surviving only in the vestigial form of 'a mere condition of acquaintance'. But it still goes on doing its job from below the threshold, providing a world for us which we can then split up. There are several experiences in ordinary life where it surfaces and comes to the fore, at any rate in part, and I have mentioned some of these in Chapter 5 on feeling.

Martin Buber gives a classic account of experiential knowledge in depth in term of his I–Thou relation, which I discussed in Chapter 2. I and Thou are only known in fullness in a direct mutual relation between two people who are genuinely open and present to each other. The reality is in the relation between them and is interdependent with the wholeness of each (Buber, 1937).

Phenomenology has also made an important contribution to our approach to experiential knowledge, since it has championed a truly radical empiricism. It exhorts a pristine acquaintance with phenomena unadulterated by preconceptions: it encourages the inquirer to sustain an intuitive grasp of what is there by 'opening his eyes', 'keeping them open', 'looking and listening', 'not getting blinded'. It opposes the use of Occam's razor at the level of phenomena because it blunts exploration of the finer structures of experience; what is needed is a spirit of generosity rather than economy. It exposes the sense organ bias which says that nothing is to be recognized as a valid datum unless it can be assigned to a specific sense organ. And it points out that this kind of bias has prevented traditional empiricism from being empirical enough, because it has proceeded too much by arguing as to what we must perceive according to some theory about the perceiving process (Spiegelberg, 1960).

One canon of validity for experiential knowledge is declarative. When I resonate with a presence, it declares itself and its nature to me through its immaterial qualities, which permeate its perceptual form. 'To declare' in this sense means 'to make clear by manifest compresence', that is, through the felt participation of a person. This, perhaps, echoes the Psalmist's use in 'the heavens declare the glory of God' (Psalms, 19: 1). The colloquial version of this canon is the statement that 'the proof of the pudding is in the eating'. Indeed, eating is so popular, as well as necessary, because it offers a regular micro-experience of compresence, in which food declares its nature in the unitive embrace of ingestion.

Declarative proof is in the palate, on the pulse, in the embrace, in the gaze. It is what Perkins crudely called 'whatlike understanding', which is 'that understanding of an experience that consists in knowing what an experience is like, and we know what an experience is like by virtue of having that experience' (Perkins, 1971). Declarative proof is transactional or interactive: it is the function of my interpenetration with whatever it is that declares itself. It does not tell us about a being out there all on its own: it tells us about a being that is in a state of compresence with whoever it makes its declaration to.

Declarative proof, when it is announced in propositional form, is also contextual: it is always relative to the conceptual definition that points towards the presence that is disclosing itself. This definition is a necessary signpost to the presence, which, however, has fundamental imaginal and affective parameters that go beyond it. A particular being, or network of beings, has dimensions that are more basic and grounded than the concepts which indicate it. If we bracket off and hold in suspension these concepts, the transaction with being can declare itself in its extra-conceptual form, in its affective and imaginal morphology. But once this declaration is translated back into language, what is then stated will have to take into account, even if in a revisionary way, the bracketed concepts. There is a dialectical tension here between the bracketed concepts and the declaration. If you suspend the concepts absolutely and utterly out of the way, then there is no determinate experience that you can pick out and ask to declare itself. If you don't bracket them off at all, the declaration is repressed by the conceptual imposition. So it's a compromise: you bracket off enough to get a declaration but not so much as to make it impossible. The result is that the declaration you get, once publicly stated, is always relative to your bracketed concepts: there is no such thing as an absolutely pristine, *stated* declaration of what the transaction is really all about. It is at most a revisionary account, set at the frontiers of, and in the context of, the belief systems of the day. There is no way in which we can avoid the historicity of our knowledge, the fact that even the most radical thought is still relative to its cultural antecedents (Gadamer, 1975).[5]

There is another supporting canon of validity for experiential knowledge. It is to do with those immaterial qualities that are felt to be present in the perceived forms but are not themselves perceived – such as the distinctive receptivity of the shape of a particular jug. I will call these qualia, to distinguish them from perceptual qualities such as colour and shape. For any given presence there is a certain fittingness, what might be called a felt appropriateness, about the way these qualia cohere within the presence they reveal. So the second canon is that of qualitative coherence. If there is lack of fittingness, of coherence, among the qualia of a presence, then we need to deepen our attunement with it and open more fully to its declaration. We need to become compresent with it.

Presentational knowledge

The world of appearance, the world that has the form of our perceptual imagery, is apprehended primarily by the imaginal mode interacting with the conceptual. It yields presentational knowledge, in which a person creates a pattern of perceptual elements – in movement, sound, colour, shape, line – to symbolize some deeper pattern that interconnects perceptual imagery of this world or other worlds. On this account of knowledge, art is a mode of knowledge. Thus a piece of music is an aural pattern made up of the basic elements of rhythm, melody, harmony and timbre (i.e. tone quality) (Parry, 1893). A painting is a visual pattern made up of the basic elements of line, massing of forms, space, light and shade, and colour (Fry, 1920). As frames of knowledge, these aesthetic patterns tell us about some unifying configurations in the world as perceived.

Perceptual images of the world are a transaction between the imaginal mode of the psyche and being. So if we say that art forms symbolize the pattern that connects such images, this pattern can be at the psyche pole or the being pole of the transaction. This corresponds to expression theories and formalist theories in modern aesthetic philosophy.

Expression theories say that the aesthetic pattern communicates, in a coherent imaginary whole, deep feeling and emotion. It discloses profound goings-on in the creative person: some heartfelt experience in the artist that is being expressed (Croce, 1953; Collingwood, 1938). Formalist theories argue that it exhibits certain inherently pleasing formal properties, some basic harmonic order in the scheme of things which is intrinsically satisfying to contemplate when we discern it in nature and when the artist embodies it in a work of art. Thus we have the notions of 'significant form' (Bell, 1914; Fry, 1920), 'configurational coherence' (Osborne, 1955), 'organic unity' (DeWitt Parker, 1926; Pepper, 1949; Beardsley, 1958).

Susanne Langer puts both theories together very neatly. First, she says that a work of art is not an *expression* of human feeling but an *icon* of it, an imaginative symbol of it, so that its design represents the dialectical tensions inherent in feeling. Secondly, she argues that human feeling, properly understood, just *is* the intensity of life process raised to a level of complexity where it becomes consciousness. It follows from these two points that the work of art is at one and the same time a symbol of human feeling and of the rhythmic structure of organic life itself. (Langer, 1952, 1988).

My own view is that the work of art symbolizes the pattern of rhythmic life inherent in the generation of perceptual imagery deep within the artist's imaginal mind, so here I agree somewhat with the expression theories and more so with Langer. I also believe that it symbolizes some deeper federal pattern inherent in the perceptual imagery itself. These federal or archetypal elements enable perception to portray a coherent and unified world. This is more in accord with formalist theories and the classical Greek tradition to do with the archetypal values of clarity, measure, balance, proportion, wholeness and harmony.

The canon of validity for a work of art as a mode of knowledge will also, of course, depend on which pole of the perceptual transaction your aesthetic theory deals with. The Chinese tradition, so ably expounded by Laurence Binyon, upholds a canon of rhythmic vitality, a harmonic principle of life. If the work exhibits this principle, then it genuinely gives knowledge of Tao, the great one and everywhere process. This is close to Langer's idea of 'vital import'. A work has vital import if it symbolizes, by virtue of its dynamic structure, the forms of vital experience, the pattern of sentience, the process of life itself as it is felt and directly known. This canon seems to me right for that aspect of a work of art that is to do with the pattern of rhythmic life inherent in the *generation* of perceptual imagery.

I think it needs complementing with a canon of formal values to take account of the archetypal, federal elements in perceptual imagery. This canon is concerned with proportion, composition, symmetry and asymmetry and such like. The vital principle and the formal principle can coexist in a work of art in varying degrees of accommodation or exclusion, of tension or repose. This all makes for the exhilaration of the artistic enterprise.[6]

Some artists have wanted to give an account of the formal, federal values of works of visual art in geometric and mathematical terms. Favourite candidates have been the logarithmic spiral, the golden section, the Fibonacci series, evident in a variety of forms in nature (Armfield, 1946). This is equivalent to some musicians' interest in the fact that the basic harmonic values of the overtone scale are also manifest in a wide range of natural phenomena. So they take the view that the patterns of music symbolize harmonic values inherent as organizing principles in the structures of nature and the universe (Berendt, 1987, 1988).

Presentational knowledge includes not only music and all the plastic arts, but dance, movement and mime. It also embraces all forms of myth, fable, allegory, story and drama, all of which require the use of language, and all of which involve the telling of a story. Storytelling is one of the two great linguistic kinds of presentational knowledge, the other being poetry. I call them forms of presentational knowledge since at their best they use language powerfully to evoke, imaginatively portray, the perceived patterns of the world of appearance.

The elements of a story include spatial settings, happenings, human characters and other entities, actions, all woven together in a temporal plot or story-line. The pattern of a good story symbolizes what the listener or reader feels is significant about the structure of the story of their own life or someone else's life or anyone's life. It also signifies something about the thrust, beat, rhythm or pulse of life as it is lived, its cycles of rise and fall, of consummation and cadence. So we have here again the same two principles of significant form and rhythmic vitality. Of course, the significance of the form is to do with the meaning of human destiny, and is of a different order to that which applies to a painting or piece of sculpture. Its federal elements are more transcendent.

The greatest stories are those that convey a story-line whose meaning illumines and transforms the meaning of one's own life. We are all, I think, looking for a greater story, the five-act drama the revelation of which will make sense of the single scene which comprises our entire life. In this connection, Jean Houston writes well about what she calls

> Great Story . . . story that enables us to see patterns of connections, as well as symbols and metaphors to help us contain and understand our existence. I mean story that contains rich mytho-poetic language whose power propels us beyond the personal-particular focus of the local life toward that realm I call the personal-universal . . . . In the mythic and symbolic dramas . . . we can discover the broad patterns of our own lives, finding ourselves changed and charged. (Houston, 1987)[7]

Finally, I come to poetry, the other main form of linguistic presentational knowledge. The speciality of the poem is metaphor and analogy, using language to evoke one image as a symbol of another image or of an idea. Here is Blake:

> He who binds to himself a Joy
> Doth the winged life destroy;
> But he who kisses the Joy as it flies
> Lives in Eternity's sunrise.

He packs six metaphors into these brief lines: 'binds', 'winged', 'destroy', 'kisses', 'flies' and 'sunrise'. The effect is to weave so many imaginal patterns together in relation to the idea of joy that both the images and the idea acquire an entirely new force and moment. This is the significant form aspect of the poem; its vital import is to do with its rhythm, rhyme, diction and sound.

There is one overall point about presentational knowledge which is important for our understanding of the world. It reveals the underlying pattern of things. And a pattern in the world has two fundamental properties. First, its parts are in relations of mutual simultaneous rapport and support; and secondly, if it is changing, its parts relate serially by exchanges of information and feedback, and presuppose a formative field which is the spatio-temporal template for such dynamic exchanges. It is only presentational knowledge, in graphics, animated film and mobile models, that can adequately symbolize these basic properties of patterns.

Propositional knowledge

The world of essence, known by the conceptual-practical modes, yields propositional knowledge, which is the main kind of knowledge accepted in our culture. This is all very familiar territory. Propositional knowledge is knowledge-about. It is expressed in propositions, statements which use language to assert facts about the world, laws that make generalizations about the facts, and theories that organize the laws. I shall also include in its meaning numerical knowledge about the world in terms of number and measure.

Propositional knowledge uses concepts that come with the mastery of language. It uses logical relations between concepts to represent experience, whereas presentational knowledge uses aesthetic relations between non-linguistic visual symbols (in the case of painting) to do so, and experiential knowledge can only point you in the direction of the appropriate kind of declarative experience.

The canon of validity for propositional knowledge is that of the logical warrant. This has two forms. Your propositions need to be coherent and consistent, free of internal contradictions. And they need to be rationally grounded in supporting evidence.

All this is fine until we realize that the use of concepts in this way divides the world up into subjects and objects, so that propositional knowledge is based on the assumption of a world out there relatively independent of the knowing subject, which we have to peer at and do experiments on in order to find out more about it. The sort of world we are examining is thus a product of the chosen tool, the concept, which we use for the purpose.

Once the conceptualized object is split off from the subject, human thinking then goes on to divide objects up into more and more conceptualized entities until the extreme is reached when the opposites start to coincide, and the object pole implodes back into the subject. This is roughly the crisis science passed through earlier this century when it was finally discovered that the electron's properties are, in important respects, a function of how it is observed. Its nature is therefore in part transactional, involving the interdependence of observer and observed. Its status can only be determined if you close the subject–object gap.

The other great or even greater crisis was when science could no longer find discrete and separate objects which it could conceptualize. For the subatomic particles turned out to be patterns of possible interconnections. Instead of minute things there were only probability patterns of contextual interdependence. There was no aggregate of little bits, but a web of interconnected dynamic phenomena determined by their relations with the whole (Capra, 1983).

This demise of the conceptual enterprise in delineating discrete objects has effectively introduced the era of what I call post-linguistic thought. By this I do not mean that we abandon language but that we need to learn to use it in a way that transcends and is not bound by its inveterate tendency to separate subjects from objects. We can, of course, make much greater use of poetic metaphor and presentational symbolism, both of which can powerfully affirm the psyche–world interpenetration. But there is still the challenge of cultivating effective unitive discourse.

The point about such discourse is that its canons of validity will have to change. One can no longer ask for supporting evidence from the facts, for the facts have now become subject–object trans-actions. The point about a subject–object transaction is that you need to go deeper into the subject in order to go deeper into the object, that is, if you want to get into the object. Physics tried going deeper and deeper into the object and simply ended up back with the subject. It has revealed not simply the observer of the electron, but by cultural induction the mystical subject immersed in the Tao (Capra, 1975). The time has now come to redress the balance.

To go deeper into the object through the subject means that we accept their total interpenetration and have abandoned the subject–object split. It means we cultivate the capacity for feeling com-present with a being; we open ourselves to participation in and with it. We let it declare itself to us as a function of our interpenetration of it.[8] Skolimowski (1990) has written eloquently about compassion-ate consciousness and the methodology of participation needed in future research.

Alongside cultivating the capacity for feeling compresence, we also need to own the great flow of imaginal creativity pouring with such formal precision into our perceiving of the world. We can be open to the imaginal power in perception by exercising imagination within perception, as Goethe sought to do in his studies of light and colour and the metamorphosis of plants (Goethe, 1820). By using the imagination to recreate the perceptual image from within it, we may learn to discover the archetypal templates, the homological principles, that our imaginal mind is already cascading into it. This is a modest methodological paradox: if you actively imagine the form of a rose while looking at it, you discover the formal principles you have already given it by perceiving it.[9] Wenger says we need to express this active imagination within perception aloud in verbal descriptions in order to unveil its disclosures fully (Wenger, 1991).

So we can no longer ask of our propositions that they be

rationally supported by the evidence. We ask that they are coherent with what beings declare themselves to be, and are imaginally grasped to be, in the context of our interpenetrating them. This is one new canon of validity for post-linguistic discourse. It requires propositional knowledge to be coherent with experiential knowledge and presentational knowledge.

The other canon is that our propositions are coherent with the logic of dialectic. For this logic the opposites are interdependent, interpenetrate and ultimately one without loss of their polar distinctness (Reason and Rowan, 1981). The old logic of contradiction, which excludes the opposites applying to the object as such, is superseded, for there is no object as such. We can no longer insist that the electron as such is either a wave or a particle. For the inquirer it only exists as how-it-is-being-observed. It falls under the logic of dialectic: it is both a wave and a particle depending on what sort of subject–object transaction it is part of.

The logic of dialectic is a necessary corollary to the practice of participative and imaginal interpenetration. It requires that we assert of any being that it declares itself to be X when we interpenetrate it primarily by participative identification through feeling, that is by attuning to its immaterial qualities and presence; and to have form Y when we interpenetrate it mainly by imaginative recreation of its perceived form through the imaginal mind, that is, when we seek to divine the deeper patterns that inform its sensory appearance. The resultant two reports will be quite different and complementary.[10] If we combine both modes of relating in equal measure then maybe the declarative and archetypal experiences themselves interpenetrate, and the final report asserts this union of opposites.

Post-linguistic propositional knowledge

Let me say a little bit more about post-linguistic thought and effective unitive discourse. As I said earlier, I do not mean by 'post-linguistic' that language is abandoned, but that it is used to give expression to a new way of perceiving the world that has liberated itself from conceptualizing objects in a manner that splits them off from subjects. Now this can mean two things, both of which are valid.

First it can mean a sort of perceiving that temporarily transcends the conceptual-linguistic layer in perception altogether. This is what Jean Wahl had in mind when he said that the philosophy of the future will return to the immediacy of extra-linguistic vision, to what has all along been present to us, hardly noticed, behind the screen of language (Wahl, 1948, 1953). There, in 'a silence of ecstasy', we recognize our participation in and communion with the world.

Secondly, it can mean a form of perceiving that has an entirely new unitive conceptual layer embedded in it. Instead of seeing the world in terms of the conceptual categories of a logic of contradiction – which separates subject from object, cause from effect, figure from ground, part from whole, process from structure – we view it in terms of categories drawn from a logic of dialectic, in which the opposites interpenetrate.

In this kind of post-linguistic perception we construe the world in terms of a whole range of new syncretistic categories. We *participate* in the presence of what there is: the interpenetration of subject and object. We become aware of the *interfusion* of dynamic events in mutual exchanges of informative feedback: the interpenetration of cause and effect. We comprehend the contemporaneous *emergence* of components: the interpenetration of part and whole. We respond to the dynamic *gesture* of a thing: the interpenetration of process and structure.[11]

These concepts, once embedded in our inquiring acts of perceiving, may then generate a truly unitive discourse, in which language as never heretofore is lifted on to a new level: it is used to evoke distinct persons and processes within a seamless whole which is our world.

Practical knowledge

The world of existence, known by the practical-affective modes, yields practical knowledge. Gilbert Ryle (1949) distinguished carefully between propositional knowledge and practical knowledge, which he called 'knowing that' and 'knowing how', respectively. He held that some philosophers, whom he called 'champions of the intellectualist legend', have tried to assimilate knowing how to knowing that. He had little difficulty in showing that this simply cannot be done. Knowing that this is how to do something, i.e. making statements that describe the skill, is not at all the same as actually knowing how to do it, i.e. having the skill.

Practical knowledge is the final outcrop of this up-hierarchy of knowledge, from experiential to presentational to propositional. It consummates the emergence of one from the other. While practical knowledge cannot be reduced to propositional knowledge, since it has a resolute autonomy of its own, it cannot exist in its extraordinary range, complexity and variety without being grounded on propositional knowledge. Without its base in language and conceptual thought, human skill would remain on a par with that of the apes.

Its canons of validity are canons of competence. Whatever the skill is, you need to be able to demonstrate that you can actually do it, over a significant time span, under all relevant conditions, and with an appropriate economy of means. What the last canon implies is that someone who, to use a physical skill as an example, can get the same effect with less movement and/or equipment has the greater skill. These can all be boiled down to two basic canons, behavioural grip and execution: that I can do it and how I can do it. Aesthetes would also want to add a canon of elegance in the delivery of a skill, not only in regard to the dancing of Fred Astaire, but also to driving a post into the ground with a sledgehammer.

Skills are a blessed relief. They bring us to the business of living. They sanctify the psyche through its apotheosis in action. A 'saint' without a comprehensive range of skills has gone too far too fast, cultivating the vertical at the expense of the horizontal, attuned to the One without expressive manifestation as one of the Many. The 'perfected master' who cannot speak one language other than his mother tongue has a lot of explaining to do.

Skills provide an important consummation for propositional knowledge. Practical knowledge does not validate propositional knowledge, but morally justifies it. Knowing *that* which never generates any significant knowing *how* is suspect.[12] We should certainly give it plenty of time to prove its applicability, but sooner or later it is called upon to account for its free reign – in terms of practice. Knowledge is for action (MacMurray, 1957). It is called upon to make a difference to what is going on in our lives. The grounding mode of feeling is not only a static delight in all kinds of being through compresence with them, it is also a dynamic delight in enhancing their uniqueness. This dynamism of delight moves upward through the hierarchy of knowledge to find its final expression in action, in competence to improve the lot of everything.

The up-hierarchy of knowledge

I have just referred to this up-hierarchy, which is a convenient metaphor for showing how the forms of knowledge and canons of validity are grounded on each other. Consider Table 8.1, which is to be read from the bottom upwards.

The artist is not going to get significant form and rhythmic vitality in the work of art unless there is some qualitative coherence and participative compresence in his or her experience of the world.

Table 8.1   *The up-hierarchy of knowledge*

Worlds	Knowledge	Canons
Existence	Practical	Execution, behavioural grip
Essence	Propositional	Dialectical logic, coherence with interpenetration
Appearance	Presentational	Significant form, rhythmic vitality
Presence	Experiential	Qualitative coherence, declarative compresence

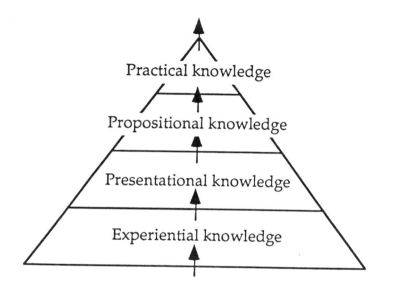

Figure 8.3   *The up-hierarchy of knowledge*

Thus Keats said the poet had to have 'negative capability', by which he meant the empathic attunement to be out there eating seed with the sparrow.

The new-age researcher will ground their inquiry in experiential knowledge of what is present, map out significant patterns and rhythms of perceptual imagery in presentational forms, then move on to propositional exposition. The new-age practitioner will simply ground their competence in everything that is below it in the hierarchy. So we have the familiar up-hierarchy diagram, as in Figure 8.3.

The inquiry cycle

Inquiry becomes more systematic if the hierarchy is turned into an inquiry *cycle*, as shown in Figure 8.4. It will begin with some seed idea at the propositional level. This is developed into an initial action-plan and practice, which will lead into the first major piece of

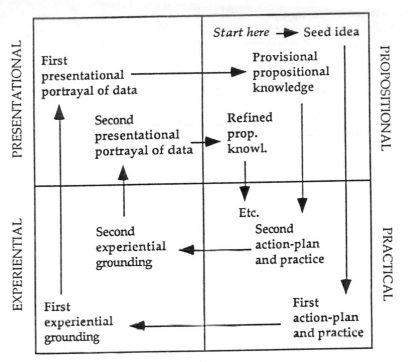

Figure 8.4 *Experiential inquiry cycle*

experiential grounding. The data from this are first explored in presentational terms, which are then formulated into propositions. This provisional body of propositional knowledge is converted into a second action-plan and second phase of action, which will reground it in renewed experiential encounter with being. The cycle can be repeated several times to enrich, refine and empower the propositional content in accord with its two canons.[13] The methodology of this experiential inquiry cycle has been used extensively in co-operative inquiry (Heron, 1981a; Reason and Heron, 1981, 1982, 1985; Reason, 1989).

The inclusion of presentational portrayal of data in this account of the inquiry cycle is an important addition to past accounts, which, while they were aware of presentational knowledge, never accorded it full status within the cycle. In only one of the co-operative inquiries in which I have been involved was presentational symbolizing of data used to any significant degree (Reason and Heron, 1981). Looking back, I think that it was valuable in its own right, not only as a bridge between experiential grounding and propositional knowledge.

If we agree that presentational symbolism is indeed a mode of knowing, then we can no longer conveniently distance ourselves from its use by delegating it to the artistic community. We need to bring it right back into the mainstream knowledge quest. Nor should it always be assumed that propositional knowledge is the only acceptable and respectable outcome of inquiry. The seed idea can start as presentational symbolism, which is taken round the cycle to become refined presentational knowledge.[14]

Whether the outcome is presentational or propositional, there are always also practical skills acquired and deeper experiential acquaintance with the world of presence.

Exercises

1   Journey through the four worlds

Sit face to face in the shade in a sunny garden (or anywhere else). Relax and let all emotional agitation become still. Breathe in unison and enter the world of presence, feeling mutual attunement through the relation of sustained and silent gazing. After ten minutes disengage from the world of presence and enter the world of appearance by attending very fully to the total image of your partner, their way of appearing in all its nuances of sound, colour, smell, form and movement, facial expression, posture, gesture. Take five minutes each to describe your partner's way of appearing as a person, as a body-mind whole, using, as well as literal description, any similes, metaphors, stories or allegories that come to mind. You might also have a sketch pad to hand to symbolize their way of appearing in a line drawing – representational or abstract. Then move on into the world of essence and take five minutes each to state whatever you know or believe to be the case about your partner, in terms both of general theory and of personal information. Finally, spend ten minutes in the world of existence, doing some work together in the garden or the kitchen. Move straight on from world to world and after visiting all four worlds, reflect together on the qualitative differences between them.

2   Discontinuity of the worlds of appearance and essence

Take twenty minutes each to explore whether how you perceive the world is consonant with what you believe about the world. Suspend all your intellectual beliefs, and just look around and listen and touch in your ordinary way, and tell your partner what kind of a world it is that you thus see and hear and have contact with. Make explicit the practical belief system involved in the very act of perceiving. Now dissociate from that process and state the beliefs about the world which you officially and formally hold as a conscious intellectual standpoint. Explore how the perceptually embedded and intellectually held belief systems are the same and how they are different. After both turns, discuss your findings.

3 Transactional grounding

Go and dig a hole in the garden, in the world of existence. Your partner then takes you into the world of essence by asking 'What beliefs are presupposed by that action?' After you have answered the question, your partner takes you into the world of appearance by asking 'What patterns in the world are presupposed by those beliefs?' After you have answered this second question, your partner takes you into the world of presence by asking 'How do you know there is a world with patterns in it?' Reverse roles with your partner, who then chooses a different action in the world of existence, and you ask the same series of questions. After both turns, discuss whether transactions in higher worlds in the up-hierarchy are grounded in lower worlds.

4 A transformational journey from presence to presence

Sit face to face; relax and let all emotional agitation become still. Enter the world of presence together through sustained silent mutual gazing. Deepen it until you are fully attuned within a unified field of togetherness. Then after ten minutes, when your timer sounds, take a short journey together. Stand up, turn round so you are back to back, spread your legs wide, bend right over and re-establish eye contact with both of you looking at each other between your legs with your heads upside down. When the laughter subsides (and let it run its full course) re-enter the world of presence together through sustained silent mutual gazing. When the timer sounds after another ten minutes (or whatever period is comfortable), sit face to face and discuss whether there were any qualitative differences between the world of presence before the journey and the world of presence after it. Some people like to re-enter the world of presence when they have returned to the original sitting position, before starting the discussion.

5 Declarative proof

Sit together at a table, relaxed and present, with two glasses and a freshly opened bottle of Vino Nobile di Montepulciano or any other distinguished wine. Pour some wine into the glasses and sip it; as you feel it lingering on the palate allow it to declare itself fully in its compresence with you. Bracket off all culturally induced wine snobbery and genuine wine lore. What does this liquid make clear – in purely qualitative, non-verbal terms – about its own nature when compresent with yours? When the wine has thus declared itself, each of you translate this into verbal terms and write it down on a piece of paper, using both literal description and metaphor and simile. Read your accounts to each other, and discuss the interactive and contextual features of the declaration.

6   Presentational knowledge
Contemplate together a good-quality reproduction of *Temple on a Clear Day in the Mountains*, a painting in ink and colour on silk, attributed to Li Ch'eng of the Northern Sung dynasty. Participate in the whole painting by holding your focus on the temple in the middle, with occasional forays to the corners and sides to establish the details there. For twenty minutes let the painting tell you – entirely in its own presentational terms – about manifest being. Then see if you can convey to each other in words what it has told you, and whether this was validated by its rhythmic vitality, its formal properties or some combination of the two.

7   Mythic transformation
Take twenty minutes each. Relax into feeling fully present, then take a few moments of silence to feel your past, present and future as one contemporaneous whole. Now tell the story of your own life recast as a *myth of descent from there to here*. Let this phrase assume its own mythic proportions in your tale. After both turns, discuss what new light, if any, the myth has thrown upon your understanding of your life.

8   Compresent rabbit
Sit together, relaxed and present, beside a tame rabbit that is feeding in the garden. Cultivate the capacity for *feeling* compresent with it. Become this particular rabbit, participate in every nuance of its very mode of being, without any loss of your own distinct presence. After fifteen minutes, discuss your findings.

9   Imaginal pot-plant
Sit together in front of a small plant embedded in a pot, relax and feel its presence. Actively imagine its total form while perceiving it: imagine its all-at-once gesture in space, imagine it from different viewpoints, imagine it at different points in its life cycle, imagine it growing and unfolding, imagine its formative dynamic; above all, follow the imaginal recreation of the plant whither it leads. After fifteen minutes, discuss your findings.

10 Polar partner

Sit opposite each other and *feel* each other's compresence through mutual gazing, synchronous breathing and deep resonance of being. Do this for ten minutes, then switch over for a further ten minutes to an imaginal recreation of the other as a particular perceptual appearance of the archetypal human. Discuss the difference between these two complementary experiences of your partner.

11 Perception of gesture

Take a walk together for ten minutes among trees, participate in their presence and practise seeing each tree not as a structure which contains processes, but as a living gesture which integrates process and structure in one dynamic whole. Share your experiences.

12 The practical justification of propositional knowledge

Take ten minutes each to think out aloud about the validity of the sentence that precedes this exercise reference number. Can it be falsified? Are there sorts of purely abstract propositional knowledge which require no practical justification whatsoever? After both turns, discuss the issue further.

13 A co-operative inquiry 1

Read this account of co-operative inquiry and study Figure 8.4 carefully. Take a seed idea such as the distinction between looking at someone's eyes as physical objects and taking up that person's gaze. Decide how to explore that distinction in practice through some structured experience with yourselves as interacting subjects, then start the practice (first action-plan and practice). Get deep into this practice, being fully open to what is going on (first experiential grounding). After the agreed time, break off from this and express your experiential findings about the eyes–gaze distinction in drawing, colour, gesture, movement or sound as you have agreed or are moved (first presentational portrayal of data). Then share and discuss your findings verbally and conceptually (provisional propositional knowledge), and consider how these findings can be refined and extended by further experience. So you devise some variation or elaboration of the original structured exercise, again involving yourselves as interacting subjects, and take this into practice (second action-plan and practice). Get deep into this second round of practice, being fully open to what is going on (second experiential grounding). After the agreed time, break off from this and express your experiential findings in drawing, colour, gesture, movement or sound as you have agreed or are moved (second presentational portrayal of data). Then share and discuss your findings verbally and conceptually (refined propositional knowledge). You have now done two cycles of inquiry, which will be enough to get a feel for the method. Between the two cycles, before devising the second action-plan, take five minutes each to review any emotional disturbances that have been stirred up by the inquiry and that may be distorting it. After completing two cycles, discuss the whole method.

14   A co-operative inquiry 2

Take the same co-operative inquiry as in the immediately preceding note, but with this difference. Start with a *seed presentation*, for example a *line drawing* which you both agree symbolizes the eyes–gaze distinction. So you start top left in Figure 8.4, moving to and fro between the presentational and the propositional, that is, discussing the drawing until you both agree with it as your starting symbol. Let this symbol determine your first action-plan for an experiential exercise. After the first practice, deepening into experiential grounding, revise the line drawing in the light of the exercise, altering it and discussing it until you agree on the revision. Then go round the cycle again, concluding with your third, agreed and refined, line drawing symbol of the eyes–gaze distinction. This drawing is your inquiry outcome. It can be prefaced and buttressed by propositions, but it is the drawing, not the propositions, which finally consummates your inquiry. Between the two cycles, before devising the second action-plan, take five minutes each to review any emotional disturbances that have been stirred up by the inquiry and that may be distorting it. After completing the two cycles, discuss the whole method.

9

A One–Many Reality

I begin this chapter with a summary statement of the metaphysical beliefs, expressed as a set of metaphors, upon which the theory of the person presented in this book is based. I then give a recapitulation of my account of the person in the light of these beliefs. The remaining sections consider some oriental views from my metaphysical standpoint.

Metaphors for a One–Many Reality

It is a central tenet of this book that Reality is both One and Many, both being and becoming, both transcendent and immanent. There are some simple metaphors for the One–Many notion. There is the polarity of plane and point: a single plane is an infinitude of points. Another is the infinite sphere whose centre is anywhere and everywhere.

The basic spatial metaphor is that there is the infinitely large – the infinitude without; and the infinitely small – the infinitude within.[1] There is only one infinitude without; there are innumerable infinitudes within. Whatever the metaphor, you can't reduce one pole to the other, for the poles are fundamental, complementary, interdependent and interdefinable.

Another radical complementarity is that of involution and evolution, expressed in the metaphors of descent and ascent. There is a descent, an involution, an embedding of the One in the embryonic Many and an ascent, an evolution, a differentiated development of the Many in the One. The One is enfolded, not dissolved, in the Many; the Many progressively manifest, and do not disappear into, the One.

The metaphor of descent, the process of involution, is further elaborated by the metaphor of a down-hierarchy. From the One consciousness-as-such emanate the formative imaginal powers, the archetypes of creation, which radiate a manifold of energies and spaces. In these are the infinitudes within, the Many, in each of which an archetype is reflected as an entelechy, the ground of an up-hierarchy.

The up-hierarchy metaphor expands the metaphor of ascent. For the entelechy emerging from the infinitude immanent within each of the Many is a godseed, a formative potential. It upthrusts this potential in successive steps of the unfolding up-hierarchy, all of whose higher levels are latent in its lowest.

In terms of consciousness, the One–Many Reality is represented as the one mind with many differentiated centres of consciousness within it. Personhood is one such centre. There is no separation between this conscious locus and its setting in universal mind. Since its consciousness is not apart from this field, it can participate in all other centres too. Each of the interrelated many is unfolding within universal consciousness: a particular focus of development and a unique perspective within it.

The separateness of egoic states of being is an illusion to do with the subject–object split. Dismantling that illusion means that personal consciousness uncovers its true heritage – that it is both distinct within, and one with, universal mind. It is involved in a set of syncretistic, dialectical or, if you like, paradoxical categories. Everything is divine, and the divine transcends everything. Perceived particulars are both Many and One, distinct and identical. My individuation is exalted in the divine, and I lose my being in the divine. The divine is dynamic and static, a plenum and a vacuum, qualitied and unqualitied, personal and impersonal (Stace, 1961).

Modern panentheism affirms the view that while all things are within the divine, the divine is not merely the whole of everything: it includes everything, is immanent in everything and transcends everything (Hartshorne and Reese, 1953). Paul Tillich's existential theology gives a special colouring to this view (Tillich, 1951–63). It propounds an ecstatic and self-transcending naturalism. The divine is not a being among other beings, but being-itself, the creative source and ultimate meaning of all natural objects: it is found in the ecstatic character of this world as its transcendent depth and ground.

The being of the world participates in the underlying being of God. The divine, the unconditioned, is to be found only in, with and under the conditioned relationships of this life as their profound significance. God is the ground of our being as persons, our ultimate concern. God, being-itself, can be described symbolically as living, personal, spirit, love. It follows from all this that through our deep concern we participate in the divine being of the world and each other. And this is close to the account of feeling which I am advancing in this book.

The person as One–Many

The One–Many Reality is reflected in the one–many structure of personhood. There is one unique, distinct potential person who is actualized both serially and concurrently in all sorts of different manifest subpersons. At a certain period of life a person may be running concurrently the spontaneous person, the compulsive person, the conventional person, the creative person, the self-creating person and the self-transfiguring person.

Of course, to say these are concurrent is not to say they are all on stage at exactly the same time; rather a person can move in and out of these different ways of being one after the other during a day, a week or a month. The same person at the same general phase of their life can be conventional in one context, creative in another, compulsive in a third, and so on. We bring ourselves on bit by bit, in an improvisatory, piecemeal kind of way, now working at this, now sorting out that, slipping back here, and moving on with swift advance there.[2]

Within each of these main substates of personhood, there are subsubpersons. The compulsive person lurches around between the distressed positions of oppressor, victim, rescuer and rebel. The conventional person moves from one stereotypic role to another, now man about the house, now young executive, now golf club member, now holidaymaker in Ibiza, now dutiful political supporter. The creative person may be innovative in several different fields: a social change agent in the winter, a writer and a painter in the spring and summer.

The self-creating person can, in their personal therapy, work with a wide array of different sets of subpersonalities, characterizing different semi-autonomous 'energy patterns' or 'operating potentials' in the psyche, getting them all into some kind of meaningful mutual adaptation. Stone and Winckelman (1985) identify here the hurt child, the playful child, the magical child; the good and the bad mother or father; the critic; the perfectionist; the pleaser, and so on. John Rowan has written a useful book outlining past and present approaches to this way of working (Rowan, 1990).

The self-transfiguring person may be the priest or hierophant, the mystic, the occultist or magus, the seer, the oracle, the healer, the representative of this, that or the other power or presence, the cosmic joker, or the lost one in the dark night of the soul.

The theory of *skandhas*, which I put forward in Chapter 5, brings in a whole new dimension of multiplicity, since it affirms that a person is born carrying other persons' unresolved behaviour patterns by virtue of some principle of affinity. If anything like this is true, then those concerned are all members one of another. The internal psychological multiplicity includes a corporate and collective one.

What I have called the entelechy – Rogers's selective and

directional 'actualising tendency' (Rogers, 1959) – which might be regarded as that principle of personhood which orchestrates and integrates the manifold of persons, subpersons and subsubpersons, itself appears as different kinds of guiding spokesperson – now affirming individuating, now participating, now proposing grounding, now reorganizing, now electing living, now learning.

In short, in a One–Many Reality, personhood is a dramatic multiplicity within a distinctive presence. And the paradox is that we find the uniqueness of that presence not by trying to restrict the multiplicity, but by celebrating its multifarious presentations.

Is there anyone there?

Some western enthusiasts for transcendence of the subject–object split in a higher non-dual awareness of reality have written as if, by dissolving the viewpoint of a subject separated from an object, that is the end of a distinct, non-separable psyche. This view it is fair to say is primarily oriental and in its extreme form Buddhist, as I discussed in Chapter 2 (pp. 38–9), although as we shall see later there are seeds of a very different account in Tibetan Buddhism.

One occidental version (Wilber, 1977) describes Awareness, or non-dual experiencing, as meaning the end of any kind of experiencer; but the universe is still all there as a diversity in unity, a seamless whole of distinct and mutually interpenetrating particulars. It is just that it is no longer objective because the subject has disappeared into absolute Mind, which is one with the universe it knows.

There is a hidden assumption, a metaphysical rigidity, in this account. It allows diversity in unity, mutual interpenetration, only to the universe. But this is an arbitrary restriction, and takes too quick a flight across the water of experience. A less hasty account is that when separate subject and separate object disappear, non-dual experiencing is revealed as a unitive field in which there is mutual interpenetration between person and world, distinct and non-separable. The end of the separate experiencer is simply the beginning of the experiencer-within-Mind, who was really there all the time, and who is of a qualitatively different order. The separation of seer from seen, and both from the One, which was the illusory outlook of the ego, gives way to the deeper and subtler realization that the differentiation of seer and seen within a unitive transactional field *is* the Many in the One.[3]

One redoubt of those who believe that there is really no such thing as an *experiencer* is the argument from transcendental subjectivity (Wilber, 1977). The argument goes like this. Whenever you look for your self, you cannot see it, because a subject cannot be an object for itself, just as an eye cannot see itself. You may say you see this or that as your self, but as soon as you see it, it has become object to a new and necessarily unseen subject. In other words, there is a transcendental subjectivity which forever remains unseen, whatever you say you see to be your self. The perceived cannot perceive. The perceiver cannot be perceived.

The argument concludes as follows. You cannot see your self because what is seeking and looking is *Brahman*, Mind itself. The seeker is the sought. Knowing this is Awareness and puts an end to the search.

This view of the matter is presented as though the Awareness that God is transcendental subjectivity is the final solution: the account with Reality is settled, the experiencer disappears into experiencing. The gap between the experiencer and God is absolutely closed simply because there is no longer an experiencer so there is no gap. The journey is over, there is nowhere else to go, no further step to take because there is no one there to buy the ticket.

This closes the gap simplistically and without paradox. Transcendental subjectivity is an infinite regress: the subject forever transcends any account that can be given of it. But the infinity of the regress does not disappear because I know its divine origin. If I become aware of *Brahman* as transcendental subjectivity, it is not that my subjectivity disappears, but that I am aware of whence it issues. This does and does not close the gap. It initiates me into yet another version of the One–Many paradox: I know I am one with *Brahman* at the same as knowing that I am infinitely other. Hence the upsurge of numinous awe, glorification and a stream of praise.[4]

The end of the search does not put an end to expansive aspiration and attunement to the One. It does not finish off the distinct experiencer, only the separate experiencer: the disconnected differentiation of the ego, which is the outcome of illusion, is not to be confused with the unitive differentiation of the transfigured person, which is a mode of divine manifestation. Now if the end of the search does put an end to the distinct experiencer, then Mind is only One and not Many. If Mind is also Many, then its Oneness will include Many distinct experiencers.

Am I distinct within Awareness of Mind or not? If I am not, how did I become Aware, let alone report the occurrence? To know Mind as absolute subjectivity, that in which experiential subjectivity is grounded, does not mean the end of the latter but the start of its absolute transfiguration. There is only an end to its separatist, dualistic illusions, and to its search for a ground which it now knows. The dew drop does not slip into the shining sea and simply disappear for ever; rather it undergoes a total alchemical transformation. It interpenetrates the ocean without any loss of its remarkable distinctness.

Dipolar unity

It is important not to be misled by the enthusiasm of the ancient texts for Oneness. There is a monopolar bias at work which really does not do justice, I believe, to the subtlety of the experiences being reported. As soon as the old mystics stepped into the domain of language and culture to write of their enlightenment (if and when it was that), they tended to fall foul of this kind of monopolar bias. Dipolar accounts of enlightenment are for the coming age; they involve a new level of sophistication in mystical reportage.

We must make a really rather obvious distinction between pernicious and non-pernicious dualities, or, if you like, between separatist, divisive dualities and unitive, complementary polarities. A couple bickering in a state of alienated hostility is an example of the former. Lovers in a profound unitive embrace, deeply and ecstatically at one with each other, is an example of the latter. The subject–object, dualistic split of ordinary concept-laden experience is an example of the former. The person–world unity of experience transfigured in the One–Many Reality is an example of the latter.

So that to say that something is dualistic is not *ipso facto* to say that it is metaphysically pernicious. We need to know whether reference is being made to a separatist dualism or a non-separate dipolarity. The One–Many Reality is a non-separatist dualism, a dipolar unity. There is the One, there are the Many, that is the duality, the dipolarity. They are in a state of mutual compenetration, so the One is in the Many, the Many are in the One, all of the Many are in each of the Many and each of the Many is in all of the Many – and that is the non-separatism, the unity. And all this is Reality, than which there is nothing other.

Blight from the East

It was from Asia that there first penetrated into Europe the world-denying concept of the religious life, as Radhakrishnan (1939) shows convincingly in his *Eastern Religions and Western Thought*. Of course, every possible school of religious thought has appeared in the East. But the most prominent regard the multiplicity of the phenomenal world as an illusion grounded on nescience, want of discrimination, or ignorance. Release and deliverance from it is the only goal, for the Real is the undifferentiated One. Variations of this view are found in the Samkhya, the Vedanta and in Buddhism (Hyde, 1949b). There is here a general metaphysical negativity and monopolar bias: a flight from the Many to the One, to God from the works of God.

'We owe to the East a conception of world denial which in its perverse form undermines most seriously the creative powers of the spirit' (Hyde, 1949b: 46). Guénon in a classic study showed that the principles of the Vedanta strictly applied mean that spirit is incapable of being expressively manifest in the human realm in any convincing sense (Guénon, 1928). The oriental sages identified with the One as a defence against coming to terms with the active creativity of the human spirit as one of the Many, within the realm of the Many.

They wanted to persuade themselves they could disappear into Oneness and write off Manyness as illusion. They tried to jump from illusory, dualistic ego-bound states of consciousness to a total identification with universal states of consciousness, irrespective of any stated position on the nature of the self. As a result they compulsively avoided the concept of personhood as a creative spiritual reality. And without a concept of personhood as that which can liberate itself from egoic illusions, and become *both* transfigured within a higher consciousness and manifestly expressive in the world, I do not think you can ever do justice to the Manyness within the One–Many Reality.

So we must ask whether the old mystics did always become universal. Did they necessarily enter Mind? Or is this sometimes an unnoticed and hopeful projection on our part? In Chapter 10 I raise the issue that the ancient sages are people who suffered from two deficits: they had no working concept of repression at all; and they lived in cultures that had a minimal, undeveloped relation to the phenomenal world. In Chapter 3 I gave reasons for supposing that their deeply repressed distress will have been relatively untouched by their meditative practices; and that its compulsive thrust will have remained, subtly distorting the whole spiritual enterprise.

Did they therefore, on occasion, displace themselves into strange mental states by sitting meditating in caves for long periods? Was it a case of compulsive transcendentalism being a castration equivalent, leading to the inner mental voice being pitched permanently an octave higher? There is a theomanic pathology in the life of the spirit that is very rarely raised by devotees of distant saints.

Lawrence Hyde is one of the few spiritually competent writers who has faced this issue squarely and fairly. In *The Nameless Faith* he wrote:

> There can be little doubt that in a large number of cases the exaltation attained by modern eastern *yogis* is nothing more than psychic in character, in spite of their own belief, and that of their disciples, that they have entered the sublime state of *samadhi*. It almost looks, in fact, as if this illegitimate mode of escaping into the subjective is the oriental equivalent of our excessive concern in the West with the realm of objectivity. (Hyde, 1949b: 49)

Asraya-paravrtti

There is, however, another side to the story from the East. Deep in the traditions of Tibetan Buddhism there are all the elements of a powerful doctrine of the self-transfiguring person. The starting point is *asraya-paravrtti*. This double-barrelled Sanskrit term means 'foundation-change'. Govinda describes this as 'a thorough transformation of our personality' that comes about through the mystical path.

For Govinda this transformation does not mean condemnation of ordinary experience, but building a bridge from it to timeless awareness. This is 'a way which leads beyond this world not through contempt or negation, but through purification and sublimation of the conditions and qualities of our present existence'. It involves an alchemical process of transmuting the base metals of everyday consciousness into the 'imperishable jewel of the adamantine mind'. Hence ordinary states of being are changed into the states of *bodhicitta*, enlightenment consciousness. The ego-bound mind becomes cosmic awareness; awareness of the individual body becomes awareness of the universal body; selfish feeling becomes feeling for others, compassion, and a feeling of identity with everything; sense perception and discrimination become inner vision and spiritual discernment; ego-bound karma-creating volition is changed into the karma-free activity of the saint.

This is a path, a progression, it takes time in the ordinary sense. It culminates in the realization of the *Dharmakaya*, the universal principle of all consciousness. This, says Govinda,

> is a living force, which manifests itself in the individual and assumes the form of 'personality'. But it goes beyond the individual consciousness, as its origin is in the universal realm of the spirit, the *Dharma*-sphere. It assumes the character of 'personality' by being realized in the human mind. If it were merely an abstract idea, it would have no influence on life, and if it were an unconscious life-force, it would have no forming influence on the mind. (Govinda, 1960: 82ff., 213ff.)

Govinda's idea of this 'personality' is pretty minimal: he thinks of it as a 'momentary form of appearance like a temporarily assumed mask'.

Suzuki also takes the view, perhaps more robustly, that the concept of *Dharmakaya* implies the notion of personality: 'the highest reality is not a mere abstraction, it is very much alive with sense and awareness and intelligence, and, above all, with love purged of human infirmities and defilements' (Suzuki, 1947: 41). He says that even the *Dhyani-Buddhas*, transcendent presences encountered in meditative vision, have all the characteristics of personality. They are not merely personifications of abstract concepts but the transformation of a universal reality in the form of human experience.

What is behind all this is the traditional doctrine that every Buddha manifests himself on three planes of reality – the universal, the ideal and the individual – and has three corresponding bodies or principles: the *Dharmakaya*, in which all Enlightened Ones are the same; the *Sambhogakaya* which constitutes the spiritual or ideal character of a Buddha; and the *Nirmanakaya*, the human embodiment or individuality of an Enlightened One.

Seeded within this doctrine is the idea of the Enlightened One as a distinct cosmic presence. If you precede it with the account of *asraya-paravrtti* then you get a very early prototype of the mystic path as one in which the potentiality for distinct personhood within universal awareness is emerging from its cocoon of illusory egoic separateness.[5] And this, I believe, is what both Govinda and Suzuki are edging towards in their interpretation of the ancient ideas.

Still, we need more than a mere edging forward. We need a positive doctrine of the charismatic *person* who is attuned to the One and who is an active, creative presence in the diverse realms of the Many.

Exercises

1 The infinitude within
Meditate together for twenty minutes. Relax and become fully present. With closed eyes, become your heart and from everywhere on its periphery move in simultaneously towards the infinitude at its centre. As you draw closer to the centre from all sides, feel the spatial scale continuously magnifying so that you are expanding into the intensely intimate, ecstatic space of the immanent infinitude, which, at a certain point on the inward journey, glows into manifestation with the energy of bliss, like a jewel. Feel the mystery

of your unity with the jewel. After the meditation, share your experiences.

2   Seven chairs

Take thirty minutes each to explore your multiple personhood, using seven chairs. The focal chair is for your entelechy, your formative potential of personhood; the other six chairs are for your spontaneous person, your compulsive person, your conventional person, your creative person, your self-creative person and your self-transfiguring person. Make sure from Chapter 3 that you have a good working grasp of these seven forms of personhood. Fix a large label on to each chair to show which person it belongs to. Start off in the focal chair and ask your six persons to share, as each is moved to do so, whether and how they are active in your current life. Move from chair to chair to give voice to each of the six. After all six have spoken, open up dialogue between them, seeing what they have to say to each other, and move from chair to chair as appropriate. Go to the focal chair whenever you feel the dialogue needs facilitation by your formative potential. If you want, arrange for your partner to keep the whole thing on the move with an occasional prompt about which chair to go to and what issue to take up. After both turns, give each other feedback, and discuss what the whole process yields.

3   Demystification

Explore together non-dual experiencing, in which subject and object remain distinct but non-separable, simply by looking at your own left hand held up with fingers extended and palm in front of and slightly to the left of your face. Now flex and extend the fingers to and fro, and feel that you are non-separable from the movement. Now stop the movement and feel that you are non-separable from the visual image of the hand – an image which your body–mind is deeply involved in generating. While focusing on the hand, attend to the visual images behind the hand and feel that you are non-separable from them since, as with the image of your hand, you are deeply involved in generating them. Discuss the experience. Did you become Mind, or enter a unified person–world transaction within Mind?

4   Meditation on transcendental subjectivity

Sit together in meditation and be aware of yourself as 'I', as subject of the first person singular. Mentally intone the pronoun 'I' as a focus for your sense of I-ness. Turn about in the very seat of your I-ness and attend to its Absolute Source, the universal I AM. As you turn about into this Origination, note the total dissolution of the separate sense of I-ness, of the egocentric focus. Note also, at the selfsame moment the egocentric chrysalis dissolves, your astonishing, exhilarating distinctness within the divine embrace. Share your experiences of this remarkable encounter.

5   Self-transfiguring mime

Play Berlioz's *Harold in Italy* and as the music sounds take it in turns to express in mime, dance and movement your emergence from the cocoon of illusory egoistic separateness into distinct personhood within cosmic awareness. After both turns, share your experiences as artist and audience.

Jung, Kolb and Wilber

This is a chapter of critical analysis devoted to the work of three inquirers whose ideas have a bearing on what is presented in this book. I start with a brief critique of Jung's theory of the four functions. While this is easy to criticize, it is difficult to overestimate its seminal contribution to psychology, education and training, partly because its pioneer spirit of holism transcends some of its limiting internal definitions. The short section on Jung ends with a side glance at Assagioli.

I then move on to examine critically how David Kolb uses a slightly different set of four psychological modes to underpin his theory of experiential learning. This theory has been very influential in higher and continuing education in recent years, and merits serious attention as a way of relating learning to its experiential base.

Finally, and in a very different vein, I look at Ken Wilber's transpersonal views on the human condition; Wilber sees the twin processes of becoming a person and generating a culture as illusory projections of a denied longing for absolute Spirit. This is a classical version of transcendental reductionism carried through with great contemporary brilliance. But, like all such reductionism, I think it is deeply flawed and that it is important to show how.

Jung's four functions

It is important not to confuse my typology of four basic psycho-logical modes in any way with Jung's theory of the four psychologi-cal functions of feeling, intuition, thinking and sensation (Jung, 1977). In my view, Jung has confused the field for too long. He never really got down to a radical phenomenology of psychological functioning, to a bedrock view of the different modes of the psyche's being. He thought there were two basic sorts of orien-tation: extraversion and introversion. Then there were the two basic functions of perceiving and judging: sensation and intuition were modes of perceiving, and feeling and thinking were modes of judging.

So his account of these last four – sensation, intuition, feeling and thinking – is entirely subverted and distorted by their being defined as species of perceiving and judging. Perceiving, he thought, was about gathering information, and judging was about resolving issues and emphasizing order. This is a curiously academic and limiting pair of definitions under which to subsume accounts of the four derivative functions. This unsatisfactory couple are really his basic modes, and cause all the trouble. Feeling, defined as a form of judging, becomes a special casualty; intuition is constricted to be a mode of gathering information; and the fundamental notion of action is absent from the whole analysis.

In any case, there is excessive repetition and overlap in the two levels: perceiving is too close to, or indeed identical with, sensation to provide a satisfactory superordinate category; and similarly in relation to judging and thinking, where one might hold that judging was a subspecies of thinking rather than the other way round.

Of course, people do a lot more with Jung's four functions than his definitions strictly allow. But then they cease to be Jungians and are smuggling in their own more satisfactory phenomenologies. Assagioli found the whole thing too limiting and went to town with six functions – intuition, imagination, thinking, feeling, sensation and desire – together with the self and the will (Assagioli, 1965). In his map of personality structure these six functions project in a star shape around the will, with the self in the centre.

This is very promising, but his six functions lack some more basic, dynamic ordering principles. They hang around the will without an adequate functional rationale. Jung tried to provide some more basic principles for his four functions, in judging and perceiving but, as we have seen, these fall far short of doing the job. Kolb, whom I consider next, tries to import some ordering principles from epistemology, but also gets into serious trouble.

Kolb's four psychological modes

David Kolb has been widely influential in recent years in higher education by virtue of his model of experiential learning (Kolb, 1984). I must stress at the outset that my critique is not directed at this model as such. It is really a model of experiential learning derived from scientific inquiry: we reflect on experience, generalize from these reflections, then test the implications of these generalizations through further experience. This is one valid model. My argument is that Kolb's account of it is too narrow and under-developed, because its phenomenal base in psychological modes is too restricted, and its philosophical justification is invalid.

Kolb's account of the psychological modes is more satisfactory than Jung's, but still too limited. He identifies, at the bedrock level, four basic psychological modes of relating to the world: feeling, perceiving, thinking and behaving. He calls these, respectively, affective, perceptual, symbolic and behavioural modes. As modes of relating to the world they are also adaptive modes, learning modes and developmental modes. But then something strange happens.

He takes the four basic modes of feeling, perceiving, thinking and behaving, and by the use of imported philosophical analysis, turns them into the learning modes, respectively, of concrete experience, reflective observation, abstract conceptualization and active experimentation. This imported analysis says there are two ways of grasping experience – directly by encounter (concrete experience), or indirectly by concepts (abstract generalization), and two ways of transforming that grasp – by internal reflection (reflective observation) or by external action (active experimentation).

There are some unsatisfactory connections implicit in all this. Feeling is correlated with concrete experience, that is, grasp of experience by direct acquaintance. Perception is correlated with reflective observation, that is, the transformation of direct experiential acquaintance by internal reflection. Thinking relates to abstract conceptualization, that is, grasp of experience indirectly by concepts. And behaviour relates to active experimentation, that is, the transformation of direct experiential acquaintance by external action. It is the first two and the last of these correlations that are particularly problematic.

Surely perception, just as much as feeling, is involved in direct experiential acquaintance. And perception itself is not just a transformational operation of reflective observation, but can be entirely intuitive and non-reflective, while behaviour is a much wider concept than that of active experimentation. What I think has happened here is that Kolb has got a reasonable set of basic phenomenal categories – feeling, perceiving, thinking and behaving – but instead of developing and expanding the set at the ground level of radical phenomenology, he has broken off prematurely to import the intellectual structure of two kinds of prehension and two kinds of transformation.

The result is four learning modes which are really cut off from a proper grasp of feeling, perception, intuition and imagination. The notion of feeling is nowhere defined or elaborated in the whole book: it is merely there in some vague, unspecified and ungrounded way to underpin the idea of concrete experience. The result is, of course, that the concept of concrete experience itself is nowhere properly explored, beyond the idea of direct apprehension. Likewise there is no adequate phenomenology of perception, which is tied far too closely to reflection by the concept of reflective observation. Intuition and imagination get exceptionally short shrift in the learning model presented. They are at best tacked on to it in ways that do not seem justified by the narrow theoretical structure. And of course intuition and imagination are excluded from the basic phenomenal set of feeling, perception, thinking and behaviour.

The model is really about reflective observation, abstract conceptualization and active experimentation – for which an indeterminate concrete experience is the necessary crude fuel. This model is a highly intellectual account of experiential learning based entirely on the paradigm of scientific inquiry, in the tradition of Dewey, Lewin, Piaget and Kelly. Kolb makes the dubious assertion that 'the scientific method provides a means for describing the holistic integration of all human functions' (Kolb, 1984: 32). It is dubious because his account of the learning cycle derived from the scientific method does *not* integrate all human functions. It rests on an inadequate phenomenal base, which has no proper consideration of the essential roles of feeling, emotion and imagination in the learning process. Let me give a further example of this lack.

Kolb has four learning styles: convergence, divergence, assimilation and accommodation. Each is a mix of a different two of the four basic learning modes. Thus convergence is a mix of abstract conceptualization and active experimentation; and so on. Now each of these styles is connected to a Jungian dimension of extraversion or introversion and to a Jungian function: for example, convergence is related to extraverted thinking. At one point in the book, this connection is achieved by a canonical correlation between the results of two psychological self-report instruments, the Myers-Briggs Type Indicator (MBTI) and the Learning Style Inventory (LSI). The first of these is used to assess subjects' Jungian types, the second subjects' Kolb learning styles.

The correlation allocates the feeling function to the learning style of divergence; but elsewhere in his text Kolb stresses imagination before feeling in his account of divergence. Likewise the MBTI/LSI result allocates intuition to the learning style of assimilation (a mixture of abstract conceptualization and reflective observation), yet elsewhere Kolb strongly stresses reasoning and theoretical competence, i.e. thinking, to characterize assimilation. In other words, basic psychological modes are being juggled around in an inconsistent way. And imagination and intuition, which were not stated in the original set of four, are introduced without any rationale.

Two things have gone wrong here. First, as long as psychological researchers put their own (or Jung's) categories into their questionnaires, and as long as research subjects oblige by making their own experience fit into these imposed categories, we shall get concoctions, not substantive findings. You can't do proper research *on* people in this way, expecting them to go along with your categories. You have to do this kind of research *with* people, co-operating with them to elicit mutually acceptable categories which honour their experience as much as yours (your experience, mind you, not your theoretical predilections). I and others have addressed this absolutely basic research issue elsewhere (Reason, 1989).

The second thing that has gone wrong is Kolb's underlying epistemology about two kinds of prehension and two kinds of transformation. He says that concrete experience is to do with apprehension, grasping experience in terms of its immediate felt qualities, and that abstract conceptualization is to do with comprehension which is grasping experience in terms of concepts. This does not stand up to analysis.

First of all, concrete experience is perceptual experience, which itself includes both apprehension and comprehension. In everyday perception there is the apprehended pattern of imagery as such, and there is the concept in terms of which we comprehend this pattern. So in concrete experience we both apprehend perceptual patterns and comprehend them in terms of concepts such as house, cat, tree, mountain. We don't just see a pattern, we also and at the same time see it as this, that or the other kind of thing.

Secondly, the distinction between comprehension and apprehension on the one hand, and transformation on the other is mistaken, because as we have seen the comprehension within perception is itself a transformation of the apprehension within perception. We transform the perceived pattern, as part of the complex process of perceiving it, by subsuming it under the concept of some class. In other words, concrete experience already involves the transformation of apprehension by comprehension.

Thirdly, since concrete experience is by its nature already transformative, there is no difference in kind between it and Kolb's reflective observation, which is one of his two kinds of transformation. It is only a matter of degree. Concrete experience is already interpretative, and reflective observation simply makes it more so. Fourthly, abstract conceptualization is not only comprehension; it is also highly transformative, both of reflective observation, and through it of concrete experience.

Indeed, the transformative process starts within concrete experience as the conceptual layer in perception, then reflective observation transforms this, abstract generalization transforms this, active experimentation transforms the generalization into testable form, and the conceptual layer in concrete experience transforms (falsifies or supports its hypothetical base) the active experimentation. In short, the whole cycle is a series of successive transformations, one of which is both within concrete experience and grounded in its imagery. This imagery is the one point of apprehension, all the rest is both comprehension and transformation.

I think I have said enough to show that the prehension–transformation distinction, as Kolb uses it, is fundamentally incoherent, and cannot be used to support his learning model. As I have said, this model is really a model of experiential learning derived from scientific inquiry: we reflect on experience, generalize from these reflections, then test the implications of these generalizations through further experience. This is one valid model, but Kolb puts it forward in a constricting form, whose phenomenal base in psychological modes is too limited and confused, and whose philosophical justification does not hold.

While all inquiry is learning, not all learning is inquiry in the sense of generating new knowledge. Learning what is known is rather different from learning about what is unknown and making it known. Kolb runs these two together in his definition of experiential learning as 'the process whereby knowledge is created through the transformation of experience' (Kolb, 1984: 38). Also there is throughout Kolb's work an unquestioned assumption that knowledge is propositional knowledge. There is no account of experiential or presentational or practical knowledge as I have portrayed these in Chapter 8.

Whereas Jung contaminates his basic four functions of feeling, intuition, thinking and sensation by imposing arbitrarily narrow limits on their definitions, Kolb takes his four modes of feeling, perceiving, thinking and behaving as basic, does not define them or augment them, but boxes them into a superstructure of inappropriate epistemology, in order to make them underpin his preferred paradigm of scientific inquiry. He then has to tack other modes such as intuition and imagination, in an unsatisfactory way, on to this structure to make up for its limitations.

Wilber's transcendental reductionism

If you believe that the actualized person is a valid part of reality and not just an illusory state, then what the person – as distinct from the limiting ego – gets up to in the way of creating cultural forms will also be a valid part of reality – a celebration, a praising, a lauding of co-creativity with the Creator. But if you believe that the person is an illusory state, an unreal separated self-substitute for the absolute Mind which alone is real, then everything a person creates will be illusory too and the whole of human culture becomes suspect.

This last is Ken Wilber's position in his account of the Atman project. What he means by 'Atman' here is not *jivatman*, the distinct spiritual monad, but absolute Mind or Spirit. The Atman project theory, as developed in *Up from Eden* (Wilber, 1983) – on which my comments below are based – is a remarkable historical foray into transcendental reductionism. But the premises are simple enough.

Absolute Spirit is all there is, says Wilber, but we develop the illusory, separate self as a defensive substitute for it. Being both a defence against Spirit and a compensation for the lack of Spirit, the substitute self embarks on the Atman project, which is a drive to recapture Spirit in illusory projected forms. It pursues false infinities – through sex, food, fame, knowledge, power – and destructively defends itself against death and dissolution. It creates culture as a world of objective substitute gratifications, for the same two purposes, to get power and defend against death. Says Wilber, 'Culture, truly, is what a separate self does with death' (Wilber, 1983: 15).

So the cultural forms of any society or epoch are substitutes for the transcendent path to Spirit, and a cost has to be paid for this substitution; and for that society or epoch there is only a tiny handful of shamans or seers or mystics who are on the true road to Spirit. Wilber then interprets the whole of human history from the beginnings until now in terms of this set of premises.

Well, the interpretation all depends on your premises; and history is a protean mass that will accommodate a wide divergence of interpretative assumptions. What is noticeable about Wilber's premises is their reductionist intent in favour of the transcendental. Both the self and culture are a deviation from, an illusory substitute for, absolute Spirit. Only a minute fraction of the human race has ever seen through all this and opted for the transcendent route to Spirit. Transcendence, could we but realize it, is what it is really all about.

This is monopolar reductionism in favour of transcendence at the expense of immanence, in favour of the Real One at the expense of the Real Many. In other words, the focus is on Spirit as the transcendent One to the exclusion of Spirit as the immanent Many – Spirit as many distinct monads, potentials for personhood, immanent within the human world. Wilber reduces all real people to unreal, separate and substitute selves: the person is nothing but an Atman project.

In truth, I believe, Spirit is One and Many depending on how you relate to it; just as the electron is wave and particle depending on how you observe it. The notion of complementarity has for some time now been an essential part of the way physicists think about nature. It is also an essential part of the way one needs to think about Spirit. We can know the Spirit as One; or we can commune with the Spirit as Many – where two or three are gathered together.

The problem with all reductionism, whether of Many to One or One to Many or matter to mind or mind to matter, is that it is primitive, uroboros-fixated – it devours itself. Thus, in its own terms, Atman project *theory* is itself an Atman *project*, that is, an objective substitute gratification put out by a substitute self, a way of avoiding Spirit while displacing the longing for it in a false direction. Wilber does not claim to write out of a state of 'non-dual awareness' giving a phenomenology of it and of how he got to it. He is interpreting and reflecting on the reports of others, his 'heroes', buttressed by hundreds of references. In his own language his theory is a high mental egoic performance; at most an exercise in vision-logic at the centaur, low subtle margin.

As such, *defined in its own terms*, it is necessarily a misbegotten enterprise, a deluded distraction from absolute Spirit, a pursuit of a false infinity, a self-defeating cosmocentric inflation, and the cost to be paid is in terms of thousands of other substitute selves who believe it, being seduced into further distraction precisely at the very moment they imagine they are being shown a way of liberation. This is deep treason indeed.

The trouble is that this castigation of the theory in its own terms is very telling. For the Atman project theory does indeed create a strong impression of cosmocentric inflation, the attempt to fit absolutely everything into it, to give an all-inclusive view of the great chain of being, metaphysically, historically, psychologically. And this is surely, *still staying within the terms of Wilber's theory*, the very trap that vision-logic falls into. The higher up the spectrum, that is, the more subtle the Atman projection as in this case, the greater the danger that it will be mistaken for the real thing and not be seen for what it is, which is an elaborately refined set of intricate ideas going away from Spirit. The more vision-logic displaces its hidden longing for Spirit into grandiose conceptual schemes, the further it is distancing itself from Spirit, claiming as victims all those who are dragged along with it. It also follows, I think, that the bigger the scheme, the greater the misrepresentation; because the further you project, the more you miss the point.

In a sense my criticism could stop here. If Wilber really believes his theory, his writing stands self-condemned as vision-logic Atman projection; and he should surely stop the ambitious manner of writing that goes away from Spirit, and just write in a very direct, simple style giving a basic phenomenology of his experience of Spirit. If, on the other hand, he thinks his own theory does not apply to his own writing, then he has the formidable task of justifying his exemption in a way that does not undermine the whole theory.

However, let's go on with a general critique. Outside its own terms, the theory can be seen as wholesale ritual symbolic murder: all actualized and potential real persons are slain. They are reduced, without remainder, to Atman projects. The innumerable corpses, the husks, strewn over the philosophical battlefield are nothing but illusory substitute selves. For Wilber, the only kind of person is the ego-persona, a sort of epiphenomenon of property ownership, property law, and mutual exchange – just another Atman project. This annihilation of the person is also the slaughter of human love. The theory is devoid of any concept of simple, everyday basic love except a derogatory one. That is the deepest tragedy of Wilber's sustained reductionism.

Because they are not real persons there is no such thing as a real personal relationship, only a synergistic overlap of Atman projects. His theory reduces human love to arranging 'for individual Atman projects to overlap each other in something of a mutually supportive way' (Wilber, 1983: 335). This cannot hold. For if it is the *projects* which support each other then this means they help each other project more and more; in other words they collude in conjoint displacement of effort away from Spirit. This is an absurd and gross misrepresentation of authentic human loving. What I think Wilber really means is that egoic self-interests (Atman projects) need to overlap in such a way that the *persons* involved are being mutually supportive (and this is still far short of an adequate account of human love). But then, of course, we have introduced real persons who have, but cannot be reduced to, their Atman projects. As we shall now see, Wilber has to feed in this way off the buried corpse of the person in order to sustain the intellectual muscle of his gargantuan enterprise.

Like all reductionism, the theory is parasitic on what it negates. It can only be made to appear plausible by the surreptitious introduction of one or more quite basic concepts that fall outside the terms of the reduction. In Wilber's case it is the concept of the person. So he says 'every person . . . intuits this Atman nature . . . cannot accept death and thus find his true Self . . . compensates with a symbolic, subjective and inward self' (Wilber, 1983: 14).

But who is this person who is doing all this? It is not absolute

Spirit; it is not the illusory self; who is it? This is not a grammatical quibble, but a fundamental ontological issue. There seems to be a real entity around, the person, who is getting into genuine difficulties about Spirit and is trying to solve them by setting up an illusory separate self. What has crept into the theory is someone, who is not absolute Spirit and not the alien self, whose substantive status is nowhere acknowledged in an argument in which it is the grounding subject. And this is the whole point. You simply cannot give an account of the Atman project without invoking a subject whose reality you must assume in order to make the internal dynamics of the Atman project appear plausible.

Once you follow this through then the whole structure of the Atman project theory collapses. You need to reinstate the personalist's distinction between the person and the egoic individual – with which the person can mistakenly identify; and the real person as the progressive actualization of an inner immanent light. There are not just Spirit and Atman projects as Wilber propounds, but Spirit and *persons* and their misguided Atman projects. And with this addition we inhabit a different kind of universe.

If persons are an expression of Spirit differentiated as Many, then there are two interdependent and complementary paths for such persons, the path of transcendence – opening to the One – and the path of immanence – creative unfoldment of the divine potential within the Many into ever greater manifest expression. Instead of seeing these two paths as concurrent and mutually enhancing, Wilber's system sees them as serial in an incoherent, discontinuous kind of way.

The *limit* of his spectrum, level 7, sees the absolute dissolution of separate self-sense, however subtle, so that's the path to the One. But suddenly there is level 8, which is the *ground* of all the levels and their resurrection embraced in unobstructed consciousness. So the ego and all the other previously illusory separate self-sense structures are back in place, 'negated but preserved' (?), and reconnected with everything, so now the Many have an acceptable status they never had before. Ultimate Wholeness suddenly becomes the 'ground' of 'egoic individuality'. Rediscovering Atman 'does not annihilate the figure of the ego. On the contrary it simply reconnects it with the rest of nature, cosmos and divinity' (Wilber, 1983: 13). Here we have a non-separate, distinct ego in a unitive state with the world and with God. What had been denied as a possibility throughout the play appears as a reality in the final act. All the levels are *only* substitutes for Atman until the last – when they suddenly become expressions of Atman.

There is a fearful, archaic-oriental, shunning of manifestation here: the real Many can only be allowed out at the very end of the road where they are rendered innocuous by being suspended in Suchness, *tathata*. This is an unnecessary mystification of the interpenetration of non-separable person and world. Awareness of this interpenetration can, I believe, be cultivated progressively from modest to magnificent states, concomitantly and in complementarity with unfolding attunement to the One. In other words, the simple idea that person and world can be distinct and not separable is not something you can only grasp at the end of the road, as Wilber seems to think; it is an idea, or rather an experience, to which everyone can have access, to some degree, right now, whatever their spiritual status. For that is what the capacity for feeling bestows and will show whenever the surface structures of consciousness allow.

Wilber's account of his levels is incoherent: none of them involves any genuine expression of spirituality until they are all over, when suddenly all of them do. This cannot properly be presented as the perennial philosophy. Indeed, the whole idea of some transtemporal, transhermeneutic philosophy which can be picked up out of any epoch and applied in any other epoch is untenable. The idea of a perennial philosophy is as outmoded in religion as it is in science: every form of knowledge is relative to the cultural setting within which it is stated.

Wilber's theory is mostly based on his and other people's interpretations of what a selection of ancient sages said. Some modern mystics are referred to, such as Aurobindo and Da Free John – both of whom were strongly influenced by the old traditions – but the real heroes are the ancients. Now I believe these ancient ones are people who suffered from two deficits: they had no working concept of repression at all; and they lived in cultures that had a minimal, undeveloped relation to the phenomenal world.

To take their accounts of their experiences at face value and make some perennial philosophy out of them, all the while ignoring the effect of these two basic deficits on those accounts, seems to me to be hazardous. In Wilber's hands it becomes extreme regressionism. He reinstates the old blight from the East: the only really important moral imperative is meditation, so that you can lift yourself out of the Atman project – which is what otherwise you will be deludedly busy with all the rest of the time. Human beings are illusions in pursuit of illusions, and are not capable of manifesting authentic expressive spirituality.

That this blight itself may be based on a combination, in the psyche of the ancient sage, of an interdependence between repression and fear of the phenomenal – this important thesis is not taken into account. So we are invited to become hostage to an ancient view of the world, with a disregard for intelligent advances – both within the psyche and in relation to the world – which we have attained since.

In other words, Wilber ignores the historicity of spiritual experience. What the ancient sages said was valid for all those other sages who shared that world at that time in history. It cannot be valid for us today without very substantial amendment. This is why Wilber's theory is a distraction from locating a phenomenology of spiritual experience which is valid for people sharing this world at this time in history. In this respect one has to be careful not to gravitate immediately to modern 'sages' who are themselves sustaining or reviving ancient traditions. They too have had a failure of nerve in embracing their own historicity, a kind of transcendental *mauvais fois*, which has led them to identify with an ancient view of the spiritual role.

Wilber's transcendental reductionism seems to be based on a simple metaphysical confusion between the notion of distinctness and the notion of separation. In an earlier work he argued that when any *distinctions* are made within being, then we have *separation* and the primary noxious dualism (Wilber, 1977: 109). He identified this primary noxious cosmic dualism with the separation of subject and object, from which he maintained all other distinctions, i.e. separations, i.e. *maya* (illusion), followed. His spectrum is the route through various structures of consciousness from noxious dualism to the One.

I have continued to make the point throughout this book that there is a fundamental metaphysical difference between being distinct and being separate. Something that is distinct may get construed as being separate, but that is to do with an error of construing, nothing to do with the distinctness that is so construed.

Multiple distinctness and oneness, diversity-in-unity, is the delightful paradox of the Real: there is no primary noxious dualism to do with there being distinctions. *Maya*, the illusion of separation, arises when people apply concepts to the world in a way that separates subject from object. It is not inherent in the multiple distinctness of being. But classic *maya* doctrine has always wanted to argue that it is inherent. This doctrine improperly projects the purely localized *maya* of human conceptual construing on to the cosmic process at large as its intrinsic nature.

Once *maya* is put back where it belongs, in errant human

construing, it becomes clear that there is no inherent separateness in the distinct centre of consciousness. It was only how the subject was construing itself that made it separate. But in reality it too is an embracing member of the unitive multiplicity. Personhood is a fundamental component of the Real, one of the authentic Many.

11
Life Cycles and Learning Cycles

In these last four chapters I take the theory of the person so far presented and apply it to processes of living and learning. So I use the four modes, the three basic polarities, the ego–person distinction, and the metaphors of the cycle and the up-hierarchy to portray these processes. The result is a series of models and maps – structural conjectures – which the reader is invited to entertain as a set of lenses through which to view different aspects of living and learning.

Because these lenses give a selective view, however much they may illuminate, they also constrain. They do not depict reality; they offer no more than possible ways of construing our experience. They focus on just one kind of story, among many other conceivable ones, about how we live and learn. But I believe the story is a useful one.

Many of the models are not only depictions of a process but also practical prescriptions about a possible way of managing some way of living and learning. Again, any such prescription is a tentative proposal, a working hypothesis, something it might be worth trying out in an experimental and critical way. It is a recommendation not a solution, an invitation to inquiry not a dogma, an exploratory project not a panacea.

An overview

This chapter reflects the dynamic interplay of life and mind, the basic polarity introduced in Chapter 2. It is about everyday living and everyday learning. The first of these is daily experience without any thought of learning from it; the second means the conscious intent to learn through such experience. I look at both these in terms of the four modes – affective, imaginal, conceptual, practical – conceived as a cycle, but with the up-hierarchy metaphor as the underlying rationale.

Everyday living cycles are called life cycles, and everyday learning cycles are called learning cycles. They may involve only the individuating modes, and then I call them cycles of the ego, since the ego is only busy with the individuating modes. Or they may engage the participatory modes as well, in which case I call them cycles of the person.

Again, cycles of the ego or the person may be basic cycles or reversal cycles, as these terms were introduced in Chapter 2. I look at some versions of these two kinds.

After discussing the life cycle and learning cycle of the ego, I explore some of the distressed states into which the ego can become locked. Then I move on to the life cycle and learning cycle of the person.

The cyclic process

In Chapter 2 I introduced the metaphor of a basic cycle, which portrays the ground process of the psyche, its flow of life through the four modes in a continuous rhythmic pulse. Derived from the up-hierarchy and its ground in affect, this cycle starts from the affective mode, and proceeds through the imaginal, the conceptual and the practical to return to the affective, and so on. Also in Chapter 2, I illustrated the individuating version of this basic cycle, which is included again in Figure 11.1. It is the cycle of the ego, busy with the individuating modes – emotion, imagery, discrimination, action – that cluster round the claims of daily subsistence; the participatory functions are minimally or tacitly involved.

In this cycle the individuating modes exclude any conscious use of the participatory modes. In the basic cycle of the person, by contrast, conscious use of the participatory modes of feeling, intuition, reflection and intention includes the individuating modes, which are thus set within an extended awareness. Life is more considered: daily subsistence is realigned within an attunement to the wider scheme of things.

When in this chapter I refer to a 'life cycle' I do not, of course, mean the course of a person's entire life, but simply the continuous cyclic succession of modes going on minute by minute and hour by hour in everyday living. The frequency of the rhythm will change a lot over any given day, with long and short cycles, and overlapping cycles.

As well as the basic cycle, to do with the psyche's ground process, there is the reversal cycle, also introduced in Chapter 2, when the psyche is reorganizing its ground process so that it functions with new content. I stress that the reversal cycle is only one form of reorganization: it just happens to be the one I choose to focus on in this book.

By using the model of the cycle, I can show the psychological modes involved with all three basic polarities I introduced in

Chapter 2. So we have ego and person cycles (individuation and participation), basic and reversal cycles (ground process and re-organization), life cycles and learning cycles (life and mind). I don't cover all possible combinations of these, just some of the ones I am more familiar with.

The basic life cycle of the ego

I introduced this basic cycle in Chapter 2. It involves the individuating modes of emotion, imagery, discrimination and action (with the participatory only subliminally involved). They are grounded in the overall emotional pattern which the person has acquired in the development of the ego and start from some immediate, active component of it. This egoic pattern is a systematic way of being fulfilled or frustrated in life. The emotional need felt now is an index of how the pattern seeks to influence behaviour in order to maintain itself. And the influence is first exerted through an image or selected percept. Once this image is launched the cycle is well under way: discrimination and action are simply means to the envisaged goal.

The ego as defined in Chapter 4 is a case of mistaken identity: the person unawarely identifies – at the expense of the whole person – with a compulsive pursuit of individuation so that it becomes distorted in the direction of separateness, alienation and rigidity of self. The life cycle here is not only conservative, it is defensively so: it is keeping the participatory modes at bay through the subject–object split; and it is also warding off the pain of primal wounding, and the deep tensions of the human condition.

Figure 11.1 portrays the life cycle of the ego in the world of existence. Remember that 'imagery' in this context basically means perception and memory. This is the cycle the ego continuously moves round in its everyday experience from hour to hour. The baseline of the cycle, and its starting point, is the individual's current emotional state, which is the felt fulfilment or frustration of its needs in the immediate world of existence. This influences perception of the present situation, within which the ego discriminates and makes relevant distinctions, to service the actions that will satisfy its needs. Such actions will modify its emotional state, leading to the generation of a new cycle.

The four stages of the cycle can be very simply illustrated. Thus (1) an individual feels hungry; (2) looks around the kitchen to see what there is to eat; (3) selectively discriminates among the items to formulate a menu; and (4) cooks a meal and eats it. Next, the same person (1) feels the need to relax; (2) looks through the television programmes in the paper; (3) selectively discriminates among the

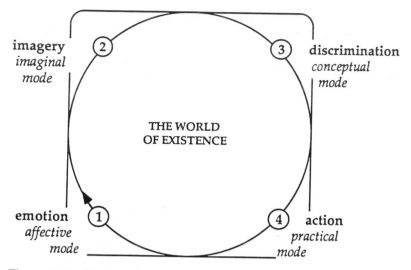

Figure 11.1   *The basic life cycle of the ego*

programmes to make a viewing schedule; and (4) turns on the TV set and watches. And so on.

In terms of basic polarities, someone in this cycle is individuating only, is identified with a restricted ground process, and is living only – with learning reduced virtually to nil.

The basic learning cycle of the ego

When its changing emotional state is relatively free from past afflictions, then the ego *can* choose to learn, by trial and error, and by social influence, what perceptions, discriminations and actions lead to felt fulfilment or frustration of its concerns. The life cycle then becomes a simple learning cycle utilizing feedback; the negative emotional outcomes of one cycle will be used to modify or change perception, discrimination or action in the next; and positive outcomes will reinforce those parts of the cycle that lead to them. Comments from others may aid this process. The individual learns through daily experience to get what he or she wants out of life.

In such ego learning, shown in Figure 11.2, the world is defined by deeds that satisfy one's needs and wants: it is the realm of everyday existence, its individual and socialized desires. The learning is mainly practical, that is, learning how to act in order to achieve these satisfactions. There is not much learning about the world as such going on, since the world is reduced by activism to those parameters that satisfy one's wants.

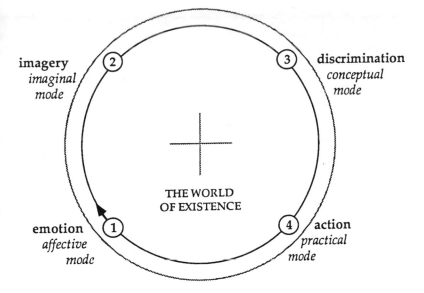

Figure 11.2 *The basic learning cycle of the ego*

For the basic life cycle to become this simple everyday learning cycle, two qualities are needed as well as relative freedom from past affliction. First, a measure of mindfulness throughout the cycle, being aware of what is going on at each stage, and of how each stage influences the next. And secondly, a sufficient concentration of attention next time round the cycle to try out alternative ways of managing each of the stages. These are the twin signs that mind is at work: some inclusive awareness and some focused awareness, both informed by the intention to grasp what is going on.

In Figure 11.2, mindfulness, the extra margin of awareness, is shown as an outer circle around the modes; and concentration as a cross in the middle of the world of existence. In terms of basic polarities, someone involved with this cycle is individuating only, but with both intuition and reflection a little less tacitly involved; is identified with a restricted ground process; and is learning as well as living, although the learning is subordinate to a restricted kind of living.

Distressed egos

The ego's changing state is from time to time afflicted by repressed distress from the individual's past. This happens when the current

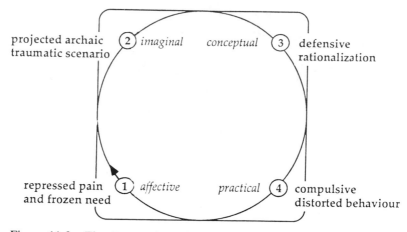

Figure 11.3   *The distressed ego life cycle*

situation echoes traumatic early life events which fixated the psyche on unmet needs and consequent pain. The ego then unawarely sees the situation in terms of these events: it reproduces in its present life a symbolic equivalent of the traumatic past, and its behaviour is compulsively distorted by the old buried longings and hurts. It is as if it is trying to create a current justification for feeling haunted by buried affliction, and for being stuck with a strategy of surviving by identifying with frustration and hurt. It is also as if it is seeking to reproduce the problem until at last it can attract the attention of someone who can come forward, interrupt the whole production and break the old spell.

In this case the basic cycle will be a treadmill, with felt need, perception, discrimination and action being unawarely caught in reproducing the closed distorted loop of the past. Figure 11.3 portrays the predicament. So, for example, a person has a repressed frozen need for the love they never got as a child; they unconsciously project this longing on to someone who cannot assuage it; they rationalize all this as meeting their adult needs; and this launches them into compulsive symbolic re-enactment of their frustrating past. Doing so displaces the frozen need and repressed pain while reinforcing them and keeping them in place. There is no possibility of learning from experience.

This pathological loop may overlap many cycles that characterize behaviour in more obvious and external terms. So however you fill out Figure 11.1 showing the basic life cycle of the ego, this distressed ego life cycle may be simultaneously involved.

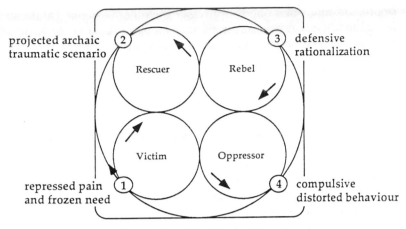

Figure 11.4   *Compulsive roles of the distressed ego*

Compulsive roles of the distressed ego

The classic roles of the afflicted ego, both in relation to itself and in relation with others, are those of the compulsive victim, the compulsive rescuer, the compulsive rebel and the compulsive oppressor. They correspond to the four stages of the distressed ego cycle, as if each stage can also turn into a subpersonality in its own disturbed right. The victim role represents the repressed distress and frozen needs. The rescuer role personifies the projection of frozen needs on to the current situation in the hope that they can be met. The rebel characterizes the defensive rationalization that refuses to acknowledge the truth of what is really going on. The oppressor portrays the compulsion to act in maladaptive and distorted ways.

Figure 11.4 shows the treadmill of compulsive ego roles. Applied within one ego on its own and not in interaction with anyone else, an individual (1) feels lowly, crushed and bad about him- or herself in some respect; (2) tries to do something about it in some inappropriate way; (3) gives this effort up with a rationalized refusal to acknowledge there is a problem; and then (4) punishes him- or herself with accusations of impotence and incompetence. He or she then (1) feels crushed and lowly and begins the cycle again. The point of the four-wheel treadmill is that each role propels the next. The victim runs the rescuer, who drives the rebel, who alerts the oppressor, who controls the victim.

If two interacting people are involved, then they share a two-person treadmill: when one is victim, the other is rescuer; when one is rescuer the other is rebel; when one is rebel, the other is oppressor; and when one is oppressor the other is victim. So if you are compulsively down, and a partner inappropriately tries to help you, you rebel, the partner then accuses you, you irrationally sink again; and so on.

There are many variations of this. You may be down, then *ask* for inappropriate help; when it is given, you reject it; your partner attacks you for this and you go down again; and so on. Or you are driven to help your partner in some ill-conceived way; the partner rebels; you accuse him or her of ingratitude; he or she sinks in compulsive guilt; and so on. So one person oscillates between victim and rebel, while the other is in a complementary swing between oppressor and rescuer; and at any point they may switch their allegiances, the one who was victim and rebel becoming oppressor and rescuer, and vice versa.

Whatever the variation, basically the two people are trading guilt and blame, passing it to and fro, because guilt and blame were imposed on them in early years, wounding their capacity for loving and congealing it in emotional pain. Thereafter the repressed pain of the wound is displaced into adult guilt and blame behaviours. The psychological colleagues of guilt and blame are collusion and denial. Two people locked into trading guilt and blame are colluding in acting out archaic scenarios, while at the same time denying to themselves and each other that it is going on.

Deeply irrational guilt makes a person identify and collude with a pathological relationship. The more collusion, the more the person has defensively to deny the pathology, leading to a build-up of repressed material which overflows into blaming behaviour, which flips the partner into their own rapid circuit of guilt, collusion, denial and counter-blame. Figure 11.5 shows this version of the cycle.

The reversal learning cycle of the ego

Here a person is interrupting the basic life cycle of the ego, using the reversal cycle first introduced in Chapter 2. So the ego's ground process is being reorganized for the purposes of learning how to live more effectively. Now I don't believe that all reversal cycles are necessarily learning cycles. For example, I think you can analyse the process of repression in terms of a subliminal reversal cycle, and that is to do with psychological survival: it is about negative living, not about learning. But here I am choosing a reversal cycle which does involve learning, not just living.

So this reversal learning cycle interrupts the first leg of the basic cycle (which moves promptly from emotion to imagery) and goes

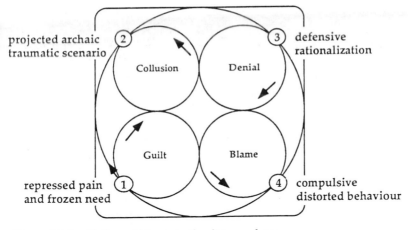

Figure 11.5   *Guilt and blame in the distressed ego*

instead from emotion to discrimination. So as soon as the current, active component of the egoic emotional pattern arises, the individual discriminates its nature and its propensity to generate a certain kind of image, and replaces this with a different kind of image, which leads directly to a different kind of action and outcome. The reversal cycle goes from emotion to discrimination to imagery to action, instead of the basic route from emotion to imagery to discrimination to action.

This goes against the grain of the basic life cycle. It is 'unnatural', revisionary, a reversal of the established, conservative scheme of things. It interrupts the normal order and coherence of the psyche, so it requires alert inward discrimination and motivation to get it going.

The cycle will be used until there is a shift in the underlying emotional pattern and its associated imagery, so that the basic cycle is re-established at a different level and in different terms. The individual is learning how to live in a way that frees behaviour from unwanted habits or the distorting effects of an afflicted past. This is a more sophisticated kind of everyday learning compared to the basic learning cycle of the ego, which simply involves learning how to act in order to achieve ego satisfactions. But note that both of them are concerned mainly with practical learning.

Figure 11.6 illustrates the reversal cycle in arrows and the old, interrupted basic cycle as a faint circle. To give an example: anxiety (1) about an impending appointment is about to launch the image of an oppressive encounter. But this image propensity doesn't get off the ground, because the aware individual spots it (2), substitutes the image (3) of a challenging meeting, follows this through into action

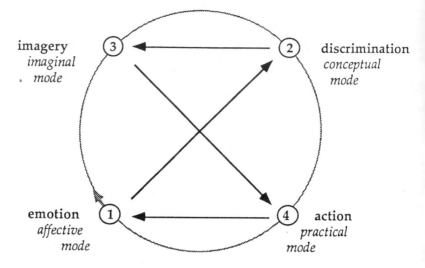

Figure 11.6   *The reversal learning cycle of the ego*

(4), and reaps its emotional rewards (1). This way there is the possibility of establishing a new kind of basic cycle with a different underlying pattern, in which the emotion of excitement generates an image of challenging encounter.

What this sort of reversal learning cycle proposes is that innovation in individuated behaviour involves a discriminating substitution of imagery. 'Substitution' is perhaps hardly the word: what is involved is the insertion of an image to banish an image propensity. And while these are not symbolized in the figure, the use of the cycle presupposes mindfulness and concentration informed by the learning intention. In terms of basic polarities, someone using this cycle is individuating primarily, but with both intuition and reflection more noticeably involved; is reorganizing a restricted ground process; and is learning through living, with the learning here widening out the living. So this is work on opening up the ego.

A classic use of this reversal cycle in everyday life is to interrupt restimulated old hurt so that it does not drive the distressed cycle of the ego, and is not acted out in compulsive behaviour. For repressed pain can be activated by those features of the current situation that are unconsciously seen as symbolic equivalents of troubled events of the past. Once aroused, it strains at the repressive barrier, generating images of driven displacement.

So the reversal cycle starts with this restimulated distress. Stage 2 is the discrimination of it, and this can have various features. It can be a simple noticing and identifying. It can develop into cognitive

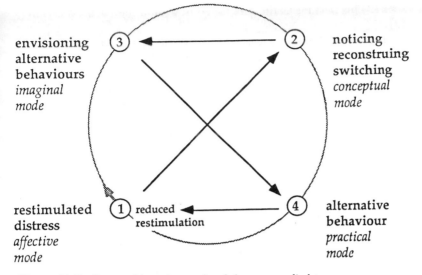

Figure 11.7 *Reversal learning cycle of the ego applied to restimulated distress*

restructuring, construing the situation in a positive light that replaces the old negative projected template.

The third stage is image insertion, a picture of alternative behaviour to the trigger-happy acting-out tendency. Attention is now switched off the agitated emotion on to a vision of a different kind of immediate future. This is taken into action in stage 4. The revised action may entirely deactivate the restimulated distress, replacing it, at stage 1 of the next cycle, with a different emotional state, in which case a new, wholesome kind of basic cycle has been launched, instead of the old distressed one. If the distress charge is reduced but still twitching, then the reversal cycle is continued until a reshaped basic cycle takes over in full swing.

Figure 11.7 shows the reversal cycle at work, interrupting a distress-driven basic cycle, which is indicated by the faint circle. Of course, it can be used to interrupt and change any kind of basic cycle, not just a distress-driven one: any life-cycle habit that is due for a shift. But remember, the use of the reversal cycle is 'unnatural', revisionary, a reversal of the established order in the psyche, so it requires inner alertness to launch it.

Given this alertness, the revisionary cycle is for use in the thick of daily egoic life. To give an example: George has an irrational impulse (1) to blame his partner. He immediately notices this (2), and instead of seeing the other as the bad parent of the past, sees (3) his partner as the one loved now, and then acts accordingly (4).

How effective this cycle is in relation to restimulated distress depends on several factors: the intensity of the restimulation; how much practice a person has had in using the cycle like this; and whether the person also has access to co-counselling or other therapy outlets for healing old traumatic memories by releasing their distress charge. I don't think it can be reliably effective without some back-up of this last kind. Given this back-up, it can be applied to dismantle many of the more gross confusions of egoic behaviour.

Everything depends on inner alertness at the point of discrimination. This is a combination of mindfulness and concentration: one needs to be aware of one's process and ready to focus thought. The person has to be immediately ready to conceptualize the irrational storm gathering on the emotional threshold *as* restimulated distress. The more it can be construed in terms of historical psychodynamics, the less its tendency to afflict the present.

A co-counselling co-operative inquiry in which I was engaged looked at a wide range of different methods for dealing with restimulated distress in everyday life. It did not explicitly identify this reversal cycle; nevertheless the inquiry findings can be seen as full of practical psychological devices for making it effective (Reason and Heron, 1982).

They made an important distinction between tactics and strategies: the former are practical methods for use in the particular situation; the latter are *policies to adopt* some preferred tactic or set of tactics. So strategies mean a greater readiness at stage one of the reversal cycle:

> They present a higher order approach to life management, rising above the purely tactical, ad hoc response to particular situations. The tactical approach is simply crisis-management: the restimulation is already upon you and you choose whatever tactic will best enable you to handle it. The strategic approach is more comprehensive: it anticipates and educates before the event. (Reason and Heron, 1982: 17)

Figure 11.8 shows the three stages of change when using the reversal cycle. The faint inner circle is the old basic cycle, changed into the new basic cycle of the outer circle by the figure-of-eight arrows of the reversal cycle.

The basic life cycle of the person

The more limited, preoccupied life cycle of the ego, shown in Figure 11.1, takes it round the individuating modes of emotion, imagery, discrimination and action. It is preoccupied with its needs and

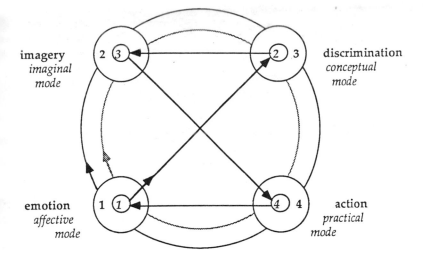

| imagery
imaginal
mode | | discrimination
conceptual
mode |
| emotion
affective
mode | | action
practical
mode |

Figure 11.8   *The three stages of change using the reversal learning cycle*

interests in the world of existence. The participatory modes remain latent, working in a tacit way, the ego feeding off their subliminal presence for its own ends, and ignoring some of their impulses.

The person, by contrast, is functioning awarely in these wider modes, including the individuating modes within them. The basic life cycle, the ground process, of the person takes into account the participatory modes of feeling, intuition, reflection and intention, as well as emotion, imagery, discrimination and action.

It is shown in Figure 11.9 as four rotating larger wheels – the participatory modes – which touch and turn each other; and within each of these is a smaller wheel – the corresponding individuating mode – influenced by the movement of the larger wheel that contains it. Each mode is shown as generating the relevant world-view of which it is the primary parent, as explained in Chapter 8.

The cycle starts with a person feeling in empathic resonance with their total situation. Out of this felt participation, the person exercises an intuitive awareness of the entire pattern of what is appearing, seeing this perhaps in terms of some metaphor, story or myth that opens up life with expansive possibilities. This in turn gives rise to reflection, taking hold of the practical issues involved in relating to the situation. And this leads to some intention to act in a way that takes account of both the possibilities and the practicalities. With such action, the situation changes and a new cycle commences.

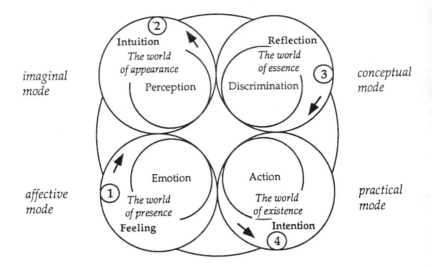

Figure 11.9   *The basic life cycle of the person*

At each stage, the individuating modes are subsumed and modified. Felt participation at stage one will influence and may alter the person's primary need, and its degree of satisfaction, and hence their current emotional state. At stage two, intuitive grasp of the total pattern of the situation will affect the imagery of what is perceived, remembered and anticipated. At stage three, discrimination will be in the service of a reflective grasp of relevant practical issues. And at stage four, action is the expression of wider purposes and intentions. What might otherwise be the more limited address of the ego at all four stages becomes transformed within a wider ambience.

As an illustration of this cycle, let us take a holistic medical practitioner relating to a client. (1) The practitioner attunes empathically to the total being of the client, realigning her own emotional needs and interests accordingly. (2) Then, as she questions, talks with and examines the client, she grasps intuitively the total imagery of spoken and bodily cues, and the story revealed by the client, and explores these imaginatively in terms of analogy and metaphor. (3) At the back of her mind, she reflects on all this imaginal data, while discriminating among it, and formulates a range of possible diagnoses. (4) Finally, she selects one of these as primary, makes a diagnosis and puts forward a plan of practical therapy.

Since she is a holistic practitioner, working with the participatory

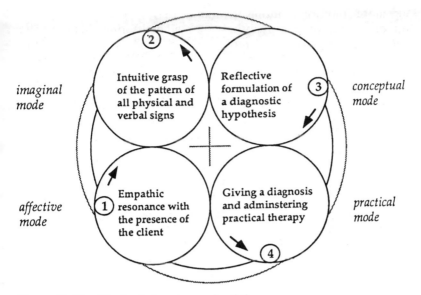

Figure 11.10   *The basic learning cycle of the person*

cycle of the person, she will want to include the client – wherever appropriate and possible – in mutuality of attunement in stage 1, in shared discussion in stages 2 and 3 and in co-operative problem-solving and planning in stage 4 (Balint and Norell, 1973; Heron, 1978).

In terms of the three basic polarities of the psyche, the person here is being participative, including the individuating modes; is involved with an expanded ground process; and is primarily living, the learning being minimal. So here is a person being consciously participative through feeling, intuition and reflection, who has an open ego and is living through the apertures but is not learning to any significant degree.

The basic learning cycle of the person

As with the ego, the life cycle of the person can become a learning cycle if, once again, the person is mindful throughout it and concentrates with the intention of grasping what is going on. Mindfulness and concentration are symbolized by the outermost circle and the central cross in Figure 11.10. In this figure I use the stages followed by the holistic medical practitioner, as outlined in the previous section.

So the practitioner in this figure may be learning about empathizing more fully, or intuiting a wider pattern of cues, or reflecting rapidly on alternative hypotheses, or administering therapy. The learning takes place by a simple feedback loop: what is noticed in one cycle is used to confirm or alter what is done in the next cycle. And what is noticed may be what goes on within a stage, or the effect of one stage on another.

Whereas the ego is learning through everyday experience how to become more effective in satisfying its individual needs, the person is learning how to become more effective in participating actively in wider and more inclusive fields of endeavour. In terms of the three basic polarities, the person here is being participative, including the individuating modes; is involved with an expanded ground process; and is learning through living, with the learning deepening the living. The person has an open ego and is living and learning through the apertures.

The co-operative reversal learning cycle of the person

The basic learning cycle of the person, just considered, can benefit from being included within a wider circle of co-operative learning, in which people meet to share their experience and reflect together on its meaning and practical implications. This is a higher-order cycle, which includes at one of its stages the whole of a lower-order cycle. Again, its effective use presupposes both mindfulness and concentration.

The model I propose for this is a co-operative reversal learning cycle. It is a reversal cycle to interrupt the social ground process that gets established when people meet together informally. Let us suppose it involves a peer professional development group of holistic medical practitioners. It is shown in Figure 11.11.

Stage 1 is the opening, affective stage. In the emotional mode, it is a time for celebration and positive encounter; and for dealing with any unresolved tensions between members of the group, and with any anxiety that any aspect of the impending process provokes. In the feeling mode, it is a time of group communion, a meditation in which members ground themselves in their mutual compresence. This nourishes the whole enterprise.

At stage 2 they share data from case histories and reflect on this together, discriminating the main issues, to get a deeper understanding of the therapeutic process, with implications for revised practice. At stage 3, practitioners reformulate their image of their therapeutic practice, in the light of their prior deliberations. This is a conscious exercise of active imagination, in which practitioners see

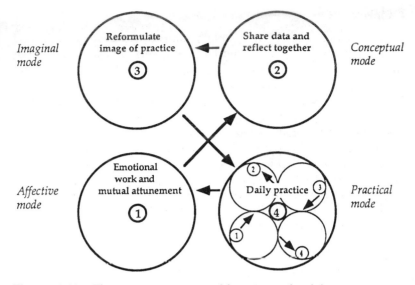

Figure 11.11   *The co-operative reversal learning cycle of the person*

themselves – each one on their own terms and in their own way going about their business in the future in ways which take account of whatever it is they wish to incorporate into their practice from the sharing of stage 2.

This active imagination can be verbalized, working in pairs or small groups. It can be elaborated through graphics, allegory, story; or demonstrated in projected rehearsal through role-play. The group then disbands and each person takes their image into action at stage 4, which is daily professional practice and consists of the basic learning cycle of the person, as described in the previous section, undertaken with many clients. After an appropriate period of daily practice, they meet again to start a second co-operative cycle.

So this is a co-operative reversal learning cycle, a higher-order cycle, which includes within it an individual basic learning cycle at stage 4. The co-operative cycle can be used by any group of people, from two to two dozen, who wish to enhance, and support each other in, their learning through living. In terms of the three basic polarities, the persons involved being participative in their way of relating, including the individuating modes, are reorganizing social ground process; and are learning co-operatively to deepen their individual living. They have open egos and are living and learning through the apertures.

Endpiece

In this chapter I have given only a sample of everyday living and everyday learning cycles, either basic or reversal ones, of the ego or the person. There are many others especially to do with interaction and relationship between persons. I have presented a sufficient number to indicate the way in which this theory of the person, with its account of the psychological modes and the three basic polarities that inform them, can illumine a variety of processes in everyday life and work.

I repeat what I said at the outset: the models shown here are like lenses which give a selective view. There are other lenses with other views. And those that are practical prescriptions are only an invitation to further inquiry.

12

A Brief Look at Learning

This short chapter makes a bridge from the previous one, which considers living as learning, to the next one, which deals with more formal learning situations in the classroom. In it I take a look at some aspects of the nature of learning.

In ordinary usage, 'learning' refers to the acquisition of knowledge or skills from experience, study or teaching. It involves interest and commitment: we only really learn what we are interested in and follow through with some degree of earnestness. Then too it supposes understanding and retention: we have learnt something if we understand it or understand how to do it (in the case of a skill) and can retain that understanding for some significant period of time.

Autonomy and holism

Learning is necessarily self-directed: no one else can do it for you. Interest, commitment, understanding and retention are all autonomous, self-generated and self-sustaining. Learning also involves the whole person, either by inclusion or by default. Either all of us is explicitly involved in the learning process, or only part of us is explicitly involved and what is excluded can be negatively influential, undermining either the content or the process.

These are the two poles of the learning process, autonomy and holism. In living-as-learning they are necessarily interdependent, to the extent, at any rate, that your living involves all four psychological modes. In educational institutions and formal courses, they can be developed in relative isolation from each other. A course can involve lots of autonomy, with student self-direction in course design, project work and assessment, yet have a rather restricted, unholistic intellectual focus.

Conversely, there can be a programme which involves all aspects of the students' psyches but which is entirely decided and managed by the staff, the students only being self-directing within set exercises. There is thus an interesting creative tension between autonomy in learning and holism in learning which educationalists are only just beginning to address, and which I believe is one of the major challenges for the next decades.

There are four levels of student autonomy. The first and minimal level is the student being self-directing only within teacher-prescribed learning activities: the teacher alone makes all the decisions about the programme of learning and its assessment. The second and more significant level is the student participating with the teacher in negotiated programme planning and assessment. The third level involves a small or large amount of exclusive student self-direction in programme planning and assessment. The fourth level, the most sophisticated, refers to student involvement in decisions with staff about whether students or staff or both shall be involved in decision-making about this or that aspect of programme planning and assessment. I have discussed all this in detail elsewhere (Heron, 1989).

Likewise there are four levels of student holism. The first involves only the four individuating modes of emotion, imagery, discrimination and action: this is limited holism at the egoic level. The second level combines the individuating and participatory modes in particular creative classroom activities where the focus is on the content of some subject matter. The third level involves the individuating and participatory modes in more person-centred concerns: personal development, interpersonal skills, professional work, group and team work, organizational structures, wider social, ecological and planetary commitments. The fourth level includes the second and third levels, integrated with development in psychic and spiritual dimensions. Levels two to four correspond to the stages of personal integration discussed in Chapter 3.

Kinds of learning

In terms of the theory of this book, just as there are four kinds of knowledge as discussed in Chapter 8, so there are four kinds of learning – experiential, presentational, propositional and practical. Experiential learning is acquiring knowledge of being and beings through empathic resonance, felt participation. Imaginal learning is acquiring knowledge of the patterning of experience through the exercise of intuition, imagination and perception. Propositional learning is acquiring knowledge stated in propositions through the exercise of the intellect. And practical learning is acquiring knowledge of how to do something through the practice of the particular skill in question.

If Howard Gardner (1983) now believes in eight kinds of

intelligence, then some *very* rough and ready correspondences can be set up with them as follows. Experiential learning: intrapersonal, interpersonal, intuitive/spiritual intelligences. Presentational learning: visual/spatial, musical/auditory intelligences. Propositional learning: linguistic, mathematical/logical intelligences. Practical learning: kinaesthetic intelligence.

However, leaving aside Gardner's scheme, I prefer to think that each of the eight modes represents a basic kind of intelligence. Experiential learning: empathic, emotional intelligences. Presentational learning: intuitive, imaging intelligences. Propositional learning: reflective, discriminatory intelligences. Practical learning; intentional, action intelligences. Which is all just another way of making the same basic point: intelligence, learning, knowing – each of these are of several different kinds, are One–Many, and need to be exercised as such. In adopting this holistic approach, I believe the up-hierarchy model is useful and I apply it in the next chapter.

Learning, inquiry and living

If learning is acquiring knowledge that is already established in the culture, it is simply learning. But if it is acquiring new knowledge that no-one else has, then it becomes inquiry or research. Learning as inquiry overlaps with learning what is known, but extends beyond it with a more sophisticated methodology.

Living-as-learning means that daily life, or some significant aspect of it, is consciously undertaken as a learning process, and I have explored some models for this in the previous chapter. This involves all four kinds of learning brought to a focus in practical learning, which in this case, and in very broad terms, means learning how to live, whether from the perspective of the ego or the person. It is ambiguous as to whether it is simple learning or learning as inquiry, since it is difficult to know what other people have or have not established as knowledge of how to live. Many people just live, as distinct from live-as-learning. And living-as-learning may be too individualistic, episodic and unfocused to count as establishing any kind of solid practical knowledge. However, if it is undertaken co-operatively with other people in some systematic way, especially from the perspective of the whole person, the enterprise is so original that it is almost certain to lead over into learning as inquiry. I put forward a model for this toward the end of the last chapter.

A special case of living-as-learning is working-as-learning, also considered in the previous chapter. Here daily work is the exclusive focus of conscious learning. At an earlier stage in working life, working-as-learning can also mean learning the job on the job, through some kind of apprenticeship or work placement or work under supervision system.

Learning how to live

It is certainly a very great mistake to see learning as either propositional learning, learning some body of knowledge set out in words and numbers, or as learning some quite specific skill, whether manual, verbal, technical, interpersonal or intrapsychic. In terms of the up-hierarchy, practical learning, based on the three other forms and construed as learning how to live from the perspective of the person, is the apotheosis, the consummation, of learning.

Our mainstream culture does not yet seem to have alighted upon this idea as having any great or special significance. But various trends are converging upon it.

1   Peer self-help groups of many different kinds have been a significant social development in recent decades. They are a focus for informal co-operative learning about how to manage some particular aspect of one's life-style such as gender, sexual orientation, racial and cultural identity, life-crisis, physical trauma and disability, addiction, psychological and physical abuse. Co-counselling offers an all-purpose peer self-help network for lifestyle growth and change.

2   Experimental communities exist which are an intense forum for co-operative living-as-learning. Thus the Life Center in Philadelphia seeks awarely to combine 'simple living, personal growth, and responsible relationships, with political and economic activism' (Gowan et al., 1979).

3   The whole of the personal and transpersonal growth movement to a greater or lesser extent considers the question of transfer: how you take the learning you have acquired in workshops and private sessions, and apply it in everyday life.

4   Learning theory is developing ideas like 'the experiential learning theory of development' (Kolb, 1984), which start to close the theoretical gap between learning and everyday life.

5   The one-world ecology crisis is starting to generate the world citizen who is learning, often with support groups, to change daily practices to take account of planetary concerns (Porritt and Winner, 1988).

13

Formal Learning Cycles

In this chapter I discuss learning that is available in a short or long course offered by an institution or private individual. I call this formal learning, simply to distinguish it from learning through living. It is holistic, involving all four modes, whether at the narrower ego level or the wider person level. I am thinking only in terms of higher and continuing education, since that is all I have had experience of as an active educator since I entered the field many years ago, although I believe the basic ideas apply at all educational levels.

I stress again that the models of practice given here are tentative proposals, working hypotheses which might be worth trying out in an experimental and critical way. They are invitations to inquiry through considered practice. Although their origin and rationale is different, the ego learning-cycle models below overlap significantly with methods used in suggestive-accelerative learning, whose effectiveness is well established, at any rate in conventional research terms (Schuster and Gritton, 1986). The person learning-cycle models I have used in varying forms over the years, and can vouch for their apparent benefits to the learner.

In higher and continuing education I think it is obligatory to introduce any method of learning only with the consent of the learner. I develop this important point in the section on holism and autonomy in learning.

The formal basic learning cycle of the ego

Formal learning in the service of the ego, as I define it, is what occurs when an individual goes to classes to acquire knowledge and skills for work or leisure in some quite specific subject area, such as astronomy, a language, geography, accountancy, or whatever. Such learning might usefully explore and experiment with a method based on the up-hierarchy of the ego, which consists of all the four individuating modes, as in Figure 13.1, which is to be read from the bottom upwards.

Translated into a learning cycle this up-hierarchy suggests the following priorities. First, a strong emotional base – in this case

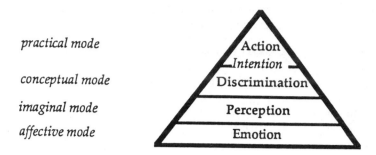

Figure 13.1 *The up-hierarchy of the ego*

confidence, fulfilment and positive arousal. Secondly, a wide range of different perceptual inputs of the material to be learned – auditory, visual and kinaesthetic – together with its imaginative development through metaphor, analogy and story. Thirdly, discrimination of the salient intellectual features of the material within a global view. Fourthly, the opportunity to rehearse and practise and discuss the material with, and get feedback from, others.

Presenting these four features in the up-hierarchy model, as in Figure 13.2 proposes that each is supported by and grounded on those below; and that the lower are the more basic and the key to the higher. This yields the hypothesis that emotional confidence, fulfilment and positive arousal are the most important for effective learning; that they constitute its formative potential.

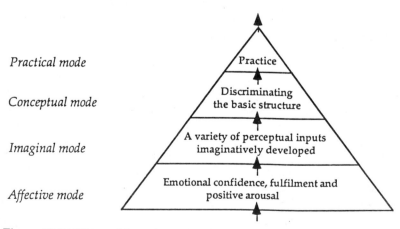

Figure 13.2 *The up-hierarchy of formal basic learning of the ego*

The importance of emotionality in learning is fundamental. It can be stated in several ways. People learn more effectively when they are enjoying themselves and what they are doing; when they are satisfying some felt need or interest, and are emotionally involved in what has personal relevance to them; when they feel good about the whole idea of learning and the exercise of their learning competence; when they feel confident, secure and in a low threat, co-operative, non-competitive situation.

It is almost naive to ask for evidence of all this. For the very notion of learning implies commitment to the content of what is being learnt and the process of learning, as well as some kind of co-operative dialogue through the written or the spoken word. This is all part of what the word means. In ordinary language, 'learning' means acquiring knowledge from experience, study or teaching; and this acquisition presupposes interest, that is, emotional involvement. Relevant evidence beyond thus grasping the meaning of the word lies first and foremost in personal, experiential knowledge: your acquaintance with your own learning process.

In terms of the correlation between mental processes and what goes on in the brain, recent research shows that the limbic system of the mid-brain has three interacting functions. It is the seat of emotional processes and their regulation; it edits incoming data, and passes on the filtered data to the new or upper brain, the neo-cortex; and it is involved in key elements of long-term memory. The result of this triadic activity is that information with emotional content, that is which interests and involves us, is both more likely to be selectively filtered (rather than discarded) and passed on to the neo-cortex, and more likely to be well remembered (Rose, 1991). Stress and high anxiety inhibit data flow through the limbic system to the neo-cortex, and cause a 'downshift' of brain function to lower levels (Hart, 1983).

Learning is enhanced when someone else, the facilitator, is confidently eliciting a positive emotional attitude within the learner; when learners generate and sustain emotional arousal among themselves; and when their learning is associated with or interwoven with art, music and drama, all of which are enjoyable activities and help to create a positive emotional response. All these methods have been used in teaching ordinary classroom subjects, and by conventional measures have been shown to be more effective than traditional teaching strategies (Schuster and Gritton, 1986).

Figure 13.3 converts the up-hierarchy model into a basic cycle. As a basis for an exploratory teaching and learning project, it suggests that when new material is presented it is grounded in this basic

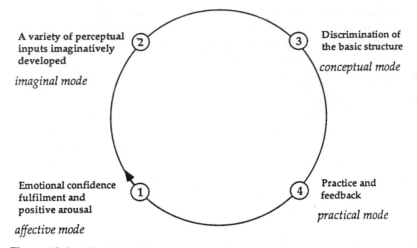

Figure 13.3   *The formal basic learning cycle of the ego*

cycle, which could include partial or complete sub-cycles. The order of the four stages could vary in major and minor cycles, but the basic thrust of the original up-hierarchy would be critical overall. I give an illustrative example of this sequence, for a two-hour adult education class on elementary astronomy, in a later section (pp. 237–8).

What traditional teaching and learning methods have massively overlooked is the vital role of the first two stages of this cycle. They have neglected any explicit use of a whole range of teacher interventions to generate and maintain a foundation state of positive emotional arousal. And they have also ignored the importance of sustained and varied presentations of the material perceptually and imaginatively – which are intended to enable the student to soak up its pre-conceptual form – as distinct from propositional exposition, which is intended to get conceptual structures directly into the learners' heads.

The point about imaginal presentations is that they contain within their patterns the latent concepts and propositions – which may precipitate themselves spontaneously into the students' minds. This kind of unforced generation of conceptual learning is the rationale for taking the learning process, in a deep and sustained way, into the affective and imaginal modes. Of course, there is still explicit cultivation to do at the conceptual level itself. But the seedling is already above ground.

This is a basic point of the up-hierarchy model of the psyche: that imaginal patterns are pregnant with conceptual content, and that to cultivate them at their own level will facilitate the later birth of that content. This phenomenological finding leads to the educational technique of an abundance of different ways of *presenting* data. The front edge of current learning theory also argues for this technique with views that overlap my phenomenological account.

The right brain, which works with form, pattern, image, space, rhythm, music, simultaneity and synthesis, also works very much faster than the left brain (language, logic, number, linearity, sequence, analysis). If it is presented with rich, complex data that also show a global overview of the subject matter, then the right brain can identify the *pattern* of this overview (Rose, 1991). It can grasp the form of a total conceptual structure simply *qua* form. In my view any conceptual structure simply is the outcrop of an underlying imaginal form.

There are primary learning style differences depending on whether your sensory intake preference is through visual, auditory or kinaesthetic/tactile channels (Rose, 1991). Hence in a classroom situation where all styles will be represented by different students, it makes sense to present material in terms of all three sensory channels. I would go further than this and say that each person, whatever their preferred style, will benefit from multi-channel presentation — to enhance the imaginal impact of the material.

Howard Gardner (1983) has a model of seven, possibly eight, different types of intelligence: linguistic, mathematical/logical, visual/spatial, musical/auditory, kinaesthetic, interpersonal, intra-personal, and, he now thinks, perhaps intuitive/spiritual. Hence if there are multiple presentations of new material which engage several of these different kinds of intelligence, learning is likely to be more satisfying and holistic, more rapid and effective (Ornstein, 1983).

In the fourth edition of his classic book on the adult learner Knowles cites Herrmann's concept of whole brain teaching and learning (Knowles, 1990). Herrmann identifies four brain quadrants: the right limbic system, the right cerebral hemisphere, the left cerebral hemisphere and the left limbic system. He correlates these, respectively, with the four specialized modes he calls emotional, holistic, logical and planned; also with four learning styles characterized as integrating experience with self; being concerned with hidden possibilities; forming theories; and attaining skills through practice. He thinks that delivery of learning needs to accommodate all these four modes and styles (Herrmann, 1987). This echoes my theory of the integration of affective, imaginal, conceptual and practical modes in learning.

Machado considers the limbic system to be 'the brain of the

brain', the seat of the 'great intelligence', which is the matrix of innate cognitive structures such as Chomsky's framework of universal grammar (Chomsky, 1985), and the generating ground of human creativity – to be reached through art, music, metaphor, stories and parables (Machado, 1991).

Suggestive-accelerative learning techniques

These techniques were developed in the early 1970s in the USA based on fragmentary reports of the work of Dr George Lozanov in Bulgaria, whose method of Suggestopedia first put together the combination of suggestion, relaxation, mental alertness and the presentation of the material to be learned to music, all before explicit conceptual elaboration of the material (Lozanov, 1978). The strict Lozanov method is still undergoing development at the hands of Lozanov himself, and there are numerous suggestive-accelerative variations of the Lozanov method which also incorporate many other developments in learning and brain science (Rose, 1991). Schuster and Gritton (1986) give a good account of the method, its underlying theory and a review of research studies that show its effectiveness.

I wish to pay tribute to the work of Lozanov and those who are developing in their own way the same terrain. There are obvious overlaps of this work with the approach to learning presented so far in this chapter, and I have learnt much from it. Yet I have to make it plain that their respective origins are *quite different*. My approach is rooted in a radical phenomenology of the dynamics of the psyche: this leads to a rationale of learning stages based on the up-hierarchy model of the psyche as I have presented it in this book. The stages and techniques I propose should not be confused with Lozanov and related methods which are based on an amalgam of brain science, conditioning theory, suggestion techniques and memory research, extending out into various theories about learning preferences, multiple intelligence and so on. The rationale of learning stages is somehow based on this amalgam; and the sequencing of stages can vary quite a lot.

The Lozanov and affiliated techniques are also much preoccupied with accelerated learning that occurs two or three times faster than traditional methods. This dramatic increase in the speed of learning is an important part of the professional and commercial presentation of their work. I have no particular interest in the acceleration of learning, only with its psychological and epistemological soundness and wholeness.

For me the important parts of the overlap to which I have

referred are a positive emotional base for learning; the use of music and relaxation and inner alertness; manifold presentations of the material to be learnt; explicit conceptual elaboration of this material at a later stage; the importance of practical exercises; the supportive and charismatic presence of the teacher.

There may be a significant difference in one important respect. I shall argue later on in this chapter that a holistic method directed by the teacher needs to be one which in principle is committed from the start to becoming one which is *eventually* self-directed by the student. It is not clear to me that this point has been fully entertained by those involved in suggestive-accelerative learning methods.

The media of holistic ego learning

By the media of learning I mean the instruments, the means, of learning. There are four classes of these, corresponding to the four stages of the learning cycle: music and celebration, presentations, propositions and activities. They are shown correlated with the world-views and their respective modes in Table 13.1, and as an up-hierarchy in Figure 13.4.

What this up-hierarchy implies is that presentations arc best grounded on music and celebration, propositions on presentations, and activities on all the preceding. What, in detail, are these four classes of media?

Music and celebration
In the field of suggestive and accclerated learning, music has long been used as the ground for the presentation of material to be learnt (Lozanov, 1978; Schuster and Gritton, 1986). In terms of my theory, music is the grounding medium, the formative potential, so to speak, of all the other learning media. Its home is the world of presence, the world of resonance, mutual attunement and positive emotional arousal; it speaks directly to the affective mode of the psyche, and to the affective-imaginal pairing that generates the world of presence. It can be played in breaks, before and after sessions; in the foreground of a session to facilitate relaxation and

Table 13.1 *Worlds, modes and media*

World of existence	Practical-affective	Activities
World of essence	Conceptual-practical	Propositions
World of appearance	Imaginal-conceptual	Presentations
World of presence	Affective-imaginal	Music and celebration

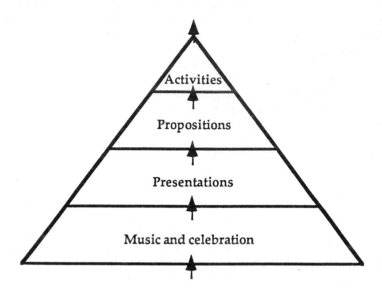

Figure 13.4   *The up-hierarchy of the media of learning*

emotional enjoyment; and as a background to the presentation of material, when appropriate, as in Lozanov's active and passive concerts, which use classical and Baroque music respectively (Lozanov, 1978).

By celebration, I mean two things. First, that a person is attuned to their feeling nature, their capacity for empathic resonance. This is one of the primary purposes of the use of music. Other processes may aid the entry into this state: these include relaxation techniques, both physical and mental, guided imagery and visualization methods, and a whole range of meditation practices.

Secondly, that a person is in a positive, buoyant, enjoyable and self-affirmative emotional state. This can be generated by the ambience of the place of learning, and by the facilitator's style of relating to the learners at every point of the course. This attitude is one that has both lightness of touch and at the same time conveys deep respect and a belief that each person has within them a remarkable, immediately accessible potential for effective and comprehensive learning.

The positive emotional state in learners can also be elicited more specifically by affirmations made to the learners as part of the way in which the facilitator – at the very outset and with reminders thereafter – sets the whole culture of the course. The use of music of appropriate kinds supports this buoyant emotional state.

In seeking to call up the feeling nature in the world of presence, through music and relaxation, we are going beyond the individuating modes of the ego to provide a deeper base for the generation of self-affirmative emotion.

Presentations
Here the material to be learnt is presented so that its pre-conceptual form can be directly grasped by the imaginal mind prior to explicit verbal and intellectual understanding. The material can be spoken aloud, with great attention paid to the use of the voice, that is, to its emotional tone and changing inflections, its volume, pitch and timbre, the use of pauses and silences. This in turn can be facilitated by background music, and attention to associated imagery.

The material can also be presented in visual paradigms incorporating colours and graphic designs that relate to the meaning of the material. It can be shown in mobile and dramatic form, through movement, dance, acting and mini-theatre. It can be elaborated through the imaginative use of metaphor and analogy. Where possible and relevant, the material in all these presentations tells a *story*. And also, where relevant, the presentations give a coherent, global overview of the subject matter, so that the basic *patterning* of its central concepts and principles stands out.

Presentations, then, are a class of media that disclose imaginal patterns in the appearance, the coming into form, of the material to be learnt. They are taken in by the learner primarily in the imaginal modes of intuition and imagery, not by premature attempts at verbal-conceptual discrimination, classification and rule-making.

Propositions
These are statements, made in words or numbers, that yield the explicit intellectual, conceptual content of the material to be learnt. Hitherto this has been regarded as the central and only medium of learning. In this scheme it is only third in importance and order, and tends to become alienated and desiccated if made the sole medium.

After exposure to the material in its imaginal form through diverse presentations, the learner is given a full analysis of its intellectual format, with salient concepts and organizing principles picked out and the detail filled in round these, perhaps with background music and with imagery and mnemonics to aid storage of the scheme in long-term memory.

It is important to note that a good deal of the intellectual, conceptual content of the material may have been released into the mind quite spontaneously in the presentational phase of learning.

And this phenomenon is indeed one of the reasons for using this four-stage approach to learning.

Activities
This class of medium includes student pairs for the practice and rehearsal of learning, simulations, role-plays, exercises, games, projects, experiments, fieldwork – all activities which enable the learner to make the material their own by incorporating it in word and deed, in interaction where possible with other learners, who can enhance each other's learning through feedback and mutual aid. Practice can be written, spoken, sung, physically active, inter-personal, graphic. It can involve extensive collaboration in peer groups, in which much co-operative and self-directed learning is going on. This is the phase in which student autonomy in learning is paramount.

The four media can also be seen as a cycle, as in Figure 13.5. Of course, there is no suggestion with this cycle that its sequence is to be followed slavishly. Many variations are possible, for example giving some degree of propositional overview of the material before the presentations, or interweaving propositional work and activity work, or delaying major propositional work until a good deal of activity work has been done. The choices are dependent on the nature of the material and the stage of learning it that the students have reached.

But the principle of the overall working hypothesis remains: learning through activity is based on prior conceptual discrimination within material which is first of all presented in its imaginal form,

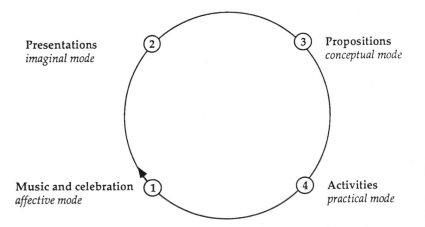

Figure 13.5   *The media of learning as a cycle*

the whole being grounded on a positive emotional foundation. As I have already said, a lot of conceptual learning may effortlessly drop out of presentational learning, in the same way that the small child, when learning its mother tongue, picks up the concepts at the same time as it acquires the sounds of words and the shape of the grammar being presented around it. So the theory proposes that the affective and imaginal phases encourage conceptual learning to emerge more readily; and that it has to emerge to some significant degree before active rehearsal and practice is of any use.

I have called this whole cycle a learning cycle of the ego because it focuses on some specific subject through the individuating modes of emotion, imagery, discrimination and action; and because it serves the needs of the ego for knowledge and skills in the pursuit of its interests. But the cycle also evokes the tacit power of feeling and intuition, so it softens the ego, and trains it to acquire attitudes of openness to the participatory modes. It therefore involves a gentle transformation of the ego.

An illustrative example

Suppose you are teaching a course on elementary astronomy as part of an adult education programme. The topic for the next two-hour lesson is the solar system. Here are some elements that can be woven into a holistic format, following the basic cycle of the modes and the media. First give your students a brief outline of your holistic strategy, its rationale, and seek their assent to it. This is very important.

Invite the students physically and mentally to relax with eyes closed and listen for a few minutes to the Jupiter music from Holst's *Planets* suite. Follow this with an affirmation and suggestion about the pleasures, the ease and fluency of learning. Present one or two major myths about the planets, sun and moon. Follow this with the story of some key discoveries about the solar system in the history of astronomy. To a background of music expressively recite out loud all the salient data about the solar system you want to include in this lesson: invite students to listen to the music and the *sound* of your words, with eyes closed, without attending to the conceptual content, and giving any imagery that is evoked free reign. At any point in this five-item sequence give space for spontaneous student-directed comment, question, answer and discussion episodes. Now have a mid-session break.

Follow this with photos and graphics that present the salient data in visual form. Then help students to portray the solar system physically in the room, with very approximate positions, motions and velocities. Let this generate questions, answers and discussion. Next, with music playing very softly, invite students to discriminate the conceptual content of your words together with evoked imagery as you state again the salient data, this time from a different perspective and in a different order. Follow this with co-operative peer teaching and learning, in which students in pairs take it in turns to share what they now know about the solar system, mythically, historically and factually, by making statements which the other agrees with or corrects, and by asking questions which the other answers or is helped to answer. Encourage them to expand this sharing from the central ground of what interests them; and to make drawings and diagrams as they explore their knowledge with each other. End with a final time for questions, answers and discussion.

This sequence starts at the affective level (relaxation, music and eliciting positive emotion), moves on to the imaginal (myth, story, vocal presentation, visual presentation, kinaesthetic presentation), thence to the conceptual (discrimination of content), and ending with practice (rehearsal of knowledge in co-operative pairs). The affective baseline of music is used to empower both the vocal presentation of salient data and the later discrimination of its content. This use of music to empower first the imaginal and then the conceptual modes is not to be confused with Lozanov's active and passive concerts (Lozanov, 1978) which are both concerned with the imaginal mode.

This follows the basic cycle closely, but I do not think there is anything specially sacrosanct about always doing so, since additions and variations and inserted sub-cycles will keep the whole thing alive with creative diversity from session to session. What is involved here, after all, is an exploratory project, an experiential inquiry in which you and your students have agreed to chart some of the depths of holism in learning.

Holism and autonomy in learning

The learning model for the classroom so far presented in this chapter is holistic: it involves all four individuating modes quite explicitly and calls up the tacit power of the participatory modes. It requires a lot of careful preparation by the teacher, who will need to direct the learning process and make unilateral decisions about the content of learning, the methods of learning and their sequencing and pacing and presentation. It is important to be aware of this, and to realize that sophisticated holistic methods imply, for the student, quite a long process of initiation which will be managed by the teacher. Of course the students will be self-directing within many of the exercises and activities that the teacher has designed and sequenced, but that is all. They will not be involved in any of the educational decision-making as such.

I believe the teacher in higher and continuing education has a deep obligation to administer this whole process on a basis of consent. The teacher must direct the initiation having obtained prior and fully informed assent of the students to be so initiated. This means explaining the holistic method and its rationale in pre-course publicity, again at the pre-course interview, where assent is sought; and again at the start of the course, where understanding, acceptance and agreement are confirmed. Without this explicit contract, the approach degenerates into benevolent manipulation and methodological indoctrination.

Such a contract honours student autonomy in learning; and unless it is honoured it is undermined and real learning suffers. We are dealing here with the dialectic of the two poles of learning – holism and autonomy – which I introduced in the previous chapter. For learning, as I said there, is by its nature autonomous as well as holistic. Learners can voluntarily surrender their autonomy in order to be initiated into holism, but only on condition that they acquire ways of exercising that autonomy, inclusive of the new holism, at a later stage.

So the direction of holistic learning is set within a contract supported by the student. If I consent to be directed in some new learning method, I agree to try out two things – the direction and the method. And there is the clear implication that I shall need a periodic review to see whether I still assent both to the direction and the method. If at such a review it becomes clear that I understand the method, find it effective and have become proficient in it, then I can claim to start participating with the teacher in the management of it. If the teacher concurs in my assessment, the direction needs to turn into consultation and negotiation, and eventually perhaps into full delegation. Then the whole point of surrendering my autonomy in the first place will have been fully justified.

A contract with students for them to be directed in holistic learning implies, as they become more competent in it, a later stage of consultative and then delegated management of that learning. This needs to be made quite explicit in the agreement at the start of the course. Teacher-directed student holism is only justified if it includes from the outset a commitment to move towards self-directed student holism. I am here writing exclusively about courses in higher and continuing education, as I made plain at the start of this chapter.

A full and satisfactory integration of holistic and autonomous learning is a sophisticated educational achievement. The principles are clear enough, the practice is at the leading edge. It is easy to sacrifice holism to autonomy and autonomy to holism. Getting them to advance each other is one of the main challenges for educationalists over the next decades.

An interesting issue arises about the integration of holistic and autonomous learning when using the formal learning cycle of the ego as I have developed it so far in this chapter. When the cycle is being directed entirely by the teacher, students can remain in the ego and have it gently softened by music, relaxation and imaginal openness. But when the cycle becomes self-directed, students emerge as conscious persons intentionally harnessing their capacity for feeling and imaginal intuition in the early phases. So as they become more autonomous in learning they also become more holistic, moving from their egohood to their active personhood, which is working on opening up the ego. This is a fairly major transition in personal development so the teacher needs to be equipped to facilitate it.

The formal basic learning cycle of the person

In the formal learning cycle of the ego, the participatory modes of feeling and intuition, especially, remain tacit in the learning process. They are, of course, evoked and involved in learning, yielding a gentle transformation and softening of the ego, but they are not brought into intentional, conscious use by the learner, at any rate as long as the learning is directed by the teacher. In the formal learning cycle of the person, they are brought forward as conscious functions. They become explicit means of learning, which extends through all the four worlds – of presence, appearance, essence and existence. The person learner is seeking awarely to integrate the four modes in their individuating and participatory forms: emotion-feeling, imagery-intuition, discrimination-reflection and action-intention. Figure 13.6 shows the sequence as an up-hierarchy for a trainee counsellor.

And whereas the ego learner needs to be open to positive emotion and emotional arousal as a precondition of effective learning, the person learner also needs to have a significant degree of emotional competence. An emotionally competent person is able to manage their emotions awarely in terms of the basic skills of control, expression, catharsis and transmutation, plus one or two others. I discussed this important notion in detail in the penultimate section of Chapter 6. It is, I believe, critical to any concept of learning which truly involves the whole person.

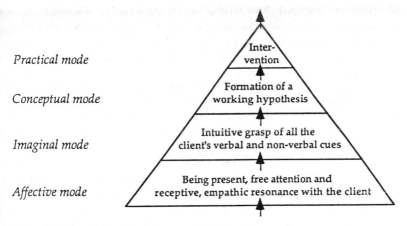

Figure 13.6 *Formal learning cycle of the person as an up-hierarchy (trainee counsellor)*

Those who attend courses for developing interpersonal skills, such as counselling, benefit, in my experience, from the formal basic learning cycle of the person. I will use counselling training to illustrate the cycle as shown in Figure 13.7. Stage 1 fosters in trainees the ability to be fully present, with attention free of

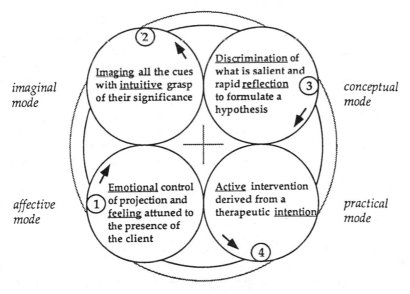

Figure 13.7 *Formal basic learning cycle of the person (trainee counsellor)*

emotional projection, and with receptive, empathic attunement to their clients. So this involves exercising both emotional competence and felt participation.

Stage 2 emerges out of stage 1: trainees exercise aware, intuitive perception of the whole pattern of their clients' behaviour – including what they are saying, but more so how they are saying it, and how they are being as evidenced in all kinds of body and breathing cues. Here trainees need to exercise attention to a wide range of perceived images of the client, together with intuitive grasp of their significance.

In stage 3 trainees learn to discriminate selectively among all this data, and evolve reflectively a provisional, working hypothesis about the client's process. So both discrimination and reflection are needed – the reflection being like quicksilver.

At stage 4, trainees acquire skill in converting this hypothesis into a practical intervention that is based upon some underlying thera-peutic purpose. Here we have both action and intention. At each stage the individuating and participative forms of the relevant modes are brought into play. Then as the client responds to the intervention of stage 4, the trainee practises deep empathic reson-ance and the cycle begins again.

Figure 13.6 brings out how the higher levels emerge out of, and are supported by, the lower levels. Figure 13.7 depicts the sequence as a cycle and brings out more fully how each stage involves both an individuating and a participatory function. It also shows the import-ance for the trainee counsellor, after making an intervention, not to be blindly attached to it, but to switch immediately into empathic resonance with the client in order to be able to pick up all the cues in the client's response, and so sustain client-centred relevance.

This cycle, too, has a positive and negative feedback loop. If the counsellor attends with great empathy to the client's response to an intervention, he or she will learn whether that intervention, the hypothesis underlying it and the selected cues, were appropriate or not. If appropriate, the next turn of the cycle may go deeper in the same direction; if not, then greater empathy and cue sensitivity, more fitting hypothesis formation and type of intervention, can be tried.

The formal co-operative reversal learning cycle of the person

If trainees learn as a peer group, then they can incorporate the basic cycle within a co-operative reversal cycle. This combination was introduced for peer professional development groups and shown in

Figure 11.11 (p. 221). It can be used equally by a group of trainees for peer training.

A trainer running, say, a counselling skills training course will also use the same kind of group reversal cycle – to launch the trainees into and bring them out of their basic learning cycle. Typically, it goes like this. (1) The trainees spend a short period doing whatever emotional or interpersonal work is needed; then ground themselves in mutual attunement by being present with each other in the mode of feeling, by some form of interactive meditation. (2) The trainer conceptually describes the up-hierarchy and the stages of the learning cycle as in Figure 13.7. (3) The trainer then demonstrates it or illustrates it, presenting a living image of it. (4) The trainees practise the whole learning cycle through its four stages, with intermittent feedback and reruns.

The second cycle starts (1) with any interpersonal or emotional work that needs to be done as a consequence of the first cycle, followed by mutual attunement; then (2) there is a return to the conceptual mode for a review of all the issues uncovered in the practice, leading to a refined account of practice, which (3) is imaged and illustrated, and so on round the training cycle. Figure 13.8 illustrates how the trainer's reversal cycle and the trainees' basic cycle interact. It mirrors Figure 11.11.

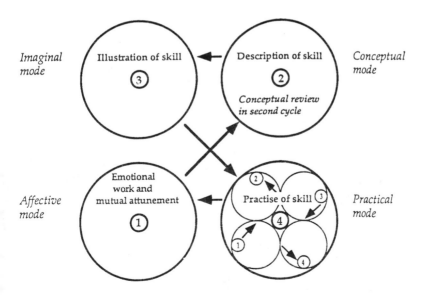

Figure 13.8 *The basic learning cycle within the reversal training cycle*

Because they mirror each other exactly, this approach to training can be used as a model to lead over to post-course peer professional development groups. And although the method clearly is more advantageous in groups, whether of self-directing peers or with a trainer, one person can use it to reflect on and re-vision their practice.

Modes and dynamic principles in learning

Figure 13.9 is intended to be a summary statement and reminder of the elements of the model of the person which I have been using in my account of learning.

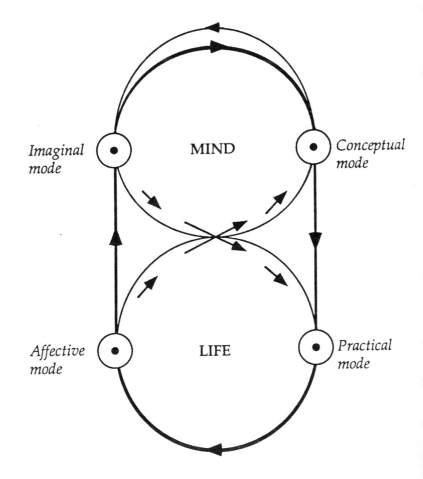

Figure 13.9   *Modes and polarities*

Here are the four modes, each with an individuating and a participatory function, symbolized by the dot within the circle, and two cycles flowing through them, one the basic cycle of the ground process, and the other a reversal cycle for reorganizing the ground process; both cycles are engaged with the polarity of life and mind.

14

The Reality-creating Learning Cycle

This short final chapter applies the learning model, in particular the reversal cycle, to the practice of 'creating your own reality' which has become a popular catch-phrase in new-age literature and seminars. This is also a way of giving another account, in rather more general terms, of the notion of post-linguistic perception discussed in Chapters 7 and 8.

By virtue of their socialization and education, each person will have fixed within them their version of the world-view imposed by their culture. The first task in reality-creating is to dismantle this way of viewing the world – which will be deeply embedded in the very act of perceiving at every moment.

One model for the old, positivist world-view, is of an up-hierarchy split into two parts that are opposed to each other, as shown in Figure 14.1. The worlds of essence and existence have

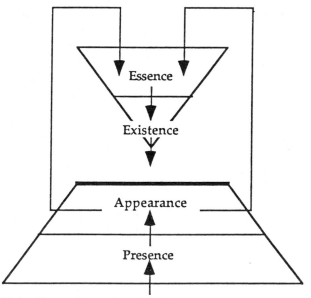

Figure 14.1 *The up-hierarchy of the four worlds split and opposed*

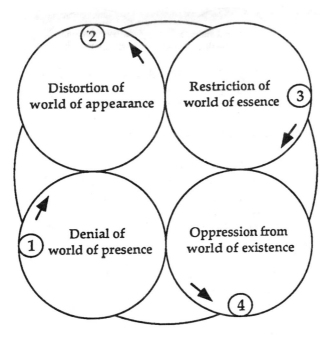

Figure 14.2 *The four worlds in a self-locking negative cycle*

become split off from the worlds of appearance and presence, and seek to oppress, control and contain them, but are still in distorted form powered by them. I refer the reader to the start of Chapter 8 for a reminder about the nature of these 'worlds'. This split between the worlds reflects the split in the world-viewers between will and intellect on the one hand and imagination and feeling on the other, the former pair dominating and controlling the latter.

Another portrayal is in terms of a self-locking negative cycle. The effect of the contracting spiral of development on a person, as discussed at the end of Chapter 2, is to bury the world of presence, and distort the imaginal power of the mind into giving a very limited account of the world of appearance. This distortion holds strongly in place the restrictive belief systems of the world of essence, which limit the range of actions that define the world of existence, which in turn sustains the repression of the world of presence. This is depicted in Figure 14.2.

The reality-creating reversal learning cycle of the person

What is needed to undo such a negative cycle is the figure-of-eight reversal cycle. It loops through the four worlds. The first step is to

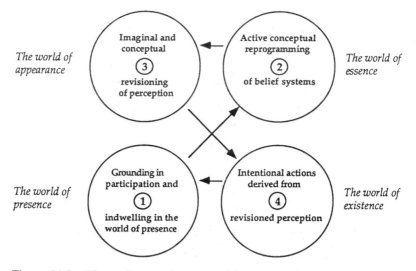

Figure 14.3   *The reality-creating reversal learning cycle*

participate in the world of presence, in order to ground the whole reversal cycle in great openness to being. This meditative starting point is the touchstone of the cycle. The second step is in the world of essence, programming the psyche with an alternative conceptual model of the scheme of things, a different world-view. This cognitive restructuring goes on not simply within the head, but within the bones, and needs to be clearly formulated in words and concepts: it is an inner propositional action, a mental posturing and speaking out of a radically changed belief system. This process creates redrawn world-maps and models – a new world of essence.

The third step is to move over into the world of appearance, bring forward actively into awareness the new belief system, and let it arouse the imagination and at the same time inform the very act of perceiving the world. The associations, classifications and categories of the new belief system are injected into perception as its conceptual component. Once these are installed in the process of perceiving, the person has engendered a new subjective–objective reality. He or she has enabled the imaginal and conceptual modes to interact creatively to generate a changed world of appearance.

The fourth step is to enter the world of existence and execute actions whose intentions derive directly from the concepts installed within the world of appearance. Then the practical and affective modes will parent a changed world of existence. Deeds with new purposes will encounter new forms of what there is. Figure 14.3 depicts the four stages of the reversal cycle. However, as we shall

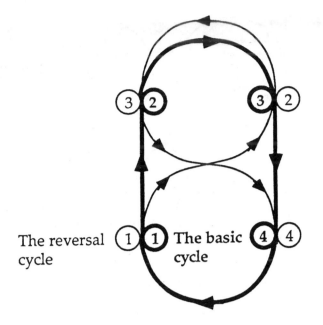

The reversal cycle

The basic cycle

Figure 14.4 *The reversal cycle with the basic cycle*

see, I believe that moving through these successive stages is increasingly a collective and consensual matter.

In daily practice, the reversal cycle will be interwoven with the basic experiential cycle as shown in Figure 14.4.

The concept of reality creation

New-age populists speak a great deal of creating your own reality. In doing so they sometimes exploit the ambiguity of the phrase in irresponsible ways and do not pause to clarify what it does and does not mean.

It clearly does not mean creating any old world that suits your fancy. It is not a formula for omnipotent solipsism except in the minds of the deranged. There is no such thing as my own reality in any absolute and exclusive sense of ownership and possession. For reality is essentially public and shared: it depends on a consensual view of its status and credentials. I can have a distinct and idiosyncratic perspective on this shared reality, but this purely personal view is interdependent with the public account.

Personal views can go beyond the reach of the public account, but only by so much. Any public account contains within it the seeds of its own transcendence; in this sense it determines how far that

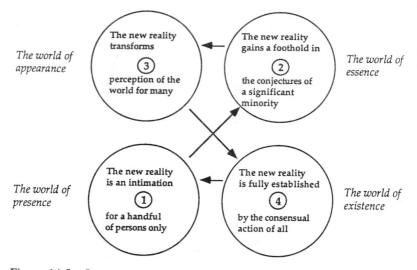

Figure 14.5   *Stages in the emergence of a new reality*

transcendence can go. When a sufficient number of personal views combine to redefine reality, then a new version of its starts to emerge, which will also contain within it the seeds of its own transcendence.

Intimations of a new view of reality probably first emerge when a very few creative persons let go their preconceptions for brief moments and attune to the world of presence in a way that is pregnant with deep intimations. After that, the new reality first emerges into some kind of explicit form at the conceptual level; and this for a significant minority of leading-edge inquirers. So today it is starting to get some ground-plans laid out in the world of essence, the world of ideas and conjecture. I think it has a long way to go to get a foothold in the world of appearance, in discriminating and immediate perception of the world. This happens when many people start to perceive the world, to image it, in terms of the new belief system. The new reality only becomes fully established when it enters the world of existence; and this is when everyone *acts* on the basis of a transformed perception. Figure 14.5 shows the sequence.

The four stages proceed by quantitative as well as qualitative leaps: from the intimations of very few, to the revised belief systems of some, to the revisioned perception of many, to the consensual actions of all. Today we are certainly in stage 2: some creative thinkers are defining a new reality in conceptual terms in an area where advanced physics, systems theory, psychical research and transpersonal psychology overlap. A more refined account would add several more fields of contemporary inquiry to the area of overlap. My guess is that no two leading-edge thinkers would have exactly the same refined map, but all of them would certainly have, at the very least, three major fields in common.

I doubt whether there are today any people continuously established in stage 3, in which the new belief system is embedded in perception as a basic conceptual layer, so that people are actually seeing the new reality as distinct from believing in it. I do not think the new belief system is developed enough or coherent enough or sufficiently well known or widespread for it to transform everyday perception in this way. Some people, however, may have transitional, hybrid perceptual schema, a sort of mix of the old and the provisionally new.

There is a significant time lag between stages 2 and 3. By the end of the seventeenth century a significant minority were already well established in the Newtonian-Cartesian belief system in the world of essence; but in the world of appearance most ordinary people were almost certainly still seeing the High Street, the sun, moon and stars in terms of the Aristotelio-medieval world-view.

In the same way, today, a significant minority have abandoned the Newtonian Cartesian belief system in favour of some elaboration of a systems theory world-view. But it may be that they, and certainly the majority of people, still *see* the world in Newtonian–Cartesian terms. It is a big shift for concepts to move from being simply beliefs held in the mind to beliefs that inform and transform the very act of perception.

To return again to the populist notion of creating your own reality. It can have a meaning in psychosocial terms. You can stop projecting distressed templates from early life upon the world and see situations for what they have to say in present time. You can visualize and affirm a positive, proactive approach to daily life which means you attract, and start to resonate with, what is positive and proactive in your world.

In more general terms, you can practise selective resonance with what there is on different levels of being. And you can realize that deep within the generative power of the imaginal mind you are co-creator, with 'something far more deeply interfused', of perceptual imagery, and so be among the emerging participants in continuous creation.

References

Alexander, C. (1979) *The Timeless Way of Building*. New York: Oxford University Press.

Armfield, M. (1946) *Tempera Painting Today*. London: Pentagon Press.

Assagioli, R. (1965) *Psychosynthesis*. Baltimore: Penguin Books.

Balint, E, and Norell, J.S. (1973) *Six Minutes for the Patient*. London: Tavistock.

Bateson, G. (1979) *Mind and Nature*. London: Wildwood House.

Bateson G. and Bateson, M.C. (1987) *Angels Fear*. London: Rider.

Beardsley, M.C. (1958) *Aesthetics*. New York: Harcourt, Brace & World.

Bell, C. (1914) *Art*. London: Chatto & Windus.

Berendt, J.-E. (1987) *Nada Brahma*. London: East West Publications.

Berendt, J.-E. (1988) *The Third Ear*. Shaftesbury: Element Books.

Bohm, D. (1980) *Wholeness and the Implicate Order*. London: Routledge & Kegan Paul.

Buber, M. (1937) *I and Thou*. Edinburgh: Clark.

Capra, F. (1975) *The Tao of Physics*. London: Wildwood House.

Capra, F. (1983) *The Turning Point*. London: Fontana.

Carrigan, P. (1960) 'Extraversion–introversion as a dimension of personality: a reappraisal', *Psychological Bulletin*, 57: 329–60.

Chomsky, N. (1985) *Knowledge of Language: Its Nature, Origin and Use*. New York: Praeger.

Clark, C.H. (1958) *Brainstorming*. New York: Doubleday.

Collingwood, R.G. (1938) *The Principles of Art*. Oxford: Clarendon Press.

Coplestone (1973) *Contemporary Philosophy*. London: Search Press.

Croce, B. (1953) *Aesthetics*. London: Peter Owen.

Cummins, G. (1967) *The Road to Immortality*. London: Psychic Press.

Das, B. (1953) *The Science of Emotions*. Madras: Theosophical Publishing House.

De Bono, E. (1975) *The Uses of Lateral Thinking*. Harmondsworth: Penguin Books.

DeWitt Parker (1926) *Analysis of Art*.

Edelman, G.M. and Mountcastle, V.B. (1978) *The Mindful Brain*. Cambridge, Mass.: MIT Press.

Fawcett, D. (1921) *Divine Imagining*. London: Macmillan.

Fawcett, D. (1931) *The Zermatt Dialogues*. London: Macmillan.

Fawcett, D. (1939) *The Oberland Dialogues*. London: Macmillan.

Findlay, J.N. (1961) *Values and Intentions*. London: Allen & Unwin.

Flavell, J. (1963) *The Developmental Psychology of Jean Piaget*. New York: Van Nostrand Reinhold.

Friedman, M.S. (1954) 'Martin Buber's theory of knowledge', *Review of Metaphysics*, 8.

Fry, R. (1920) *Vision and Design*. London: Chatto & Windus.

Fulcanelli (1984) *Le Mystère des Cathédrales*. Albuquerque, NM: Brotherhood of Life.

Gadamer, H.G. (1975) *Truth and Method*. New York: Seabury Press.

Gardner, H. (1983) *Frames of Mind*. New York: Basic Books.

Gendlin, E. (1981) *Focusing*. London: Bantam Press.

Goethe, W. (1820) *Anschauende Urteilskraft*.

Gordon, W.J.J. (1970) *Synectics: The Development of Creative Capacity*. New York: Harper & Row.

Govinda, A. (1960) *Foundations of Tibetan Mysticism*. London: Rider.

Gowan, S., Lakey, H., Moyer, W. and Taylor, R. (1979) *Moving Toward a New Society*. Philadelphia: New Society Press.

Grof, S. (1976) *Realms of the Human Unconscious*. New York: Dutton.

Grof, S. (1988) *The Adventure of Self-Discovery*. Albany: State University of New York Press.

Guénon, R. (1928) *Man and His Becoming According to the Vedanta*. London: Rider.

Hadamard, J. (1945) *The Psychology of Invention in the Mathematical Field*. New York: Dover Publications.

Hall, C.S. and Lindzey, G. (1957) *Theories of Personality*. New York: Wiley.

Harding, R.E.M. (1942) *An Anatomy of Inspiration*. Cambridge: Heffer.

Hart, L.A. (1983) *Human Brain and Human Learning*. London: Longman.

Hartshorne and Reese (1953) *Philosophers Speak of God*. Chicago: University of Chicago Press.

Heron, J. (1970) 'The phenomenology of social encounter: the gaze', *Philosophy and Phenomenological Research*, 31: 2.

Heron, J. (1977) *Catharsis in Human Development*. Guildford: University of Surrey.

Heron, J. (1978) *Humanistic Medicine*. London: British Postgraduate Medical Federation.

Heron, J. (1979) *Co-counselling*. Guildford: University of Surrey.

Heron, J. (1981a) 'Experiential research methodology', in P. Reason and J. Rowan (eds), *Human Inquiry*. Chichester: Wiley. pp 153–66.

Heron, J. (1981b) 'Philosophical basis of a new paradigm', in P. Reason and J. Rowan (eds), *Human Inquiry*. Chichester: Wiley. pp. 19–35.

Heron, J. (1982) *Education of the Affect*. Guildford: University of Surrey.

Heron, J. (1987) *Confessions of a Janus-Brain*. London: Endymion Press.

Heron, J. (1988) *Cosmic Psychology*. London: Endymion Press.

Heron, J. (1989) *The Facilitators' Handbook*. London: Kogan Page.

Heron, J. (1990) *Helping the Client*. London: Sage.

Herrmann, N. (1987) 'Brain dominance technology', in R.L. Craig (ed.), *Training and Development Handbook*. New York: McGraw-Hill. pp. 349–58.

Houston, J. (1987) *The Search for the Beloved*. Los Angeles: Tarcher.

Huxley, A. (1970) *The Perennial Philosophy*. New York: Harper & Row.

Hyde, L. (1949a) *Spirit and Society*. London: Methuen.

Hyde, L. (1949b) *The Nameless Faith*. London: Rider.

Hyde, L. (1954) *I Who Am*. Reigate: Omega Press.

Hyde, L. (1955) *An Introduction to Organic Philosophy*. Reigate: Omega Press.

Jackins, H. (1965) *The Human Side of Human Beings*. Seattle: Rational Island Publishers.

Jackins, H. (1973) *The Human Situation*. Seattle: Rational Island Publishers.

James, W. (1890) *The Principles of Psychology*. Vols 1 and 2. New York: Holt, Rinehart & Winston.

Janov, A. (1983) *Imprints: The Lifelong Effects of the Birth Experience.* New York: Coward-McCann.

Jantsch, E. (1980) *The Self-Organizing Universe.* Oxford: Pergamon.

Johnson, R.C. (1957) *Nurslings of Immortality.* New York: Harper & Row.

Jung, C.G. (1977) *Psychological Types,* in *Collected Works,* Vol. 6. Princeton: Princeton University Press.

Kitselman, A.L. (1953) *E-Therapy.* New York: Institute of Integration.

Knowles, M. (1990) *The Adult Learner: A Neglected Species.* Houston: Gulf Publishing.

Koestler, A. (1964) *The Act of Creation.* London: Hutchinson.

Koestler, A. (1978) *Janus.* London: Hutchinson.

Kohlberg, L. (1981) *The Philosophy of Moral Development.* San Francisco: Harper & Row.

Kolb, D.A. (1984) *Experiential Learning.* Englewood Cliffs, NJ: Prentice-Hall.

Krishna, G.H. (1970) *Kundalini: The Evolutionary Energy in Man.* London: Stuart & Watkins.

LaBerge, S. (1985) *Lucid Dreaming.* New York: Ballantine.

Lake, F. (1980) *Studies in Constricted Confusion.* Oxford: Clinical Theology Association.

Langer, S.K. (1951) *Philosophy in a New Key.* London: Oxford University Press.

Langer, S.K. (1952) *Feeling and Form.* New York.

Langer, S.K. (1988) *Mind: An Essay on Human Feeling,* abridged edition. Baltimore: Johns Hopkins University Press (original volumes 1967, 1972, 1982).

Leonard, G. (1978) *The Silent Pulse.* New York: Dutton.

Liebert, R.M. and Spiegler, M.D. (1990) *Personality: Strategies and Issues.* Pacific Grove, Calif.: Brooks/Cole.

Loevinger, J. (1976) *Ego Development: Conception and Theories.* San Francisco: Jossey-Bass.

Lozanov, G. (1978) *Suggestology and Outlines of Suggestopedy.* New York: Gordon & Breach.

Machado, L. (1991) 'The theory of the great intelligence', *Multi-Mind,* 1: 9.

MacMurray, J. (1957) *The Self as Agent.* London: Faber & Faber.

Maslow, A.H. (1955) 'Deficiency motivation and growth motivation', in M.R. Jones (ed.), *Nebraska Symposium on Motivation,* Vol. 3. Lincoln: University of Nebraska Press.

Maslow, A.H. (1970) *Motivation and Personality.* New York: Harper & Row.

Merleau-Ponty, M. (1962) *Phenomenology of Perception.* London: Routledge & Kegan Paul.

Moody, R. (1977) *Life After Life.* Atlanta: Mockingbird Books.

Mookerjee, A. (1982) *Kundalini.* London: Thames & Hudson.

Noyes, R. (1980) 'Attitude changes following near-death experiences', *Psychiatry,* 43: 234–41.

Ornstein, R. (1983) *Multi-Mind.* London: Papermac.

Osborne, H. (1955) *Aesthetics and Criticism.* London.

Parry, C.H.H. (1893) *The Art of Music.*

Partridge, B.L. (1982) Quoted in *Der Spiegel,* July.

Paul, L. (1961) *Persons and Perception.* London: Faber.

Penfield, W. (1975) *The Mystery of the Mind.* Princeton: Princeton University Press.

Pepper, S. (1949) *Principles of Art Appreciation.* New York: Harcourt, Brace & World.

Perkins, M. (1971) 'Matter, sensation and understanding', *American Philosophical Quarterly*, 8: 1–12.

Porritt, J. and Winner, D. (1988) *The Coming of the Greens*. London: Fontana.

Postle, D. (1991) *Emotional Competence*. London: Wentworth Institute.

Pribram, K.H. (1979) 'Holographic memory', interview in *Psychology Today*, February.

Prigogine, I. (1980) *From Being to Becoming*. San Francisco: Freeman.

Radhakrishnan, S. (1939) *Eastern Religions and Western Thought*. London: Oxford University Press.

Radhakrishnan, S. and Raju, P.J. (eds) (1960) *The Concept of Man*. London: Allen & Unwin.

Reason, P. (1989) *Human Inquiry in Action*. London: Sage.

Reason, P. and Heron, J. (1981) *Co-counselling: An Experiential Inquiry (1)*. Guildford: University of Surrey.

Reason, P. and Heron, J. (1982) *Co-counselling: An Experiential Inquiry (2)*. Guildford: University of Surrey.

Reason, P. and Heron, J. (1985) *Whole Person Medicine: A Co-operative Inquiry*. London: British Postgraduate Medical Federation.

Reason, P. and Heron, J. (1986) 'Research with people', *Person-Centred Review*, 1(4): 456–76.

Reason, P. and Rowan, J. (1981) 'On making sense', in P. Reason and J. Rowan (eds), *Human Inquiry*. Chichester: Wiley.

Reinert, C.P. (1989) *Increasing Intelligence by Imaging*. Garvin: Glenview Press.

Ring, K. (1984) 'The nature of personal identity in the near-death experience', *Anabiosis*, 40(1): 3–20.

Rogers, C.R. (1959) 'A theory of therapy, personality, and interpersonal relationships, as developed in the client-centred framework', in S. Koch (ed.) *Psychology: A Study of a Science*, Vol. 3. New York: McGraw-Hill.

Rogers, C.R. (1980) *A Way of Being*. Boston: Houghton Mifflin.

Rogo, D.S. (ed.) (1978) *Mind Beyond the Body*. New York: Penguin.

Rose, C. (1991) 'The state of the art', *Multi-Mind*, 1: 1–7.

Rowan, J. (1990) *Subpersonalities*. London: Routledge.

Ryle, G. (1949) *The Concept of Mind*. London: Hutchinson.

Sacks, O. (1990) 'Neurology and the soul', *The New York Review*, 22 November.

Schuster, D.H. and Gritton, C.E. (1986) *Suggestive Accelerative Learning Techniques*. New York: Gordon & Breach.

Skolimowski, H. (1990) 'The methodology of participation and its consequences', *Collaborative Inquiry*, 3: 7–10.

Spiegelberg, H. (1960) *The Phenomenological Movement*. The Hague: Nijhoff.

Stace, W.T. (1961) *Mysticism and Philosophy*. London: Macmillan.

Stone, H. and Winkelman, S. (1985) *Embracing our Selves*. Marina del Rey: Devorss.

Suzuki, D.T. (1947) *The Essence of Buddhism*. London: The Buddhist Society.

Tholey, P. (1983) 'Techniques for inducing and maintaining lucid dreams', *Perceptual and Motor Skills*, 57: 79–90.

Thompson, W.I. (ed.) (1987) *Gaia: A Way of Knowing*. Great Barrington, Mass.: Lindisfarne Press.

Tillich, P. (1951–63) *Systematic Theology*, 3 vols. Chicago: University of Chicago Press.

Torbert, W.R. (1987) *Managing the Corporate Dream*. Homewood, IL: Dow Jones-Irwin.

Tyrrell, G.N.M. (1948) *The Personality of Man*. London: Penguin.

Underhill, E. (1927) *Man and the Supernatural*. London: Methuen.

Wahl, J. (1948) *Philosophers' Way*. New York: Oxford University Press.

Wahl, J. (1953) *Traité de Métaphysique*. Paris: Payot.

Wenger, W. (1991) *How to Image-stream*. Gathersburg: Psychegenics Press.

Whitehead, A.N. (1926) *Science and the Modern World*. Cambridge: Cambridge University Press.

Whitehead, A.N. (1928) *Symbolism*. Cambridge: Cambridge University Press.

Whitehead, A.N. (1929) *Process and Reality*. Cambridge: Cambridge University Press.

Whitehead, A.N. (1938) *Modes of Thought*. Cambridge: Cambridge University Press.

Wilber, K. (1977) *The Spectrum of Consciousness*. Wheaton, Illinois: Theosophical Publishing House.

Wilber, K. (1983) *Up from Eden*. London: Routledge & Kegan Paul.

Wilber, K. (1990) *Eye to Eye*, expanded edn. Boston, Mass.: Shambhala.

Yates, F. (1964) *Giordano Bruno and the Hermetic Tradition*. London: Routledge & Kegan Paul.

Zener, K. (1958) 'The significance of experience of the individual for the science of psychology', in *Minnesota Studies in the Philosophy of Science*, Vol. 2. Minneapolis: University of Minnesota Press.

Index